THE WRITING OF MELANCHOLY

ROSS CHAMBERS

THE WRITING OF MELANCHOLY

Modes of Opposition in Early French Modernism

Translated by Mary Seidman Trouille

THE UNIVERSITY OF CHICAGO PRESS
Chicago and London

Ross Chambers is the Marvin Felheim Distinguished University Professor of French and Comparative Literature at the University of Michigan. Mary Seidman Trouille is a lecturer in French and the humanities at the University of Chicago.

Except for chapter 4, which appears here for the first time, this work was originally published as *Mélancolie et opposition: Les débuts du modernisme en France*, © Librairie José Corti, 1987

THE UNIVERSITY OF CHICAGO PRESS, CHICAGO 60637
THE UNIVERSITY OF CHICAGO PRESS, LTD., LONDON
© 1993 by The University of Chicago
All rights reserved. Published 1993
Printed in the United States of America
02 01 00 99 98 97 96 95 94 93   1 2 3 4 5
ISBN: 0–226–10070–7

Library of Congress Cataloging-in-Publication Data
Chambers, Ross.
    [Mélancolie et opposition. English]
    The writing of melancholy : modes of opposition in early French
modernism / Ross Chambers : translated by Mary Seidman Trouille.
        p. cm.
    Translation of: Mélancolie et opposition.
    Includes index.
    1. French literature—19th century—History and criticism.
    2. Modernism (Literature)—France.   3. Melancholy in literature.
    4. Polarity in literature.   I. Title.
PQ295.M63C5313   1993
840.9′1—dc20   92-27590
                                                                CIP

In memoriam

Michel de Certeau
Sonia Marks

D'où viennent les mélancolies historiques, les sympathies à travers siècles, etc.?

[Whence come these fits of historical melancholia, these affinities from century to century, etc.?]
  Gustave Flaubert, Letter to Louise Colet, 26–27 May 1853

Alles Ständige und Stehende verdampft, alles Heilige wird entweiht, und die Menschen sind endlich gezwungen, ihre Lebenstellung, ihre gegenseitigen Beziehungen mit nüchternen Augen anzuschauen.

[All that is respectable and upright melts into fog, all that is holy is desanctified, and humans are finally forced to look soberly on their life situation and mutual dealings.]
  Karl Marx and Friedrich Engels, *The Communist Manifesto* (1847)

Wir fragen uns nur, warum man erst krank werden muß, um solcher Wahrheit zugänglich zu sein.

[We only wonder why it is necessary to become ill in order to have access to such truth.]
  Sigmund Freud, "Mourning and Melancholia" (1916)

CONTENTS

PREFACE

This book is drawn from a series of seminars and reflects that manner of working, which is as distinct as it is invaluable. One should not expect to find here the rigorous presentation of a central argument or exhaustive analysis of a complete corpus. An argument I find suggestive is developed, in a rather sinuous manner, through "readings" of texts that I propose as representative, although I fully recognize the lacunary, even arbitrary, nature of this method. As is often the case in the critical genre of "readings," remarks of the most specific and pertinent nature are at times found side by side with generalizations that, for lack of elaboration, may appear tenuous. These readings are meant to be suggestive and to serve as working hypotheses that provide the framework necessary for more detailed analyses, as well as subjects for future research and reflection by myself or by others. In a seminar one does not seek to conclude discussions or to close lines of research; one tries to open them. The reader who finishes this book with a sigh of discontent, feeling that "there are some good ideas there, but the real work remains to be done," will have my full approval, especially if he or she is led to initiate analyses or pursue reflections that my essay has in some way inspired.

My book can pass as a study in literary history, but it is not the work of a historian. The material presented here is not the result of painstaking archival research or of new interpretations based on specific historical documents. The decline of the Second Republic, Louis-Napoléon's rise to power, and the coming of the Second Empire are not viewed as the "framework" within which one can situate, as secondary phenomena, the literary texts produced during that period. Quite to the contrary, the self-situating devices within the texts themselves, their situational self-reflexivity, constitute the focus of my analyses. That is to say, the historical "context" will be treated not as an independent object of inquiry, but as a *product of reading* produced by the interaction of an actual reader in possession of a certain

number of codes, conventions, techniques, and interpretive presupposi-
tions (including certain "historical" knowledge drawn from other French
texts of the mid-nineteenth century) with a group of texts that I regard—
based on what is itself a major presupposition—as *situationally marked*.

In other words, the texts are understood not as *énoncés*, statements that
might be studied objectively, but as *énonciations*, utterances whose essential
trait is to produce—as a necessary precondition to their existence as
texts—a certain interpretive context, without which the communicational
act they presuppose cannot take place. The assumption this study is based
on is therefore the idea that texts continually propose a contextualizing
interpretive act as necessary to complete their reality, and that by figuring
in various ways the interpretive contract they presuppose, texts not only
anticipate the situation and role of the reader—a reader who is necessarily
situated in their future—but at the same time provide clues concerning the
context of production that reader will be encouraged to take into account.
An interpretive context is inevitably *dual*, since it leaves space for a reading
that is necessarily extrinsic to an enunciatory context—a "locus" from
which the text speaks—that the text alone can evoke.

We must therefore have confidence in texts. They know, they respond.
They understand far more than we do about the issues we debate; and if
one questions them with a minimum of tact and attention, the answer they
provide is substantial, profound, and at times surprising. Nevertheless, the
questions texts respond to are still those that we as readers formulate; it is
only once we have asked them that we realize these questions were somehow anticipated from the start. I originally sought to develop the theory
of textual self-contextualization—concerning the way a text anticipates its
interpretation by self-reflexive figuration, but within a context evoked if
not determined by the text—in a book titled *Story and Situation: Narrative
Seduction and the Power of Fiction* (Minneapolis: University of Minnesota
Press, 1984). The analyses we will consider later are based on a version of
this same theory, which is briefly outlined at the beginning of the first
chapter.

My analyses are also based on a conception of the social function of
"textuality" that was barely touched on in the book mentioned above. This
concept is developed in another work titled *Room for Maneuver: Reading
(the) Oppositional (in) Narrative* (Chicago: University of Chicago Press,
1991), which serves as a companion piece to the present book. If, as I
suggested in *Story and Situation*, the text-reader relationship seems to be
one of "seduction" in the case of certain modern texts, one must search for

the reasons behind this need for seduction in the context of their production. Only texts that are alienated from the context they presuppose need to seduce their readers. Accordingly, it is in the form of an "oppositional" relation that the texts studied here enable us to read the context of production they propose as pertinent to their reading. It is because these texts stand in opposition to their context of production that they must appeal to a reading instance that might allow them to transcend this initially unfavorable context, making themselves seductive to an implied reader (a reader always figured as future). The book I am presenting here on the new writing of the 1850s in France may therefore be considered a chapter drawn for closer scrutiny from a more general study of the oppositional social function of literature.

Opposition, I know, is a fashionable topic these days. (So, if it comes to that, is seduction.) Readers will judge for themselves what this book owes to the philosophically more refined and rhetorically shrewder essays of people like J.-F. Lyotard or Gilles Deleuze and Félix Guattari. I clearly owe a great deal to Michel de Certeau; my intellectual debt to him is heightened, moreover, by a debt of friendship more difficult to acknowledge in a scholarly study of this kind. For it is not as a mere trend of fashion but as a manifestation of community that I would interpret the current convergence of thought around the notion of opposition. Just as a whole generation in France, and indeed through much of Europe, shared the exaltation and disillusionment of 1848, so too an international generation experienced together the enthusiasm and frustration of 1968. Is it not because we ourselves live in the wake of 1968—somewhat disillusioned about the possibilities for collective action but unable to accept the legitimacy of an alienating status quo—that collectively we have become so interested in the concept of the oppositional? It is certainly for that reason that I have been led to read certain texts of the 1850s in the same light.

In any case, it is with a certain melancholy, but also in the spirit of friendship, that this book on historical melancholy has been written: Friendship for writers long since dead and for a new generation of students who, in 1968, were less than ten years old. (My thanks go to the students who took my seminars in Ann Arbor, New York, and Baton Rouge, in the winter, spring, and autumn of 1986.) Friendship above all for the critics (Françoise Gaillard, Naomi Schor, Barbara Johnson, Shoshana Felman, Edward Ahearn, Dolf Oehler, Nathaniel Wing, Richard Terdiman, and many others) whose exciting work on the nineteenth century in France has nurtured my own thinking. Finally, I wish to thank the friends I think of whenever

I sit down at my desk, those I write for. I will mention here only Marie Maclean, herself a distinguished Baudelaire specialist, who reads all my drafts so carefully and discerningly, and Ian Reid, who continually reminds me how far texts go beyond the readings we try to make of them.

Such intellectual debts and debts of friendship are indistinguishable. It is for that reason that on my dedication page, next to the name of Michel de Certeau, there appears the name of another departed friend, Sonia Marks. The act of mourning that leads me to dedicate this book to them is also an expression of the warmest thanks.

PREFACE TO THE ENGLISH TRANSLATION

Working with Mary Trouille on an English version of *Mélancolie et opposition* has been an enriching experience. It has taught me something I was unable to acknowledge five years ago: that in the melancholy experience of writing about melancholic writing there was also an intense pleasure, derived in large part from devising critical texts whose own linguistic texture had something in common with the texts they were about. In aligning my own writing on certain of the lexical and semantic resources of the French language that seemed in part to have generated the poetry and prose of Nerval, Baudelaire, and Flaubert, I was extending the chain of writing and confirming in a minor way the theory of collective textuality the book proposes.

Inevitably, the evidence of that collective production has largely disappeared in translation, to the extent that it depended on the French language. On the other hand, Mary Trouille has disentangled my embedded syntax and hypotactic style, turning some rather dense thickets of prose into more acceptable English sentences. From them an argument emerges that is perhaps a bit less suggestive, unable to rely on the connotations of some key French words, but that has gained, I think, in clarity and concreteness.

The Writing of Melancholy differs from *Mélancolie et opposition* in one more substantial respect. I have written an entirely new chapter 4, on Nerval's "Sylvie," to replace the readings of the same author's "Angélique" and "Aurélia" that migrated in 1991 from *Mélancolie et opposition* to *Room for Maneuver*. The most obvious point of intersection between the two books now lies, therefore, in the more developed treatment of the work of Nerval as a case of writerly "suicide" that straddles them.

My warmest thanks go to Mary Trouille for her fine work; and for their enthusiastic support of this project, to Michel Jeanneret, Françoise Meltzer, and Alan Thomas.

ONE

ON BEING *NOUVEAU*

A reader's task is not to serve as the addressee of a message, but to read a text. Yet in many, if not all, narrative or poetic texts a "place" is reserved for the reception of a message: that of the narratee.[1] As Gerald Prince explains, the narratee is a partner in a narrative act—or more generally speaking in an elocutionary act—whose subject is referred to as the narrator in the case of a narrative account (or *récit*) and as the lyrical "I" in the case of poetic writing. The main argument presented in this chapter and in the chapters that follow is grounded in the crucial distinction between such a "narrative function" and what I will call the "textual function." The latter is perhaps best understood as a collaborative event that arises from the relation between a text and its reader or, more precisely, from the relation between a piece of writing and an instance of reading.

In my discussion of texts, I will therefore refer to a double system of address that involves both a narratee and a presupposed instance of reading. But every text also involves a third function: the function of referentiality, which produces a "world" that is to varying degrees fictive or familiar and that is understood as the text's world of reference. This referential function shares a subject with—and in fact coincides with—the text's narrative function. It is well recognized in narrative theory that the narrator participates in a double relation: a relation with the narratee, but also with the text's narrated world. Within narrative discourse (or what Genette calls "le discours du récit"), there occurs a filtering of information such that the referential object is produced according to the Genettian categories of time, mode, and voice.[2] This framework allows us to define the "I"-narrator or poetic "I" as the site of an ideological production that addresses a "you"-narratee whose role is to receive, and even to share, the narrative subject's "perceptions"—that is, his or her productions of the world. (Note, however, that even third-person narration implies an "I"-narrator.)

Contrary to certain somewhat oversimplified views, the narrative function is not an actual enunciation; what is generally referred to as the narrative discourse is merely the *representation* of a discourse. That narrative discourse constitutes an *énoncé* (or discourse-as-structure), rather than an *énonciation* (or discourse-as-event), is demonstrated by studies such as Genette's that show it to be susceptible of grammatical analysis.[3] Readers of a text would therefore be mistaken to believe themselves *directly* implicated in the narrative function's production of a slot for the narratee. It is true that in the simplest case—that of a "naive" reading of a literary text or in everyday communication (which is not as simple as one might think)—the textual function more or less coincides with the narrative function; that is, it is limited to an "instruction" given to readers to put themselves in the place of the narratee and to become the addressees of a message whose subject is the narrative "I." In this case the text produces an instance of reading that coincides with the position of the narratee.

But this "zero degree" of textual function could only correspond to an absence of self-reflexive figurations in the text. It is only to the extent that a text is perceived as *not* speaking of itself and *not* representing itself that it is not considered "readable" (in a sense that distinguishes it from the narrative function). In literature, however, such a perception is extremely rare, if not nonexistent. From experience we know that there is no easier interpretive strategy than to read a text as a commentary on itself as a literary production.[4] Once that strategy is adopted, the text produces itself as meaningful only in relation to a context of reading, as I tried to show in an earlier study.[5] In this way the text becomes an *énonciation*—a "message" whose meaning is situational and that therefore involves the active intervention of an instance of reading, an intervention that leads not to the mere reception of a message, but to an act of interpretation. In this case the narrative function becomes part of the text, but only as an object of reading; it is no longer a true communicative act having the reader as its direct addressee.

However, the duplicity or "play" of the texts we will examine in this book stems from a certain ambiguity in their narrative function—from the possibility of confusing a representation of discourse with an actual enunciation. These texts take advantage of the reading habits of their period (which tended to confuse textual and narrative functions) in order to convey a seemingly reassuring message through the narrative function while using the textual function to call for a more subversive reading. I would even argue that the message conveyed by the narrative function is always a reassuring one in bourgeois culture; for the communicational context implied by the narrative function—a context that in fact constitutes the true content of the message—serves only to reinforce the prevailing ideology, which presupposes the existence of an autonomous subject and the instrumentality of discourse. Conversely, these ideologemes are undermined by the phenomena of writing and reading mobilized by the textual function.

It goes without saying that the possibilities for textual self-figuration are virtually unlimited and that consequently it is always possible to read in terms of the textual function. What interests us here, however, is how these self-figurations, once they are perceived by a reader, produce a kind of split or fold within the text through which it undergoes a process of self-differentiation, becoming both subject and object of the interpretive act. This split within the text gives rise to the instance of reading that is both anticipated and generated by the text. This instance of reading should in no way be confused with the passive addressee of the narrative message, and it should also be distinguished from the specific personality characteristics of the empirical reader. Within the textual function there are no "subjects" like the "I"-narrator and "you"-narratee of the narrative function, coinciding with the predications through which they are produced. There are instead *enunciatory subjects* or subjects of writing, which are split, multiple, and traversed by multiple codes—languages of desire, sociolects, idiolects—although coinciding with none of them, to the point that ideally they are identifiable only with the text itself—with the text as it is *read*. Within this textual function, the act of reading consists of becoming not the "I" or narrative subject of the text, but what is called its *sujet d'énonciation*—a "deeper" subject that is manifested only in the form of traces: signs to be deciphered, writing.

In the context of our discussion, language should not be viewed as a self-contained system of expression or nomenclature, as a tool at the disposal of human subjects who are somehow independent from it in a world existing prior to discourse, which language would then "name." The referential function does in fact produce the "world of the text," but it produces it *as if*—as if that world existed prior to the text, as if language were simply naming it, instead of producing it. Yet that world exists only as a function of linguistic and cultural codes operating in the text; it is the product of a "dictionary" and an "encyclopedia"—that is, of other texts that the text assumes are common to itself and its readers. The referential world therefore not only is, in a precise sense, "proper" to the text, but is a function of the reading activity implied by the text. In other words, the textual function is hierarchically superior to the referential function.

One can say much the same thing about the relation between narrator and narratee that constitutes the narrative function. The narrative function seems to imply the existence of communicating subjects whose relation might appear to be both the origin of and the precondition for discourse. Yet the narrator and narratee (and the relation between them) are in fact products of their own discourse—of linguistic predications in which they serve as "shifters" ("I," "you," *je, tu,* or *vous*) in grammatically determined slots. Their "existence" is a function of reading, since their mode of representation is the simulacrum. Narrator and narratee are simulacra produced by an interpretation of the signs that they themselves are supposed to generate through their interaction. As a result, there is a narrative function and an "I"-"you" narrator-narratee relation, even when this relation is not made explicit in the discourse by the presence of first- and second-person pronouns (in a third-person narration, for example).

As for the textual function, through which the text "represents" itself and calls forth an act of reading (while the act of reading symmetrically produces the text as a textual self-representation), its mode of representation can be described as figural. By this I mean that a text can represent itself only by being perceived to produce images of itself, in a play of reflections that frequently leads commentators to speak of a mirroring effect. Not only are these images interpretable (and so, as I have said, dependent on an instance of reading), but they are interpretable as allegories of the text, in the precise sense in which Mallarmé declared the sonnet "Ses purs ongles . . ." to be "allegorical of itself." For allegoresis implies textual enunciation in the form of the act of allegorizing, but the allegorized (whether as "what the text is about" or the allegorizing subject) can be identified only as an object of interpretation and is therefore open to unlimited reading and infinite interpretability—the defining characteristic of textuality, as we know empirically and are beginning to understand theoretically.[6]

It is important to understand that these three functions all generate contexts, although each in a different way. All present the text as identical to the contexts produced by the text. The context of reference (produced by the referential function) and the communicative context (produced by the narrative function) are so familiar that they present little difficulty; let me simply reiterate the crucial theoretical point that these contexts must be thought of not as independent of the text and existing prior to it, but as products of textual discourse (which is itself the product of an interpretive act). The greatest challenge is to conceive of reading not as an act exterior to the text, but as a self-contextualizing function that is anticipated, produced, and controlled by the text and yet, at the same time, is produced as the *producer* of the text. I am not denying the freedom of empirical readers; however, their reading is always foreseen and "situated" by the text itself, regardless of the interpretative grids, codes, and methods that they might bring to the text and that remain "foreign" to it (such as the psychoanalytic code I will use in chapter 5 to interpret a nineteenth-century text). This interpretive gesture is necessarily anticipated and oriented by the text, to the extent that its self-reflexive apparatus serves to define the text as a *text* only by presenting it as a discourse to be interpreted. Thus the reader is that indispensable "stranger" without whom the text would not exist and whose position is anticipated textually (in the form of the presupposed reading instance) by the way the self-figurative apparatus introduces a split or fold into the text, a split that is therefore constitutive. The narrative and referential functions—the "world" the text produces and the "normal" communicative situation that it simulates between conventional "subjects" discussing something—should therefore be themselves situated as a function of the interpretation of the text within a context of reading. For that reason, the self-contextualizing function—which I call the "textual function," but which might also be referred to as the "reading function"—should be considered hierarchically superior to the other functions I have discussed. For the text can generate contexts—referential, narrative, or textual—only when it is *read*, yet at the same time it is a text only insofar as it is *readable*.

*

Let us consider, by way of example, the opening scene of *Madame Bovary*:

> Nous étions à l'étude, quand le Proviseur entra, suivi d'un *nouveau* habillé en bourgeois et d'un garçon de classe qui portait un grand pupitre. Ceux qui dormaient se réveillèrent, et chacun se leva, comme surpris dans son travail.

> [We were in class when the headmaster came in, followed by a new boy, not wearing the school uniform, and a custodian carrying a large desk. Those who had been asleep woke up, and every one rose as if just surprised at his work.][7]

The referential function of the text is clearly provided here by the strongly redundant use of school terms: *à l'étude* ("in class"), *le Proviseur* ("headmaster"), *un nouveau* ("a new boy"), *habillé en bourgeois* ("not wearing the school uniform"), *garçon de classe* ("custodian"), *un grand pupitre* ("a large desk"). These terms are part of what one might call "the school code" (*le code scolaire*); they situate the action in a classroom and give an immediately recognizable meaning to statements that might at first glance appear less strongly coded. The phrases "ceux qui dormaient," "chacun se leva," and "surpris dans son travail" are based on cultural assumptions concerning schoolboys. What do they do during class? They sleep, they sit (but stand up when an authority figure enters the room), and they pretend to be working.

As for the initial "we" (*nous*) that introduces the subject of the narration, it is immediately clear that this figure is entirely accustomed to the school setting and is at home with everything I have just enumerated, handling with ease the vocabulary corresponding to it. The narrative "I" is not a member of the school hierarchy, however, since during the period evoked by the terms "garçon de classe" and "un *nouveau* habillé en bourgeois," such a person would have referred to the headmaster more respectfully as "*Monsieur* le Proviseur." The narrative "I" is therefore a student (or former student) who assumes as his narratee another former student, for whom it is unnecessary to provide any specific information concerning classroom customs. The narrative discourse of the text is therefore easily classifiable in the well-known genre of "schoolday memories" (*les souvenirs de classe*), as culturally familiar in France as the "army tales" (*histoires du régiment*) that former soldiers enjoy telling each other.

But is that all there is to the text? Suppose that, alerted by the parallel between this "entrance" into the text and the new boy's entrance into the class, accompanied by instruments of writing (and notably the desk), it should occur to some reader that the text may be figuring itself in this way? In that case certain hypotheses of an interpretive nature are bound to arise. Here is a text that seems to present itself—in a routine, uniform world plunged into the lethargy and boredom of work that is a mere semblance of work—as the equivalent of the *nouveau* (a "new boy," or more generally a newcomer), and therefore as capable of waking up those who are sleeping and of surprising those who pretend to be working. In that case, the *nouveauté* or newness claimed by the text is strongly relativized by the institutionalization implied by its classroom setting. The new student enters the classroom under the guidance of an authority figure, the headmaster, whose presence justifies and legitimates his own; he is also accompanied by an acolyte of the school system, the custodian (*le garçon de classe*). Moreover, his status as a *nouveau* is anticipated by school language, just as the ceremony marking his integration into the school environment is provided for by institutional authority. *Un proviseur* ("headmaster"), if one considers the etymology of the word—which derives from the verb *pourvoir* ("to provide")—is indeed someone who *provides* for all eventualities, in the double sense of *prévoit* ("to foresee") and *prévient* ("to anticipate so as to forestall"). In these circumstances *être nouveau* ("to be a new student") means filling a well-established slot and being unlikely to remain new for very long.

And indeed, the "surprise" produced by Charles's entrance into the classroom is not genuine. Are those who stand up "*comme* surpris dans [leur] travail," *as if* they had been interrupted in their work, pretending to *work* or to be *surprised* or both? The word *comme* ("as if") is ambiguous and can apply either to *surpris* or to the whole phrase. It is common knowledge, moreover, that a self-respecting student is never surprised and is always prepared for the possible entrance of an authority figure. Finally, although being dressed *en bourgeois* (in street clothes worn by the bourgeois class) distinguishes the new student from those in school uniform and is a point worth noting, *l'habit bourgeois* can itself be seen merely as another type of uniform: a *class* marker in a different but subtly linked sense of that word. The "textual function" here can therefore be summarized in this way: that the text raises the question of *nouveauté* or "newness"—including that of the text itself—in a universe so rigidly structured that everything is always already *classé*, that is, *identified by class*. Not newness, then, so much as novelty.

*

The main argument of my book is that in nineteenth-century France there emerged a kind of literary *nouveauté* whose distinguishing feature was a certain way of playing with the relation between the narrative and textual functions and with the construction of communicational contexts in general. As a result of this development, the textual function, or what might be called the text-reading relation, took on unprecedented importance. This is not to say that the narrative function disappeared from the texts; on the contrary, it continued to be clearly present, and indeed *highlighted*, in the texts. From that time on, however, there developed a space of play, a duplicitous gap between the narrative and textual functions of such importance that a reader who missed it would also misinterpret the meaning of the texts, which derived to a large extent from the disparity that became readable between the two functions. Owing to this new predominance of the textual function, the narrative function could no longer be considered a simple "model" of communication more or less backed up by the textual function. Literary communication henceforth became more complicated, since the narrative and textual functions were no longer in alignment and since the relation between them had become a duplicitous one—duplicitous both in the etymological sense of yielding a double reading of the text (a reading simultaneously narrative and textual) and in the more common sense (whose relevance will become clear in due course) of deception or disguise.

This new literary trend emerged in the 1850s. This was not of course an absolute point of origin: in literature and the arts there is never an absolute origin. One could easily identify the "ancestors" of the texts I am about to discuss, even if they did not themselves point intertextually to various predecessors dating back to earliest antiquity. In chapter 3, for example, I will probe certain parallels (as well as some significant differences) between certain texts of the 1850s and others belonging to the 1830s—a decade in some ways comparable. The *nouveauté* of these texts, like that of Charles Bovary, was already anticipated then and was to be quickly categorized or "classed" according to the tradition(s) it perpetuated. Their novelty bears a curious resemblance in this way to the capitalistic commercial practices characterizing the same period—such as the invention of "novelty items" (*articles de Paris*) and the extension and democratization of fashion— which are reflected in the purchases made by Emma Bovary. And finally, the novelty was limited, since the literary trend in question involved a relatively small number of texts produced during the 1850s. Works of a conventional nature continued to be written, along with other, more innovative texts that reflect trends quite different from those I will be discussing here.

The heroes of my book are therefore Nerval, Baudelaire, and Flaubert. The principal texts in my discussion—"Sylvie," *Les Fleurs du mal*, and *Madame Bovary*—have been chosen because of the (relative) "originality" they display in the duplicity of their writing. Although during the early years of the Second Empire it is possible to distinguish a political "Left" and "Right" in French literature, the great texts that I call modernist[8] resist such categorization (which is approximate at best) because of their duplicity. For example, with his revival of political satire in *Les Châtiments* during his exile, Hugo is more openly engaged politically than certain of his contemporaries, but this work reflects more traditional stylistic options. In contrast, Gautier often appeared on the verge of following modernist tendencies; but in opting for a more formalist approach, he assured himself of government approval as well as leadership of the Parnasse group and the "art for art's sake" movement.[9]

By contrast, early modernist texts in France are not openly engaged politically like Hugo's works and may appear—and even be intended to appear—apolitical like the aestheticist writing of the period (and also following the dictates of prudence under so authoritarian a regime). When one knows how to *read* them, however, these texts nevertheless bear witness against a social system and a political regime that together constitute the ruling order: the cultural hegemony of the bourgeoisie, the reign of capitalism in the economic sphere, and an authoritarian style of government. The duplicity of these texts can be described as "oppositional," to echo Michel de Certeau's use of the term;[10] for though they do not directly challenge the dominant social order, they nevertheless offer "readable" evidence of fidelity to alternative values. It does not make much sense to ask whether their duplicity is the product of conscious strategies, since (as in the case of any oppositional behavior) their disguise is the result of a certain "knack" or savoir-faire, a trick of writing that could not be theorized then (and is perhaps not fully theorizable now) but that was far from being naive.

Literary duplicity of this kind arises in reponse to repressive social forces, a sense of being under surveillance or even censorship. I am using this last term in its broadest sense to refer to all the various means of repression—whether legal, institutional, judicial, economic, or cultural—that a society like that of the Second Empire could bring into play. But institutional censorship is itself revealing, since authoritarian governments generally have two options to choose from. Under a system of direct censorship, before an author can publish or produce a text, the text must be submitted to an official censor for approval. This gives the author some leverage to "play" with the system and, paradoxically, encourages a certain spirit of resistance. The other method of censorship is initiated only once a text has been published. The author, publisher, journalist, or director of a magazine or newspaper can be prosecuted and sentenced to imprisonment or fines for having published a work that is judged *after the fact* to be subversive, immoral, or criminal. This "indirect" method of censorship is illustrated by the lawsuits brought against *Les Fleurs du mal* and *Madame Bovary*.

Under either system, certain individuals are held responsible for a discourse that is attributed to them, which explains why the subject position tends to disappear or else to multiply or disguise itself under such regimes. Because of its greater arbitrariness and unpredictability, however, the indirect censorship that characterized the Second Empire encouraged, and often resulted in, *self-censorship* by writers. And when self-censorship becomes habitual, spontaneous, almost "second nature" in this way, it can lead to forms of textual duplicity that resist it, to an artfulness that is never closely examined and does not become fully conscious, despite the technical skill it requires.

To put it in Freudian terms, the repression that is self-censorship is manifested only through the return of the repressed in modified form. That is why the new kinds of modernist writing emerging in the 1850s can be seen as evidence—or more precisely as a trace—of the general atmosphere of censorship and resulting self-censorship during that period. As ironic as it may seem, authoritarian regimes and strict social control over art can be thought to have a "good side," since they foster literature that is complex, ambiguous, and highly readable. Take for example, in Baudelaire's highly ironic prose poem "Une Mort héroïque," the favor (*faveur*) enjoyed by the mime Fancioulle, an artist condemned to silence but in possession of means—those of pantomime—in which the author of "La Fanfarlo" and "De l'essence du rire" surely saw a figure for an antirealistic and "modern" mode of artistic production.

In "Une Mort héroïque," Fancioulle participates in a plot against the Prince. When the plot is uncovered, the mime is condemned to death, but also is ordered to give a final performance to the court before his execution. He succeeds at his performance in a masterly way and proves that "l'ivresse de l'art est plus apte que toute autre à voiler les terreurs du gouffre; que le génie peut jouer la comédie au bord de la tombe . . . perdu dans un paradis excluant toute idée de tombe et de destruction" ["the intoxication of art is more apt than any other to veil the terrors of the abyss; that genius can play comedy on the brink of the tomb . . . lost in a paradise excluding any idea of tomb and destruction"].[11] Everyone is deeply moved by the performance: the public, the narrator, even the Prince himself. But the Prince's admiration is poisoned by jealousy and by fear that his own powers have been surpassed: "Véritable artiste lui-même, . . . se sentait-il vaincu dans son pouvoir de despote? Humilié dans son art de terrifier les cœurs et d'engourdir les esprits?" (pp. 126, 132) ["Himself a true artist, . . . did he feel defeated in his despotic power? humiliated in his art of terrifying hearts and numbing minds?"] (pp. 63, 66). He therefore orders a young page to brutally interrupt the mime's act with a long, shrill blast of a whistle, which causes the artist to collapse stone dead on the stage. The relation between the Prince and Fancioulle as artists suggests that the mime's artistic success results from a certain collaboration or even complicity between them (since they are old friends), but also from mutual hostility and conflict (since they are *frères ennemis*). The Prince's political power is identified here with the power of death itself, which is capable of "terrifying people's hearts and numbing their minds." (As I suggest in chapter 5, there are other texts in which Baudelaire attributes metaphysical dimensions to social apathy and the autocratic regime that fosters it, defining poetic production by its resemblance and simultaneous resistance to regimes of this type.) And the construction of a relation between children in "Une Mort héroique" suggests that the power relations between the Prince and the artist are played out at a "prelinguistic" or *unconscious* level, in any case on the level of the *unspoken*, since the page chosen by the Prince stands opposite Fancioulle, whose name is a gallicized form of the Italian *fanciullo* and so derives from the Latin *in-fans* (meaning "not speaking," and hence "child").

Brought on by the blast of the whistle, Fancioulle's death, then, signifies less the power of art than its defeat. Fancioulle has no effective means of resisting the Prince's power or the power of death. The favor distinguishing an artist under the rule of a Prince is paradoxically that of *failing*. The consciousness of failure is the distinguishing mark of any oppositional practice that is at all aware of itself and of the difficult conditions under which it operates: it must try to outmaneuver a force that, like death, is by definition *insurmountable*. The case of the modern artist—confronted by bourgeois society and conscious of its tremendous power to co-opt any type of challenge or any attempt at singularity or originality—is a clear, albeit somewhat hackneyed, example of this. An author like Flaubert, for example, attempting to produce "new" writing in a mercantile and expansionist society that had invented "novelty" as a means of producing profit and expanding markets, cannot have been unaware that his book was itself a literary commodity participating in the very economy he despised. Nor could he have overlooked the way that, in the cultural and commercial marketplace, his novel replicates the seductive means deployed by the merchant Lheureux who, in order to sell Emma his goods (*nouveautés*), exploits her desires no less surely than her lovers do. Thus—long before Kafka and Beckett—Flaubert and Baudelaire, as well as Nerval (the apologist of madness in a society in which madness was strongly repressed), were fully conscious of their inevitable failure as they wrote.[12]

Yet as a result, these authors established failure as one of the positive values and even as one of the sources of pride of European modernism. For it is certain that, when faced with certain audiences and certain historical circumstances, failure becomes a kind of a moral obligation while success becomes a source of shame. One might almost say, for example, that Gautier's reputation today has suffered because of the relative success he enjoyed with the readers of his time. And in literature, just as one can (like Gautier) succeed in the short term and fail in the long term, it is possible, conversely, to be a relative failure in the eyes of one's contemporaries and yet win the esteem of future generations (as would Nerval, Baudelaire, and Flaubert). The secret of this delayed success lies of course in the phenomenon of readability, which is a function of the duplicity and complexity of these texts—that is, of the reserves of interpretability they derive from the oppositional situation in which they were produced. That is why the first phase of French modernism was in many ways a game of "win who loses"—a game whose basic rules I hope to trace in this book.

*

Today the term "modernism" is generally *not* linked with duplicity, opposition, or failure; it is associated above all with what has come to be called "textual autonomy"—that is, a text's supposed liberty to conform to its "own laws," independent of mimetic, moral, or political requirements. The text is self-referential and concerned only with itself; it reveals its laws through its self-referentiality. In January 1852, a few weeks after the coup d'état, Flaubert—who had begun *Madame Bovary* the previous September—expressed his desire and dream to write "un livre sur rien, un livre sans attache extérieure, qui se tiendrait de lui-même par la force interne de son style" ["a book about nothing, a book dependent on nothing external for its support, which would be held together by the internal strength of its style"].[13] In Baudelaire's famous tribute to Gautier of 1859, we read the equally memorable lines: "La Poésie, pour peu qu'on veuille descendre en soi-même, rappeler ses souvenirs d'enthousiasme, n'a pas d'autre but qu'Elle-même; elle ne peut pas en avoir d'autre, et aucun poème ne sera si grand, si noble, si véritablement digne du nom de poème, que celui qui aura été écrit uniquement pour le plaisir d'écrire un poème." ["If a person is willing to probe within himself and to recall the enthusiasm of his youth, he will find that poetry has no end but itself; it can have no other purpose. No poem is so grand, so noble, so completely worthy of being called a poem, as the one that has been composed simply for the pleasure of writing poetry."][14]

There is therefore a strong affinity between the writers I see as the first modernists and the advocates of "l'art pour l'art," the aesthetic movement that began in the 1830s and that grew under the Second Empire into the apoliticism of Gautier, Banville, Leconte de Lisle, and others of the Parnasse group, who created poetry that was technically polished but thematically removed from the realities of the period. The two groups should not be confused, however. The facile identification of one group with the other is clearly mistaken; it results from an oversimplified and erroneous view of the phenomenon of self-reflexivity. So, at least, I shall argue in this book. For effects of self-figuration, by which a text folds back on itself, do not *close* the text in relation to its context but, quite to the contrary, *open* it to history in two ways. First, self-figuration splits the text into an object of interpretation (on the one hand) and an interpretive agent (on the other) that furnishes the context on which a grasp of the text's "meaning" depends. In this way the text defines itself as an enunciation by drawing attention to the pertinence of the situation from which it speaks to an appropriate reading of the text. And the second way the text is "opened" to history is therefore through the instance of reading presupposed by the text's self-figuration; it is the text's readability that guarantees its interpretive history (or "fortune," one might say) among successive groups of future readers. I will therefore argue that self-figuration is always readable as an index of historicity and that its readability always functions as an invitation to interpret the textual enunciation (or "speech act") in a historical manner, in relation to its social positioning. The paradox of modernism is that by marking itself in this way in relation to its historical context, the modernist text also calls attention to its desire for autonomy and to its attempt to escape from history by showing the contextual reasons that underlie them.

In this respect the "art for art's sake" movement and the Parnasse group are themselves symptomatic. Their texts affirm and call attention to their apoliticism by presenting themselves as objects among objects and by striving to attain the neutrality of an *énoncé*, a statement that would be pure structure (in contrast to an *énonciation*, which would be "oriented" and contextualized). But as a result, these texts betray the strength of the desire for neutrality and autonomy that animates them. Historically situated in spite of themselves, they speak of the presence and obsessive power of a social context that they conjure up by their very attempts to deny it, by their refusal to acknowledge it. In chapter 2 I will analyze one of Gautier's texts from this perspective.

Gautier and the Parnassians represent an extreme case, however. The modernists differ from them in that their desire for literary autonomization leads them not to avoid the contemporary context, but rather to call attention to it; they speak of it no less obsessively than "l'art pour l'art" attempts to ignore it. My point, however, is that this self-contextualizing is more the product of the *textual* function than of the *referential* function (i.e., part of the narrative function), even though in the work of authors like Nerval, Baudelaire, or Flaubert the referential function itself clearly addresses contemporary reality. Moreover, it is by figuring *the alienated situation of literary production* that the textual function makes it possible to infer its condemnation of the social context in which literature finds itself isolated and autonomized.

It is not enough, then, for a reader to pay close attention to the narrative message in these texts, since their true relation to history is readable only in their textual function. More precisely, it becomes fully apparent only through the *duplicitous relation* between textual and narrative functions. For in the final analysis it is this relation of duplicity that reveals the range of conflicts and contradictions within the text, the unresolved or only partly resolved tensions at work in it, that in turn constitute its elocutionary context. We can begin to see this if we continue our reading of the opening passage of *Madame Bovary*. If we pursue the hypothesis that the character of Charles is the site of the text's self-figuration, we are led to the following observations: (1) that there is a discrepancy between two contextualizations depending on whether one reads in terms of the narrative or the textual function; and (2) that in the textual function, the text is figured as an alienated discourse with respect to social language.

> Le Proviseur nous fit signe de nous rasseoir; puis se tournant vers le maître d'études:
> — Monsieur Roger, lui dit-il à demi-voix, voici un élève que je vous recommande, il entre en cinquième. Si son travail et sa conduite sont méritoires, il passera *dans les grands*, où l'appelle son âge.
> Resté dans l'angle, derrière la porte, si bien qu'on l'apercevait à peine, le *nouveau* était un gars de la campagne, d'une quinzaine d'années environ, et plus haut de taille qu'aucun de nous tous. Il avait les cheveux coupés droit sur le front, comme un chantre de village, l'air raisonnable et fort embarrassé. Quoiqu'il ne fût pas large des épaules, son habit-veste de drap vert à

boutons noirs devait le gêner aux entournures et laissait voir, par la fente des parements, des poignets rouges habitués à être nus. Ses jambes, en bas bleus, sortaient d'un pantalon jaunâtre très tiré par les bretelles. Il était chaussé de souliers forts, mal cirés, garnis de clous.

On commença la récitation des leçons. Il les écouta de toutes ses oreilles, attentif comme au sermon, n'osant même croiser les cuisses, ni s'appuyer sur le coude, et, à deux heures, quand la cloche sonna, le maître d'études fut obligé de l'avertir, pour qu'il se mît avec nous dans les rangs. (p. 3)

[The Headmaster motioned to us to be seated; then, turning to the teacher, he said to him in a low voice:

"Monsieur Roger, here is a pupil whom I recommend to your care; he'll be in the second. If his work and conduct are satisfactory, he will go into one of the upper classes, as becomes his age."

The new boy, standing in the corner behind the door so that he could hardly be seen, was a country lad of about fifteen, and taller than any of us. His hair was cut square on his forehead like a village choir boy; he looked reliable, but very ill at ease. Although he was not broad-shouldered, his short jacket of green cloth with black buttons must have been tight about the armholes, and showed at the opening of the cuffs red wrists accustomed to being bare. His legs, in blue stockings, looked out from beneath yellowish trousers, drawn tight by suspenders. He wore stout, ill-cleaned, hob-nailed boots.

We began reciting the lesson. He listened with all his ears, as attentive as if at a sermon, not daring even to cross his legs or lean on his elbow; and when at two o'clock the bell rang, the master was obliged to tell him to fall into line with the rest of us.] (pp. 3–4)

The referential function relies here on a certain number of conventional codes operating between narrator and narratee that allow us to identify Bovary as a *déclassé*, or social misfit. A new student (*un nouveau*) among the old ones (*les anciens*) in the class, he is also (as we now learn) a country boy (*un gars de la campagne*) in an urban milieu, since this *collège* (like other boarding schools of its kind) was probably in a moderately large town. As a bumpkin in town, he is no doubt uncomfortable dressed *en bourgeois* (that is, in middle-class town clothes). His clothes bother him physically as well: his heavy shoes and tight clothing reveal a boy who is in an adolescent growth spurt and remind us that adolescence is a difficult age in terms of both physical and social adjustment. Finally, he is out of place by virtue of being several years behind his classmates: a fifteen-year-old allowed to enter only *cinquième* (the French equivalent of seventh grade, and hence normally for twelve-year-olds). The disparity between his age and his intellectual capabilities is measured by the embarrassing shortness of his sleeves and pants.

From the beginning of his novel, Flaubert therefore presents us with the portrait of an *inadapté* or social misfit, about whom the narratee is assumed to share the point of view of the narrator, whose own perspective clearly identifies him with the group of students or *anciens* already fully assimilated to the school system. This identification is made clear by the fact that the narrator, who does not feel any need to explain the role of a headmaster or custodian, or the meaning of phrases such as *récitation des leçons* ("reciting lessons") or *se mettre dans les rangs* ("to line up"), does feel compelled to describe in some detail the new student (*le nouveau*), who constitutes the only element out of the ordinary in the eyes of the regular schoolboys (*les anciens*). It is of course Charles's character as a social misfit—out of his place and out of his "class"—that the students, with the active complicity of their teacher, will gleefully adapt to social conformity through various methods of hazing. Charles must learn to "line up with the rest of us" (*se mettre avec nous dans les rangs*).

On an ideological level, the narrative (in its narrative function) never questions the finality of the school as an institution that functions to identify misfits and make them conform to social codes and norms. By dutifully "reciting," "copying," and "memorizing" his exam answers—that is, by dint of repetition—Charles soon becomes practically indistinguishable from the others, except perhaps for the truly unusual quality of his very banality and mediocrity. His complete assimilation is confirmed a few chapters later, where we read: "La conversation de Charles était plate comme un trottoir de rue, et les idées de tout le monde y défilaient dans leur costume ordinaire, sans exciter d'émotion, de rire ou de rêverie" (p. 38) ["Charles's conversation was flat as a sidewalk, a place of passage for the ideas of everyman; they wore drab everyday clothes, and they inspired neither laughter nor dreams"] (p. 46). Here, of course, Charles is seen from Emma's point of view, whereas in the opening passage of the novel cited earlier, he is contextualized from the perspective of a narrator and narratee that situates him in terms of the school, its codes, and its social authority (represented by the headmaster). From this perspective he has only to learn "to line up with the others," and he will in due course pass into the class of older students or "grown ups" (*les grands*)—that is, he will be considered an adult.

The situation changes, however, and Charles is viewed with greater sympathy when he is considered in terms of the textual function, where he is no longer the referential object of the narrator-narratee relation but a more positive figure through which the novel represents itself. In this reading the place of the *nouveau*—a socially designated slot for people who are not (yet) in their place—is occupied by a character who is present but *scarcely there*. The new student is so dominated by the intimidating presence of the headmaster that he remains "back in the corner so that the door half hid him from view" (pp. 3–4). Barely visible, he remains immobilized, not daring to "even cross his legs or lean on his elbow," and plunged into a trancelike attention so deep that the teacher must rouse him from his daze to tell him to line up with the others. Moreover, he remains utterly silent until he is finally asked to give his name.

Charles's zero degree of presence exerts a power to surprise and to disturb the flow of everyday affairs no doubt to the extent that it manifests a kind of absence: an absence of interiority, an intellectual vacuum reflected in his clumsy exterior and absentminded look, but also in his anxious efforts to absorb the words of others through his rapt attention to his lessons: he is "all ears." By metonymic transference, the new student's cap will shortly be described as having "les profondeurs d'expression du visage d'un imbécile" (p. 4) ["unplumbed depths, like an idiot's face"] (p. 4). But already Charles appears here as the village idiot come to be educated in town—and as a Gilles-like buffoon mocked by the crowd.

Charles's idiocy and his quasi invisibility are clearly figurations of the Flaubertian ideal of "le livre sur rien": the book about nothing. But this unpolished, imbecilic bumpkin is simultaneously filled with good intentions that make him educable. Like a sponge soaking up water, Charles is eager to learn and to recite his lesson, to absorb the words one needs to know (and repeat), and to acquire the established customs that everyone is expected to follow—everything that can be learned without intelligence simply by imitating a standard model. In this regard his *vide intérieur*, or inner emptiness, is wonderfully adaptive, since it enables the perfect assimilation of this *déclassé* to the norms of society. This is the irony implicit in Charles's function as a self-reflexive figure of the text. For like Charles's idiocy, Flaubert's "book about nothing" can also be said, mutatis mutandis, to be always open to the repetitive, the banal—in short, to the forms of stupidity Flaubert calls *bêtise*. The *will not to be present* (while still continuing to exist) that is evident in the novel's style (and notably in the various techniques of impassibility that almost efface the narrator) seems to open up a kind of vacuum within the space of the text that is then filled by the language, thoughts, viewpoints, and judgments of *others*—that is, by the clichés, the vulgarity, sentimentalism, banality, egoism, and pettiness of the various characters. To these can be added all the equally conventional literary codes—codes of representation and narration—whose function is to ensure the intelligibility of the text as a "realist" discourse capable of mimetically reproducing "actions" within a certain "universe."

Yet this assimilation to banality that Charles desires so intensely poses a problem for the text. *Madame Bovary*, as a "book about nothing," must resolve the problem posed by the invasion of its own blankness, its "idiocy," by the stupidity, banality, and vulgarity—the *bêtise*—of a world that is foreign to it. It must assure itself of a margin of independence that will allow it to exist (unlike Charles) as an autonomous entity, despite its quasi invisibility and quasi absence. How could this be achieved? One might think of the "internal strength and cohesion" that Flaubert expects to derive from the formal network of "style"—something like what Proust called "le vernis des Maîtres" ["the polish of the Masters"]. But if *Madame Bovary* can claim the status of an autonomous text, this can in the end only be by virtue of the ironic reading it calls for, the kind of ironic reading that is illustrated by the way we have just been led to read Charles's character ironically as a self-reflexive figure. It is of course through the character of Emma—another crucial self-reflexive figure—that the novel expresses its desire for individualization and adventure in a world where it is not easy to distinguish between the romantic and the banal, individuality and cliché, adventure and repetition.

The implications of the text's self-figuration through Emma are extremely complex; I will therefore save my discussion of this aspect of *Madame Bovary* for the final chapter. Let me simply state here that the novel resembles its heroine (and differs from Charles) in its desire to distinguish itself and in its belief in the possibility of a certain "happiness" that nevertheless eludes it—the happiness of an autonomous existence different from and superior to the everyday world from which it necessarily draws its raw materials. Yet though the novel shares Emma's *bovarysme*, the distancing techniques by which her character is presented on the narrative level suggest that the text possesses a certain ironic knowledge of itself, a *vedersi vivere* as Pirandello would say, that distinguishes it, as self-ironic, from the way it appears to be submerged in its own contradictions and to share the insurmountable blindness of the nonironic Emma. Although its narrative detachment or "impassibility" produces a vacuum that allows the text to be invaded by everything it despises—to be overwhelmed by all the horror of modern life—irony (which is a product of reading and a manifestation of the textual function) comes to the rescue, exploiting this narrative discretion as a means of guaranteeing the text a certain margin of inviolable autonomy.

As I will demonstrate later, Flaubert's use of irony is far more complicated than this initial and somewhat schematic analysis might suggest. For the moment, let it suffice to say that the textual function serves above all to "ironize" (to undermine through the use of irony) the notion of "textual autonomy," while at the same time retaining—through this very same use of irony—a small margin of autonomy after all. So we have here a text that expresses its autonomy only through a language of emptiness and nothingness, a language of idiocy that throws into question any possibility of individualism in relation to its invasive context. Can idiocy easily be distinguished from sheer stupidity? *Le nouveau* knows that he can be assimilated rapidly into his new context, indeed that he is "always already" integrated into the known, the familiar, the usual. Similarly, the marginal—"resté dans l'angle, derrière la porte" ["standing in the corner behind the door"]—is destined like Charles to disappear into that other form of invisibility: the normal and the banal. Of course the greatest irony is that *Madame Bovary* is now a text that we read in class and that we refer to (for that reason) as a *classic*. The text's alienation derives therefore from the great difficulty it faces in trying to *distinguish* itself, to differentiate itself from what is not it. Flaubert's text suffers from an identity problem—from a malaise whose name, as I shall try to suggest, is melancholia.

*

Although the textual function in *Madame Bovary* forces us to problematize the whole notion of "textual autonomy," the duplicity of that text—whose meaning arises from the relation between narrative and textual functions—still emerges intact from our analyses. The character of Charles, for example, appears in a quite different light depending on whether he is read in terms of the narrative function or the textual function. Whereas the narratee is expected to approve (and in a sense to participate in) the series of hazings that mark Charles's initiation into student life and that force this *déclassé* to conform, the textual reader sees him instead as a figure whose value lies in his difference and his alienation. His assimilation therefore appears *normal* in the narrative function; but in the textual function it raises the question of textual autonomy in order to *problematize* it. Moreover, in an overall reading of Charles's character, it is his gradual conformity to social norms that allows us to articulate these two functions of the text with each other and to grasp the tensions they generate.

This latter point raises the crucial question of the relative weight one should give to the narrative and textual functions. One could, of course, point to Charles's marginal status to argue that a correspondingly insignificant role should be ascribed to the textual function he represents. In that case the reading of the novel would focus above all on the narrative function. This is, in fact, the way *Madame Bovary* has been read by most readers and notably by those who view the novel as a well-crafted "realistic" text about Charles and Emma's unhappy fate in rural Normandy. The documents from the 1857 trial of the novel clearly show that this was the usual reading of *Madame Bovary* among Flaubert's contemporaries. Indeed, the judicial examination was limited to whether the novel condemned Emma's "immorality" strongly enough to discourage other women from following her example. Given the absence of a readily identifiable narrator, this was of course difficult to demonstrate.

Pointing to the production of other similarly realistic and "immoral" works during the period, Dominick LaCapra suggests that *Madame Bovary* in fact drew the authorities' attention by virtue of the distinctive qualities and effects of its writing, whose *nouveauté* would have provoked a sense of vague discomfort, disturbance, and surprise that no reader could have been in a position to analyze.[15] This hypothesis is entirely plausible; but its implication is that even when the novel first appeared, its duplicity was already fully operational and caused the narrative function to overshadow and marginalize the textual function, whose concealed presence ("half hidden by the door") was nevertheless somehow still perceptible and could not be totally ignored.

Today this is no longer the case, and the current tendency is instead to give greater weight to the textual reading of the novel as opposed to a purely narrative reading. The text, of course, favors such a reading by the various ways it *perturbs* a narrative reading (by its free indirect style, the "absence" of a narrator, etc.). For example, although Charles is described as a marginalized character, the *description* of his marginalized status—motivated as it is by the surprise his entrance produces, the attention given him by the other students and hence by the narrator—dominates the textual space. It is Charles we are invited to read, and this highlighting of Charles as the focus of the text leads to a parallel highlighting of the textual function that is figured by him; its marginality, in short, accounts for its prominence. Seen in this light, the novel no longer reads as the story of the necessary assimilation of a *déclassé* but appears as a text bearing witness to the social conditions of its own production—conditions of alienation such that, in order to distinguish itself from the world of the headmaster, a text must resort to the idiocy of a "book about nothing." And because of the vacuum it creates, this idiocy in turn runs the risk of being invaded (and seems in fact to *call* for its own invasion) by the banal, everyday world where people sleep, pretend to work, and even when they are interrupted by something or someone *new*, pretend to be surprised. In this world, there is always an authority figure like the headmaster to quell excitement and restore order, "motioning to us to be seated."

The case of *Madame Bovary* therefore raises the question of the text's historical survival, since the court case brought against it shows that serious efforts were made to suppress it soon after its publication. If LaCapra's interpretation is accurate, one might conclude that, without resorting to direct deception, the novel (and other texts of its kind) employs a duplicitous strategy that makes use of the narrative function to deliver a relatively reassuring message while a more subversive and disturbing textual function hangs back, like Charles, half hidden but not completely out of sight. Yet this latent function can later become activated, thereby making the historical context of the text and the circumstances of its production readable for future generations of readers.

This is the strategy employed in both *Madame Bovary* and *Les Fleurs du mal* with such a close calculation of effect that they came very near to being suppressed by the courts. In keeping with the oppositional spirit, Baudelaire viewed this persecution as a mark of honor. Had his work been completely suppressed, however, any oppositional project it might have represented would have been neutralized. (As for "Sylvie," it was protected by its author's reputation as a harmless eccentric, which seems to have made its troubling textual characteristics—like the subversive complexity of "Aurélia"—invisible.)

This strategy of "readability" enables such texts to survive by outmaneuvering the alienating conditions in which they are produced, so as to make that production context available to future readers. They outlive their own alienating conditions of production. The success of this strategy depends on a writerly phenomenon: on a duplicitous gap set up between the narrative and textual functions, a discrepancy that makes reading the text an experience of instability and uncertainty. An empirical reader cannot avoid reading in terms of the narrative function; he or she would be mistaken not to pay attention to the textual function; yet these two functions are incompatible. Between them is a tension that is impossible to resolve, since what constitutes "normality" in the narrative function—Charles's conformity to social norms—is precisely what becomes problematic in the textual function. Reading the text thus becomes the experience of a certain decentering and of a kind of vaporization, since there is no central "subject" upon which to build a coherent structure that will *hold*. "Alles Ständische und Stehende verdampft," reads a famous line in the *Communist Manifesto* (1847) in its denunciation of bourgeois society: "All that is upright and substantial melts into fog."

It was, moreover, in the context of a historical analysis of the progressive "etherealization" of artistic discourse that Flaubert had proposed "the book about nothing" as an artistic ideal:

> Je crois que l'avenir de l'Art est dans ces voies, je le vois à mesure qu'il grandit s'éthérisant tant qu'il peut, depuis les pylônes égyptiens jusqu'aux lancettes gothiques, et depuis les poèmes de vingt mille vers des Indiens jusqu'aux jets de Byron; la forme en devenant habile s'atténue; . . . elle ne connaît plus d'orthodoxie et est libre comme chaque volonté qui la produit.
>
> [I believe the future of Art lies in this direction. I see it, as it has developed from its beginnings, growing progressively more ethereal, from Egyptian pylons to Gothic lancets, from the 20,000-line Hindu poems to the effusions of Byron. Form, in becoming more skillful, becomes attenuated; . . . there is no longer any orthodoxy, and form is as free as the will of its creator.][16]

Thus in art the increasing skill of craftsmanship brings about a progressive attenuation or "etherealization" of its substance, while the erosion of authority (or what Flaubert calls "orthodoxy") leads to a kind of randomness, a dispersion of individual or free will on the part of the artist. These formulations clearly have political resonances. For in the same letter of 16 January 1851, writing in the aftermath of the coup d'état and the inescapable evidence of the failure of 1848, Flaubert adds: "Cet affranchissement de la matérialité se retrouve en tout, et les gouvernements l'ont suivi, de-

puis les despotismes orientaux jusqu'aux socialismes futurs." ["This progressive shedding of the burden of tradition can be observed everywhere:
governments have gone through a similar evolution, from Oriental despo-
tisms to the socialisms of the future."][17] Flaubert cannot escape drawing a
parallel between the "etherealization" of art and the pulverizing of socialist
hopes, which by 1852 had been irreparably shattered and pushed into the
future. (But he may well have been thinking also of the effects on "public
order" of the events of February 1848 themselves, and of the instability
they introduced into government affairs of whatever political stamp.)

Like Flaubert, his exact contemporary Baudelaire associated the Second
Empire with Oriental despotism, but he compared it even more directly to
the experience of vaporization characteristic of modernity. As I will propose in chapter 5, Baudelaire saw the reign of Napoleon III as the embodiment of a social repression capable of vaporizing, like Satan, "le riche
métal de notre volonté" [the precious metal of our will"].[18] It is within the
context of this dual vaporization—of defeated socialisms gone up in smoke
and willpower fogged by torpor—but also in the nausea and instability
induced by a decentered discursive world that one must situate the form of
historical melancholy of which the etherealized texts of modernism are for
us both the symptom and the trace.

ANGER VAPORIZED

Writing on Gautier's poem "Tristesse en mer," Madeleine Cottin astutely remarks that "Gautier transcends ordinary seasickness [*mal de mer*] by transforming it (and with such art!) into a *mal du siècle*."[1] I am not sure, however, that it is completely accurate to speak of transcendence and transformation. The poem perhaps implies, more simply, a metaphorical equivalence between melancholy and nausea, which have in common a certain decentering of the world, an instability of being, and even the desire to end it all that seems to result. Rather than hyperbolizing—a hyperbolical transformation of seasickness into *spleen*—this poem seems, in my opinion, to reflect a desire for euphemizing, treating melancholy as a simple case of nausea.

It is by attributing these two phenomena—sadness and nausea—to weather conditions during a crossing of the English Channel that Gautier's text brings about its real transfiguration. For through the description of a rough sea crossing experienced by an individual traveler, the poem manages both to naturalize and to personalize a social phenomenon of "historical" melancholy that, in certain texts of the 1850s, seems to stand in opposition to the official values of order and conformism, as well as to the unofficial value of pleasure, in a way that appears quite specific—although generally camouflaged as personal experience and with frequent recourse to meterological alibis. It was, for example, in the midst of the new Paris, crisscrossed by the "strategic" boulevards of Baron Haussmann and filled with a populace given over to the whip of Pleasure ("le fouet du Plaisir"), that the Baudelairean poet would carry his spleen.

Yet the epidemic of ennui experienced by that society (at least by its bourgeoisie)—the ennui denounced by Baudelaire in "Au lecteur," reflected in Emma Bovary's "exile" in Normandy, and depicted in Daumier's drawings of couples at the theater, in their parlors, and in their beds—seems less an oppositional phenomenon with respect to the conditions of

Honoré Daumier, "Six Mois de Mariage" ["Six Months of Marriage"]. Notice the thematization of yawning, a pictorial representation of emptiness capable of swallowing the universe, as the Baudelaire of "Au lecteur" might say. Also notice the figuration of ennui as uniformity, repetition, and "in-difference" reflected in the symmetry and resemblance between the figures of the couple, their clothing, and their expressions. From *Mœurs conjugales*. Reproduced by permission of the Huntington Library, San Marino, California.

bourgeois existence than their direct outcome. This outbreak of ennui is a straightforward symptom of the bourgeois "order"—of the regularity and uniformity of existence, the absence of adventure and of risk, required for the smooth functioning of industry and commerce. It took the perspicacity of certain artists to sense the strength of the anger and revolt hidden or repressed beneath the calm surface of ennui and to transform it from a manifestation of official order into an oppositional *spleen*.

This word "spleen," while it expresses the English (and hence modern) character of this malaise, also permits us to probe the characteristics of this "new" *vague à l'âme* by referring back to the ancient medical theory of humors. Etymologically related to French *colère* ("anger") and to the English word *choler*, both derived from *cholē*, the Greek term for bile, melancholy was viewed as an invasion of the brain by mists or vapors rising from the spleen, the source of black, bilious humor. Melancholy was thought to result from the rising up of lower forces from within that people sought to suppress, as they would a vomiting of gall (or yellow humor). It was seen as an attack that endangered the seat of reason and order, causing dizziness and nausea, fainting spells and weakness (commonly referred to as an attack of "the vapors"). In the more serious cases, these vapors produced a state of "madness" that we would now call angst or depression, but that nineteenth-century doctors diagnosed as "melancholia." Nerval viewed Dürer's angel as a figuration of this melancholy, which he in turn emblematized in the image of *le soleil noir* ("the black sun") in his poem "El Desdichado":

> Ma seule *étoile* est morte, — et mon luth constellé
> Porte le *soleil noir* de la *Mélancolie*.

> [My one *star*'s dead, and my constellated lute
> Bears the *Black Sun* of *Melancholia*.][2]

If the sun is black, it is because it is covered by a veil of mourning. Nerval naturalized his vision of a melancholy-prone universe by alluding to overcast weather conditions: for example, to mist or cloudy skies in France (or to dust in Cairo). Similarly, Emma Bovary's vision of the city of Rouen ("noyée dans le brouillard, elle s'élargissait au-delà des ponts, confusément" ["smothered by fog, it spread in a blur beyond the bridges"]) and the frequent allusions in Baudelaire to Parisian fog "inondant tout l'espace" ["flooding all space"], refer meteorological representations to mental and psychic space, as Arden Reed has argued,[3] and more specifically to invasions of the "vapors." The precise meaning and function of these allusions to weather vary, of course, from one author to another. Nerval's Valois, for example, represents a space that is poeticized or euphemized in response to a space that is increasingly invaded by the utilitarian needs of industrialization and rationalization (railways, factories, urbanization); corresponding to these misty landscapes are the quavering, modulating voices of peasant women, figuring a certain poetics of indeterminacy and instability, which is that of the texts themselves (see chapter 4). In *Madame Bovary*, on the other hand, the fog over Rouen can be read as an emanation of collective passion: "comme si les cent vingt mille âmes qui palpitaient là eussent envoyé toutes à la fois la vapeur des passions qu'[Emma] leur supposait" ["as if the one hundred twenty thousand hearts that beat there had all at once exhaled the vapor of the passions that (Emma) imagined them to feel"]. Much like the surroundings of Yonville (which are transformed into a quasi-marine landscape during Emma's horseback ride with Rodolphe), the foggy city is an index of the intensity of Emma's romantic vision as it struggles against the dominant mood of ennui (see chapter 7).

As for fog in Baudelaire's poetry—"sale et jaune" ["dirty yellow"] in "Les Sept Vieillards," "muraille immense" ["immense wall"] in "Le Cygne"—it is an urban smog whose essential component is factory smoke, those "fleuves de charbon" ["streams of coal smoke"] that in "Paysage" rise upward toward what is called, with nicely ironic anachronism, the "firmament." In "Les Sept Vieillards," this invasive fog results in the decomposition of space and in the blurring of spatial distinctions, such as those between street and river, as well as between the exterior landscape of the city ("le décor") and the inner landscape of the poet's soul ("l'âme de l'acteur"):

> Un matin, cependant que dans la triste rue
> Les maisons, dont la brume allongeait la hauteur,
> Simulaient les deux quais d'une rivière accrue,
> Et que, décor semblable à l'âme de l'acteur,
>
> Un brouillard sale et jaune inondait tout l'espace,
> Je suivais, roidissant mes nerfs comme un héros
> Et discutant avec mon âme déjà lasse,
> Le faubourg secoué par les lourds tombereaux.
>
> [One morning, while in the grim streets
> The houses, which appeared taller in the fog,
> Resembled the two banks of a swollen river,
> And when, like stage scenery matching the actor's mood,

A dirty yellow fog flooded all space,
I roamed, steeling my nerves like a hero
And talking with my already weary soul,
Through the old city neighborhood shaken by each heavy
      van.][4]

There is, then, an effect of generalized indifferentiation that is confirmed and intensified by the sudden appearance of the first old man, and even more so by the frightening proliferation of sameness to which the unhappy "I" of the poem is then subjected as the old men multiply:

Tout à coup, un vieillard dont les guenilles jaunes
Imitaient la couleur de ce ciel pluvieux, . . .

M'apparut. On eût dit que sa prunelle trempée
Dans le fiel. . . .

[Suddenly, an old man whose yellow rags
Imitated the color of that rainy sky

Appeared to me. It looked as though the pupils
Of his eyes had been soaked in bile. . . .]

It is the threatening nature of this apparition and proliferation that the poem emphasizes, interpreting it as a reminder of mortality, a memento mori—"Aurais-je, sans mourir, contemplé le huitième . . . ?" ["Could I have survived an eighth such apparition . . . ?"]—and above all as a danger to reason and its authority:

Vainement ma raison voulait prendre la barre:
La tempête en jouant déroutait ses efforts,
Et mon âme dansait, dansait, vieille gabarre
Sans mâts, sur une mer monstrueuse et sans bords.

[Vainly my reason sought to take the helm:
But the storm's antics foiled its efforts,
And my soul went dancing on, an old and mastless scow,
Across a monstrous and shoreless sea.]

In writing "Les Sept Vieillards," did Baudelaire perhaps recall the image of the boat tossing on the stormy sea in Gautier's 1852 poem "Tristesse en mer" ("le vaisseau danse, l'eau tournoie")? Despite important differences in tone, the two poems have in common the theme of threatened identity.

By blurring distinctions, the Baudelairean fog creates effects of resemblance that the poem depends on for its very unity; yet at the same time it threatens the stability of a well-ordered world, in which essential differences would be maintained, as well as the identity of an ego that wishes to control that world and "to take the helm." Under the influence of these foggy "vapors," space decomposes, since it is no longer centered around a stable ego and hence no longer "oriented." That is why, in cases of melancholy, there is always a feeling not only of indifferentiation, but also of lack or loss; it is always a state of mourning, similar as Freud says to *Trauerarbeit*—even if the cause of grief remains obscure. Nerval's nostalgia ("Ma seule *étoile* est morte"), Baudelaire's remembrance of "le vert paradis des amours enfantines" ["the green paradise of childish loves"], the "happiness" to which Emma aspires, and aesthetic aspirations to an *ideal* acknowledged as unattainable (Gautier's ideal of beauty, Baudelaire's "anywhere out of this world")—all these vague, objectless desires betray the feeling that something essential is henceforth lost and imply a sense of irreparable *rupture*, a feeling of discontinuity between a past in which enthusiasm was still possible and still made sense and a present that labors instead under a painful consciousness of lack.

The poets personalize and privatize this lack. The irreparable loss or frustrated desire that characterizes their existence always arises either as a personal matter—as in Nerval's claim never to have seen his mother ("Je n'ai jamais vu ma mère") or Baudelaire's nostalgic dream of lost bliss ("J'ai longtemps habité sous de vastes portiques . . . " ["I long dwelt beneath spacious porticoes . . ."])—or else as an aesthetic matter: the obsession with absolute beauty in Gautier, Baudelaire, and Flaubert. However, this *privatization* and *aestheticization* of frustration and alienation can themselves be read as symptoms of the period and specifically as a consequence of a phenomenon of depoliticization that does not prevent these vague individual nostalgias from betraying a feeling of collective loss. Although obviously such phenomena are always overdetermined, if there is an aesthetics and an erotics of *lack* during this period, it is in part because a certain portion of the population, comprising those who had been young and enthusiastic in the 1840s, had lived through a bitter experience of loss in the political sphere.

Indeed the year 1848, between February and June, was a time of massive disillusion for this generation. Nerval was about to turn forty, Gautier was three years younger, and Baudelaire and Flaubert were both twenty-seven.

The "June days" ended the dreams of love and harmony, the enthusiasm
for social reform and the utopian projects of the previous decade, which
had been a time of "secular religions"[5]—all these hopes for the future were
definitively crushed. June 1848 marked the end of a universalizing fantasy
as the bourgeoisie realized that it constituted a class, with class interests to
defend against other interests—and notably against those of the working
class, which consequently began to acquire its reputation as a "dangerous
class" to be kept in check by means of vigilant oppression. When, in a letter
of March 1852 explaining his nonparticipation in the plebiscite, Baudelaire wrote "LE 2 DECEMBRE m'a *physiquement dépolitiqué*" ["What happened on the 2nd of December *physically depolitified* me"], it is not difficult
to hear in the coined word *dépolitiqué* ("depolitified")—which is not the
same as *dépolitisé* ("depoliticized")—an echo of the word *dégoûté* ("dis-
gusted").[6]

Physically repelled, the poet then added in characteristic fashion: "If I
had voted, I could only have voted for myself. Perhaps the future belongs
to the *déclassés*."[7] In chapter 1 we saw in Flaubert's text something of this
feeling of—or desire for?—alienation or *déclassement*, which in Baudelaire's case is accompanied and supported so clearly by a parallel desire for
privatization. It is a double alienation, since in breaking his class ties the
déclassé knows that he remains vulnerable to a second alienation, which is
an unwanted or undesirable class identification (*classement*). This question
aside, in "Le Voyage" Baudelaire was soon to intensify—but also to continue to privatize—the expression of this disillusionment concerning earlier utopian hopes:

> Notre âme est un trois-mâts cherchant son Icarie;
> Une voix retentit sur le pont: "Ouvre l'œil!"
> Une voix de la hune, ardente et folle, crie:
> "Amour . . . gloire . . . bonheur!" Enfer! c'est un écueil!
>
> Chaque îlot signalé par l'homme de vigie
> Est un Eldorado promis par le Destin;
> L'imagination qui dresse son orgie
> Ne trouve qu'un récif aux clartés du matin.
>
> [Our soul is a schooner seeking its Icaria;
> A voice resounds from the deck: "Open your eyes!"
> A voice from the topmast, ardent and wild, cries:
> "Love! . . . glory! . . . happiness! . . ." Damnation! It's a reef!

Each small island hailed by the lookout,
Is an El Dorado promised by Destiny;
But the imagination, readying its orgy,
Finds only a sandbar by the morning light.][8]

(Here again the poet makes use of metaphors drawn from sea travel to express the destabilization of a universe in which the loss of illusions is inevitable:

Et nous allons, suivant le rythme de la lame,
Berçant notre infini sur le fini des mers.

[And we go on, following the rhythm of the waves,
Rocking our infinite on the finite sea.][9])

It is easy to imagine that the sense of temporal break brought on by such disillusionment must have shaken the identity of those who experienced it: they no longer recognized themselves, and at the core of their being, memory revealed only a lack. But in such circumstances memory also becomes a source of unhappiness and perturbed consciousness by virtue of the very continuity it provides. On the one hand, nostalgia for a lost past is compounded by the feeling of having lived through a period of rupture and of having become a site of fragmentation, dispersal, and scatter. The memory of people who have, in this sense, survived their own death seems to consist only of residues and remains, the "bric-à-brac confus" described in "Le Cygne," and therefore raises the question of its relevance to the new reality that emerged after the rupture. Nerval was the poet of memory in this sense—a memory that was both nostalgic and fragmentary, incomplete and out of touch with the present.

At the same time, however—and this is the second source of troubled consciousness—memory is haunted by the specter of remorse, of regrets that one cannot forget or break free from and that continually resurface. Although Nerval, perhaps more than any other of his generation, is the poet of guilt and of lost opportunities, and although the "bric-à-brac" theme emerges also in Baudelaire, the latter's truly obsessional theme is that of memory as the burden of remorse—an oppressive, corrosive *excess* of memory. In "Spleen" 76 ("J'ai plus de souvenirs que si j'avais mille ans"), he would write:

Je suis un cimetière abhorré de la lune,
Où comme des remords se traînent de longs vers
Qui s'acharnent toujours sur mes morts les plus chers.

[I am a graveyard abhorred by the moon,
Where, like bitter regrets, long worms crawl about
And continue to feed hungrily on my dearest dead.][10]

And again, in "Le Cygne":

Et mes chers souvenirs sont plus lourds que des rocs.

[And my fond memories weigh heavier than rocks.][11]

Memory is therefore a double or even triple source of painful self-consciousness, since the remembrance of lack and loss is accompanied by the burden of an obsessive sense of irreparable failure, as well as by a lightness of being, a sense of fragmentation and dispersion of identity, that makes one feel like a living residue.

Who can judge the effect of the missed opportunities of 1848 and the failures of 1848–51 on the emergence of this thematics, clearly overdetermined as it is? Those who lived through the events of May 1968 and who—like the generation of 1848—experienced, in the space of a few weeks, the dramatic swing from enthusiasm and exaltation to disillusion and the sense of an irreparably lost opportunity could perhaps bear witness to the effect of such an experience. In any case the Second Empire, given its historical character, could only inspire bitter and disillusioned reflections regarding the relation of modernity to time, history, and "progress." By actively prolonging the social and economic policies of the July Monarchy (industrial, commercial, and colonial expansion as well as modernization, urbanization, and the development of an infrastructure), the government pushed aside and ignored the enthusiastic desire for social change that had marked the spirit of February. Instead, the new regime underlined the continuity of capitalist history as a steady march toward "progress" (which was quite understandably the object of Baudelaire's rage). During the same period Paris was transformed into a huge construction site, a visual image of entropy and disorder, which Baudelaire describes in "Le Cygne": "palais neufs, échafaudages, blocs, / Vieux faubourgs" ["new mansions, scaffolding, blocks of stone, / Old neighborhoods"].[12] The transformation of the capital suggested the possibility of constructing a new world; at the same time, however, it cast doubt on the quality of this new construction in relation to a past considered finer and nobler.

For like Marx witnessing the coup d'état, the French had the feeling that history was repeating itself and maintaining its continuity only by growing steadily worse, presenting itself "the first time as tragedy, the second time as farce," as Marx put it in the famous line from *Dix-huit Brumaire*. Under such conditions, confronted by such a model of history, writers naturally asked themselves *how* to write and what *kind* of work to create that would convey the feeling of dislocation and lack of center, the dispersion of being, the haunting sense of failure, error, and wasted opportunities. Such writing could only be a work of melancholy.

Later, in his notebooks, Baudelaire recalled the rage he felt in 1851: his "fureur au coup d'état." [13] We can easily imagine this anger; but at the same time we perceive how difficult it was for it to achieve direct expression in a France that had become "depolitified" and dominated by censorship. The only available outlets for this rage lay in turning it inward against oneself (giving rise to a thematics of remorse) or (as was notably the case of Flaubert and Baudelaire) in transforming it into a loathing for politics in general and, in particular, for any type of socialist "daydreams" or revolutionary efforts. (See, for example, Baudelaire's diatribe against utopian authors at the beginning of his prose poem "Assommons les pauvres!" and Flaubert's treatment of the feverish agitation of 1848 in *L'Education sentimentale*.)

Anger at the 1851 coup d'état could be openly expressed only by those living outside France, and Hugo would be the only writer to do so, reviving political satire on the model of Juvenal from his exile in Jersey. In France, where such violence was blocked by self-censorship, this anger could be expressed only in a sublimated (and hence repressed) form by becoming a writing of melancholy. For melancholia is anger vaporized, the result of repression and a sign of the return of the repressed. In the writing of melancholy, the violent reaction of rage to the 1851 coup d'état, itself violently repressed (remember what happened in June), could "express itself" in a way that partly eluded the censor, that is, by becoming readable. At the center, where the melancholic is aware of lack, we shall therefore read unexpressed anger, and we shall see the uncentered universe of melancholy as a site of repressed violence (see especially chapter 5). In other words, melancholy is not a "message" to receive but a text to interpret.

For melancholic writing is not necessarily writing that thematizes sadness; rather, it espouses the decentering and the vaporization of being that are the principal features of melancholia. Arden Reed was the first to decipher Baudelaire's meteorological mists as the figure of a kind of writing that was itself vaporized, shifting, and unstable—as a textual smoke screen that would fulfill the opium dream alluded to in *Les Paradis artificiels*, in which the author, instead of smoking his pipe, would be smoked by it (as in "La Pipe").[14] I will draw on Reed's argument to advance my own that modernist writing is a writing of melancholy by virtue of the split between the narrative and textual functions that defines it. This gap or "play" in the text allows for the ideological construction of a communicative discourse (it does not deny the power of the narrative subject). At the same time, however, it produces a form of textuality that is more diffuse, more mobile, and more difficult to grasp because of its *missing center*—that is, because there is now only a readable subject of enunciation, in lieu of the so-called *sujet d'énoncé*. In my discussion of the opening passage of *Madame Bovary*, I pointed to the instability arising there from the conjunction of a narrative discourse that is centered and a textuality that undermines any notion of center. In Flaubert's novel the "idiocy" of the text is in conflict with the invasive stupidity of the outside world, from which it must distinguish itself at all costs. We will see that the fundamental problem of literary "spleen" is likewise one of identity: to distinguish itself from the "social" discourse of ennui.

Since it is the site of a faltering individual identity, it is not surprising, then, that modernist writing, as a product of vaporized anger, is also the site of a fascinating exploration of the relations between what must inevitably be called (almost without anachronism) the conscious and the unconscious. As an outcome of political trauma, the repression that followed, and the self-censorship that was practiced thereafter, people seem to have become gradually aware of a fundamental split and of a play between the "I" (the seat of consciousness and reason) and certain psychic depths (the repository of repressed thoughts and feelings). There is an abyss that the conscious self is unaware of or that at most it dimly senses; but it is the source of destabilizing vapors that rise up and invade the mind in a way that cannot be ignored. The double, duplicitous nature of the literary discourse of the period—faithful to the narrative function (with its knowable, centered, and fully locatable subject) but already beginning to probe in its textual function the liberating yet frightening implications of the uncentered signifier—consequently had the character, already, of an "awareness" of the unconscious. Or perhaps of an awareness of the "unconscious"?

*

What characterizes a text like "Tristesse en mer" (and by extension the work of Gautier, of which I take it to be representative) is a kind of double self-censorship. In this poem melancholy is understood as an outcome of the repression of violent forces, just as seasickness results from an effort to keep one's balance when a ship is agitated by the movement of the sea. But this melancholy itself is the object of an attempt at inhibition and euphemization, in the way a seasick passenger will try to suppress nausea and the urge to vomit, while feeling tempted to put an end to the struggle by jumping into the sea. In Gautier's text the rise of violent forces characterizing melancholy is felt both as a temptation and as a danger—as a temptation to end it all and to annihilate an identity that is already weakened and suffering, that is, the identity of the melancholic, yet at the same time as a danger of "drowning" a social self that, as we will see, the poem refuses to renounce. Reading this strikingly beautiful poem, we therefore witness a drama: the identity struggle of the lyrical "I" (the equivalent here of the narrative "I" of prose writing) as it resists a tempting textual dissolution of the self by clinging to the *garde-fou* or handrail provided by social communication. It is this clinging to social identity that gives significance to the work of euphemization and to the deployment of understatement (litotes) we observe in the poem.

We realize this, moreover, as early as the title, where *tristesse* ("sadness") scarcely captures the distress bordering on suicidal longings expressed in the poem itself. Similarly, the phrase *en mer* ("at sea"), which might suggest a simple pleasure excursion, hardly gives an inkling of the turbulent waves encountered during this stormy crossing of the English Channel— a storm that itself, no doubt, bears little comparison to the gales of the open sea.

> TRISTESSE EN MER
> Les mouettes volent et jouent;
> Et les blancs coursiers de la mer,
> Cabrés sur les vagues, secouent
> Leurs crins échevelés dans l'air.
>
> Le jour tombe; une fine pluie
> Eteint les fournaises du soir,
> Et le steam-boat crachant la suie
> Rabat son long panache noir.
>
> Plus pâle que le ciel livide,
> Je vais au pays du charbon,
> Du brouillard et du suicide;
> — Pour se tuer le temps est bon.

Mon désir avide se noie
Dans le gouffre amer qui blanchit;
Le vaisseau danse, l'eau tournoie,
Le vent de plus en plus fraîchit.

Oh! Je me sens l'âme navrée;
L'Océan gonfle, en soupirant,
Sa poitrine désespérée,
Comme un ami qui me comprend.

Allons, peines d'amour perdues,
Espoirs lassés, illusions
Du socle idéal descendues,
Un saut dans les moites sillons!

A la mer, souffrances passées,
Qui revenez toujours, pressant
Vos blessures cicatrisées
Pour leur faire pleurer du sang!

A la mer, spectres de mes rêves,
Regrets aux mortelles pâleurs
Dans un cœur rouge ayant sept glaives,
Comme la Mère des douleurs.

Chaque fantôme plonge et lutte
Quelques instants avec le flot
Qui sur lui ferme sa volute
Et l'engloutit dans un sanglot.

Lest de l'âme, pesant bagage,
Trésors misérables et chers,
Sombrez, et dans votre naufrage
Je vais vous suivre au fond des mers!

Bleuâtre, enflé, méconnaissable,
Bercé par le flot qui bruit,
Sur l'humide oreiller du sable
Je dormirai bien cette nuit!

. . . Mais une femme dans sa mante
Sur le pont assise à l'écart,
Une femme jeune et charmante
Lève vers moi son long regard.

Dans ce regard, à ma détresse
La Sympathie aux bras ouverts
Parle et sourit, sœur ou maîtresse.
Salut, yeux bleus! bonsoir, flots verts!

Les mouettes volent et jouent;
Et les blancs coursiers de la mer,
Cabrés sur les vagues, secouent
Leurs crins échevelés dans l'air.

[SADNESS AT SEA
The seagulls fly and play;
And the white coursers of the sea,
Straining against the waves, shake
Their tangled manes in the air.

Night falls; a misty rain
Puts out the furnace blazes of the evening,
And the soot-spitting steamboat
Lowers its long black plume.

And I, paler than the livid sky,
For the land of soot and smoke,
Fog and suicide am bound;
— The weather is just right for suicide.

My burning desire drowns
In the bitter white swirling waves;
The boat dances, the water churns,
The wind grows suddenly cooler.

Ah! I feel sick at heart;
The Ocean swells its grieving breast,
Sighing like a friend
Who understands me.

Away! lost love's despair,
Worn-out hopes, illusions
Fallen from their pedestals!
One short leap into the deep, wet furrows!

Into the sea! past sufferings
That continually return to haunt me,
Pressing on your scabby wounds
To make them weep fresh tears of blood!

Into the sea! specters of my dreams,
Deathly pale regrets buried
In a crimson heart pierced with seven swords,
Like the Mother of all Sorrows.

Each ghostly grief sinks and struggles
A few moments in the swirling waves
Which then close in
And swallow it with a sob.

Soul's ballast, heavy baggage,
Miserable, precious treasures—
Sink! and in your shipwreck,
I'll follow you to the bottom of the sea!

Deathly blue, swollen beyond recognition,
Rocked by the sounding waves,
I'll sleep well tonight
On the damp pillow of the sand!

. . . But then a woman wrapped in a cloak
And seated by herself on the deck,
A young, charming woman,
Turns her gaze toward me in one long look.

In her eyes Sympathy with outstretched arms
Speaks and smiles to me in my distress,
As would a sister or a lover,
Welcome, blue eyes! Adieu, green waves!

The seagulls fly and play;
And the white coursers of the sea,
Straining against the waves, shake
Their tangled manes in the air.][15]

The first three stanzas situate the "I" of the poem in a quasi-impressionist landscape—a moving seascape (perhaps recalling some painting by Turner) depicting the flight of seagulls and the clippers "shaking their tangled manes" as they strain against the high waves. It is a landscape in which distinctions—between air and water, above and below—are blurred, since the seagulls fly low to play with the waves rising in the air. To this are added weather descriptions that give an overall impression of darkness and enclosure: the misty rain that "puts out the furnace blazes of the evening," the "soot-spitting steamboat" lowering its "long black plume." There is a hint of Nerval's "black sun" and of the Baudelairean landscape of spleen: the fog and the lowering sky bearing down like a cover. At the same time, Gautier represents a world that is unbalanced, destabilized, fluid. In this context the "pallor" of the "I" winds up signifying something other than a Byronic temperament or incipient seasickness—something like an identity that has been invaded and weakened in the individual moving toward the "land of soot and smoke, fog and suicide," that is to say, toward the modern. (England as the most industrialized country of the world, the land of spleen and pea soup fogs, was a cliché of the period.) The "steam-boat" (a recent loan word in French) struggling in the turbulent waters of the Channel is an obvious incarnation of this English-style modernity.

The long development that follows (in stanzas 4–11) explores the theme of suicide introduced in the last verse of stanza 3: "—Pour se tuer le temps est bon" (literally, "it's good weather for killing oneself"). There, aboard a ship floundering in a stormy sea, we find a disheartened soul in the grip of an intense desire to drown himself. The relation—etymological, semantic, or poetic—between the words "désir avide," "âme navrée," "se noyer," and "naufrage," points to *un désir du vide* beyond the "désir avide"—a desire for obliteration into nothingness. For it is indeed the temptation of suicide as a flight into the void that the ocean represents; the despair of that "friend who understands me" is in fact a projection of the subject's own despair. (Moreover, alongside the subject's narcissism, the substitution of the word "ocean" for the English Channel indicates on his part a certain tendency toward hyperbole and dramatization, a sign of the somewhat excessive importance the subject gives himself and that the poem subtly deflates.) In other words, for the subject of the poem, yielding to the temptation to throw himself into the sea is the same as yielding to his own despair—obliterating the self that suffers by giving in to the source of that suffering as it wells up within.

Thus the poem concerns an inner drama. That is why, in stanzas 6–8, it takes stock of the melancholic subject's memories in order to explore his troubled identity—a present identity that consists of disillusion ("lost love's despair, / Worn-out hopes, illusions / Fallen from their pedestals"), but also of past sufferings that continually return to haunt him. A locus of loss and simultaneously of continuity—hope is worn out, past suffering survives—the self is haunted by *ghosts*. The "specters of my dreams" in stanza 8 recall the disenchantments evoked in stanza 6, just as the "deathly pale regrets" recall the painful obsessions of stanza 7. But spectral dreams and pale regrets share a ghostlike quality, in the faded reality of the first and the refusal to die of the second, as well as in their power to inflict suffering by transfixing the subject's heart as if (another piece of self-aggrandizement) he were Our Lady of Sorrows.

In stanzas 9–11, a change of theme is introduced by the dream of casting these ghosts into the sea and watching them disappear in the swirling waves, swallowed up by a sob (a liberating explosion of tears rising from the diaphragm, not unlike vomiting). The contents of memory—earlier described as insubstantial and ghostlike—now become heavy ("Soul's ballast, heavy baggage"), the better to imagine them swallowed up by the waves: what earlier lacked consistency becomes a heavy burden to make it easier to dispose of. Thereupon the identity of the "I"—earlier experienced as weakened and attenuated, reduced to ghostlike memories—becomes a heavy object in turn, able to disappear beneath the waves just as easily as the memories that compose it: "Sink! and in your shipwreck, / I'll follow you to the bottom of the sea!"

The reverie of an easy death ("une mort facile") is therefore succeeded by a dream of a happy death ("une mort heureuse"), as Bachelard would have said: a short plunge to the bottom of the sea. A stanza with almost Rimbaud-like resonances (as in "Bateau ivre") sounds the climactic note, or rather reaches a suspension point that indefinitely prolongs and defers resolution of this suicidal train of thought. In a dreamlike trance, the "I" imagines itself "Rocked by the sounding waves," sleeping "On the damp pillow of the sand." Note that the subject does not imagine himself *dead*, but sees himself transfigured into a new identity that one might call "abyssal." It is an identity of the depths, in which one is saturated with water and—"deathly blue, swollen beyond recognition"—given over to the sea and to sleep.

However, the suspension points also close the parenthetical reflection on suicide that began at the dash preceding the last verse of stanza 3: "— Pour se tuer le temps est bon" ["— The weather is just right for suicide"]. The "I" of the poem is roused from his suicidal reverie by the figure of a woman—a vision of stability (the word *assise* has connotations of firmness) amid the movement of the boat and the sea. This female figure restores a sense of center and balance to the situation, despite (or perhaps because of) the fact that—in accordance with the masculinist ideology of the nineteenth century—she remains modestly to the side, apart from the others, as one would *expect* a respectable woman to do. No longer abandoned in a universe in disarray (like the "Mother of all Sorrows"), but the object of a female gaze, the subject is silently greeted and—by virtue of the play on words evoked by the word *salut* (which means both "greetings" and "salvation")—*saved* by the virginal figure of the charming young woman. (The iconographic details of the woman's cloak and blue eyes clearly contrast with the images of the seven swords and the "Mother of all Sorrows" in stanza 8.) In the long look of sympathy that the woman gives him, the subject of the poem finds an *amie*, a female friend whose reassuring presence contrasts with the desperate yet reassuring swell of the Channel, the male *ami* whose "grieving breast, [sighs] like a friend who understands." Thus, at the climactic moment, in place of a metaphysical distress arising from the blurring of difference and the narcissistic temptation of solitary despair (the "friendly" ocean as a projection of the melancholic self), there is now spiritual (and specifically religious) consolation and the recovery of inner serenity through the social communicability that is established with the woman (the sympathy in her smile and the exchange of greetings implied by the "Salut, yeux bleus" that responds to her gaze). All this is a function of the restoration of sexual difference and the conventions of gender.[16]

So the initial quatrain, which was troubling and vaguely threatening in the somber context of the beginning, takes on a new meaning and a joyous tone when it recurs at the end, transformed by the changed mood of the subject, whose feeling of gaiety is now projected into it. The poem mobilizes the pathetic fallacy for a wittily ironic demonstration that the same meteorological setting can appear somber or gay depending on the gloomy or serene mood of the observer. It also shows that sudden mood swings of this kind can quite easily be triggered, for instance, by a chance encounter and a simple exchange of glances.

As a result, the poem casts a retrospectively reassuring light over the earlier description of the subject's despondent mood: his "black humor" was merely a passing feeling of "sadness" due to the circumstances of the moment (seasickness brought on by the rocking of the ship), and it was then quickly dissipated by another, purely chance circumstance (the encounter with the woman). Moreover, the rhythm of the octosyllabic verses, which always seems sprightly compared with the solemnity of alexandrine verse, had from the very beginning supported the *denial of depth* that characterizes the poem's overall tone—a kind of forced glibness that is encapsulated also in certain mock-tragic lines such as "Pour se tuer le temps est bon." The same subject who earlier took himself for a Byronic hero (a Corsair or a Giaour) now figures in an ironic, playful, and disenchanted perspective that amusingly deflates his importance (in a tone that itself recalls *Don Juan* as well as Musset's *Namouna*). We realize that he has never been anything other than a respectable traveler who, in the course of a mundane crossing of the English Channel, is cured of a banal case of seasickness thanks to a chance meeting—itself entirely stereotypical—with a woman. The romantic cliché of "love stronger than death" is operative in the end only *as* a cliché that the poem gently mocks (yet subscribes to at the same time).

In the verse "Salut, yeux bleus! bonsoir, flots verts!" there is then a *mise en abyme* of the poem and a certain self-reflexivity, not only because the sense of the whole text is recapitulated there—the rejection of despair and death and the welcoming acceptance of smiling friendship, love, and sociability—but also because the greetings exchanged with the woman define the overall tone of the poem as *mondain*, or worldly. For the salutation "Salut, yeux bleus! bonsoir, flots verts!" is addressed not only to the eyes of the woman that rescue the subject from his distress, but also to the waves that were the vehicle of his despair, thereby incorporating the waves into the worldly tone of the text. It should also be pointed out that, because of their phatic character of pure address, salutations can be thought to have one function and one alone: that of acknowledging individual *persons* as social identities. By naming the addressees "yeux bleus" and "flots verts," the speaker "I" reestablishes himself as a subject, and as the sole subject of a dual discourse, addressing first the woman on the deck and then the ocean, which has now ceased to be threatening. The allure of the waves is in this way exorcised, and with it the temptations of textuality and blurred identity. On the verge of succumbing to these temptations, the weakened identity of the melancholic individual has recovered its strength by affirming its oneness with a type of narrative subject or *sujet d'énoncé*, proffering a worldly discourse of pure communicability.

Whereas the smile of "Sympathy with outstretched arms" is associated with the verb *parler* ("to speak"), the waves are associated with verses (*vers*) by their green color (*vert*) and swirling, turning motion.[17] These waves are the site of a *bruissement*—a gentle, steady background surge of sound that is not exactly noise (*bruit*) but close to it. This *bruissement* "rocks" the subject—another figure of the rhythmic nature of verse—as he sleeps in the depths, transfigured by immersion. The poem presents and activates in this way two conceptions of identity: the social "I" and the self of the depths (*le moi abyssal*), as well as two conceptions of poetry: the communicative smile of greeting and the melancholic sounding and rocking of a dispersed self. However, the second is evoked only as a temptation or danger from which the first can attract us away and rescue us. For that reason the poem as a whole conforms to a wordly aesthetics, by turning away from a textual identity that it denies and rejects. The recourse to humor and to euphemism is a stylistic sign of this poetic allegiance to the values of respectable society (*la bonne société*).

Yet doesn't the emptiness of this social identity, as well as the phatic form of communication (the salutation) it employs, have something in common with the background noise (*le bruissement*) that the subject fears, but that attracts him so strongly? How can communicability without real substance (minimizing, for example, the reality of melancholy and its underlying violence) be valued more highly than a text that is all *bruissement et bercement*—background noise and rocking sensation? The friend with the breast swollen with despair bears a curious resemblance to the smiling, communicative "Sympathy with outstretched arms," if only because each serves to allay the same problem of disequilibrium, decentering, and disgust. Yet for Gautier the first is a dangerous friend, while the other offers hope and salvation.[18]

*

That there are political implications in Gautier's rejection of noise and furor in favor of a more measured and coded discourse is not immediately obvious in "Tristesse en mer." But it is easily perceived in another text written in the spring of 1852: the opening sonnet of *Emaux et camées*, titled simply "Préface":

[PRÉFACE]
Pendant les guerres de l'empire
Goethe, au bruit du canon brutal,
Fit le *Divan occidental*,
Fraîche oasis où l'art respire.

Pour Nisami quittant Shakespeare,
Il se parfuma de çantal,
Et sur un mètre oriental
Nota le chant qu'Hudhud soupire.

Comme Goethe sur son divan
A Weimar s'isolait des choses
Et d'Hafiz effeuillait les roses,

Sans prendre garde à l'ouragan
Qui fouettait mes vitres fermées,
Moi, j'ai fait *Emaux et Camées*.

[PREFACE]
[During the imperial wars,
Amid the noise of brutal cannon fire,
Goethe wrote *West-Östlicher Diwan*,
A cool oasis where art breathes.

Leaving Shakespeare for Nisami,
He scented the air with sandalwood
And adopting an Oriental meter,
Recorded the chant that Hudhud sighs.

Just as Goethe on his couch
Isolated himself from things in Weimar
And plucked the petals of Hafiz's roses,

Without taking notice of the hurricane
Beating against my closed windows,
I composed *Emaux et camées*.][19]

Given that "the hurricane / Beating against my closed windows" clearly alludes to the events of 1848 and the following years, the "I" of the preface (who claims not to *take notice*) enacts a gesture of repression considerably more readable than was perceptible in the rejection of the storm and of melancholy that we just traced in "Tristesse en mer."

Yet the seeds of agitation and disorder cannot be expelled from a text with impunity, for those same repressed elements return with a vengeance to disrupt the very text that has tried to exclude them. Just as "Tristesse en mer" cannot express the rejection of the "oceanic" urge without making it the focus of the poem, so too Gautier's "Preface" to *Emaux et camées* cannot affirm poetry's autonomy in relation to the "hurricane" of events without that storm's making its presence felt in the text. Nor can the subject who claims to take no notice of events in fact fail to demonstrate, in insisting on his desire to exclude them, that they have penetrated his attention.

In his preface Gautier asks whether it is better to emulate the Shakespeare of the great tragedies and historical dramas—and not, it seems, the romantic comedies praised in *Mademoiselle de Maupin*—or whether one should follow Goethe, who deviated from Shakespeare's example and turned away from the noise and agitation of the military campaigns of Napoleon I's empire in order to adopt other poetic models (such as those of Persian classicism). Although the poem clearly opts for Goethe's model, in the phrase "moi, j'ai fait *Emaux et Camées* ("I composed *Emaux et camées*") it nevertheless affirms the specific role of the poetic subject "I" in a way that is symptomatic because the emphasis on "I" implies both his comparability with and his difference from Goethe. The poem therefore affirms and safeguards the individual identity of the subject in relation to the models it invokes (Goethe, Nisami, and Hafiz) in the way it affirms and safeguards its own artistic autonomy in relation to wars and the unfolding of history. Nisami and Shakespeare are clearly presented here as extremes: of pure poetry, on the one hand, and of historical poetry, on the other. But what of the other two writers—Goethe (who "during the imperial wars" followed Nisami's model) and Gautier (who, "without taking notice of the hurricane" that marked the rise of the Second Empire, followed Goethe's model)? Are they as "pure" as one might believe? Isn't there some Shakespeare in them after all?

To refuse history is to opt for an artistic autonomy figured by the "cool oasis" in the middle of the desert; but such autonomy also sets up a dichotomized universe in which the rhythm or "breathing" of Oriental meter, the scent of sandalwood, and the chant inspired by Hudhud contrast with the noise of brutal cannon fire, just as the roses characteristic of Persian poetry contrast with the material "things" from which Goethe tried to isolate himself. Consequently the sonnet that affirms this autonomization of art is not made up solely of roses, perfume, chants, and breathing. As one might expect, it deals as much with what it claims it wishes to exclude—wars, noise, the desert (inseparable from the evocation of an oasis), Shakespeare, "things," and hurricanes—as with what it proposes as the ideal material for making poetry. Thus isolation from the world is by no means a sure way to protect the roses of poetry from contact with the reality that might wilt them (especially since poetry like Hafiz's and his followers' is supposedly written by "plucking petals off roses"). Here we find ourselves confronted with a variation of the same problematic we encountered with *Madame Bovary*, a text that can become autonomous only by opening itself up to invasion by the mundane world—the world of *bêtise* from which it wished to distinguish itself.

As Gautier's sonnet enacts it, this problematic is resumed in the opposition between the words *divan* ("couch") and *ouragan* ("hurricane") set up by the rhyme that governs the tercets. The storm beating cruelly against the windowpane contrasts with the stability and calmness of the *divan*—a couch on which one is comfortably seated and, at the same time, the name (in Arabic and Persian) for a body of poetic work. Following Goethe, Gautier would like to situate *Emaux et camées* on the side of the latter. We are clearly dealing with an "Orientalist" reverie, as Edward Said would call it, in which the Orient is constructed both as the absence of history and as an aestheticizing culture, thus providing a model of poetry as pure codification (for example, the "notation" of a chant magically inspired by some legendary bird)—that is, a kind of musical score composed according to strict rules and conventions, from which the materiality of referential content would be excluded. Thus the invariability of this poetic style with its strict exclusion of realism would mirror the supposed historical immobility of the Orient. Marx too characterized "Oriental despotism" as a regime of unchangeability, and Gautier notoriously enjoyed imagining himself a sultan, seated on his divan, isolated and immobile, abandoning himself to the poetic reveries of happiness inspired by his hookah.

The very words of the text, however, betray this idealization of the Orient and this sublimation of the poetic. *Un divan* is not only a place of rest, but also a study and council chamber where the sultan withdraws for political consultations with his ministers. Similarly, *un canon* is not only a weapon of war; in art, it is also a standard and a measure of beauty—an artistic ideal. By alluding to the models (Goethe, Nisami, and Hafiz) to which he aspired in writing *Emaux et camées*, Gautier indicates the canon by which he wishes his collection to be measured. Thus the poem announces its allegiance to a poetics of purity and "textual autonomy" in language that betrays this ideal by underlining the inseparability and the mutual involvement of the divan/poetic work and the divan/council chamber (on the one hand) and of the war cannon and the artistic canon (on the other). Through a kind of return of the repressed, the "noise" of history the poem wishes to exclude from its aesthetic "oasis" returns to disturb its harmony and purity according to a mechanism that Michel Serres describes as communicational "noise" parasitizing a host discourse.[20]

Consequently the true figure of *Emaux et camées* is not the divan comfortably isolated from the world, nor the "cool oasis where art breathes," but the closed window—the protective glass or shield erected against a threatening world by a self that has taken refuge in his work. This glass does not fit into either the paradigm of the hurricane or that of the divan. It does not fall into the category of noise and wars or into the opposite category of songs, perfumes, and breathing. For the window is not an immaterial essence like the fragrance of a rose, but a material *thing* with certain traits in common with the enamels and cameos evoked by the title: a smooth surface, hardness, firmness, and durability against attack from the storm outside. Closed like the text-oasis, the window nevertheless remains permeable to the noises outside; indeed, it is the means of their transmission (since it is by means of the window that the "I" of the poem becomes aware of the hurricane he declares he has ignored).

It is because of its permeability to the outside, then, and indeed its fragility and brittleness, that the window most closely resembles Gautier's text, whose vulnerability we have just seen to the world of history and to the noises that it wished to exclude. It is moreover by its resemblance to the window that *Emaux et camées* manifests the considerable difference that distinguishes the collection from the models it claims for itself, whether Oriental (Nisami and Hafiz) or Western (Goethe). For Gautier's text is not a soft, luxurious *divan*, but a hard and clear surface behind which the poetic subject has taken refuge, a subject who is far from being insensitive to the storm that is threatening and beating against the transparent glass. That is the "secret" the text both hides and reveals, the difference from its models that marks it as modern, the crack in the system that makes the whole system vulnerable. For like the steamboat in "Tristesse en mer," the window in "Préface" is clearly fragile; both are threatened with shipwreck by the storm that beats against them.[21]

The appropriate conclusion seems to be that Gautier's aestheticism, and perhaps (subject to verification) the whole aestheticizing movement derived from his work—a movement characterized in point of content by hyperexoticism and formally by poetic codification pushed to the extreme—produces the text not as an autonomous "oasis," but rather as a protective pane of glass. Permeable to the "noise" of history, this text is readable as a function of the duplicity characteristic of modernism: as the product of a gesture of repression, the poem possesses an unconscious that is psychological and ontological in kind as well as political. "Tristesse en mer" represses the seasickness and the nausea of the soul, along with the violence of which they are the symptoms; but the repression of all these disturbances constitutes the subject of the poem. Similarly, the poem titled "Préface" represses the noise of the cannon only to better show how this disorder (which is both communicative and political) returns with a vengeance.

But there is a difference with respect to the texts I am examining more closely in this book, which is that aestheticizing texts like Gautier's do not wish to "take notice of" the complexity that makes them readable *as* texts. The aestheticizing text presents itself as an object, as the product of craftsmanship that, because it is supposedly as transparent as it is brilliant, pretends to offer nothing to read other than the work that produced it—work conceived not as the work of writing but as the labor of an *author*. Thus the role of the text-window is not only to protect a social "I" against the storm raging outside, but also to serve as a transparent showcase through which to present to an admiring readership a craftsmanlike "subject" corresponding to the poet's social identity.

In other words, in its textual function a text like Gautier's "Préface" asks that the poem be read only in its narrative function and that the lyrical "I" appear, therefore, only as the subject of the verb *faire* ("to compose or make"): "Goethe . . . / Fit le divan occidental, / . . . Moi, j'ai fait *Emaux et Camées.*" ["Goethe . . . wrote (made) *West-Östlicher Diwan*, / . . . I composed (made) *Emaux et camées.*"] Besides the half-boast of the comparison of *Emaux et camées* to Goethe's poetry and the difference I have already discussed between Goethe's Orientalism and the modernity of Gautier's collection (a difference marked by the text itself), it should also be pointed out that the textual self-reflexivity serves here only to stress a *fecit* that is the signature of an artist (as in the painting and high craftsmanship of the Renaissance). There is perhaps no more effective way to telescope the textual and narrative functions or to present the poetic "I" as identical to the social persona whose name appears on the cover of the collection as that of the person who "made" *Emaux et camées*. The text is produced as the object of an act of fabrication, just as that fabrication is presented as the product of a subject—of a subject that is readable only through that fabrication and whose being is limited to this act and even exhausts itself in performing it. In the way that the narrative "I" is identical to its predications, the poetic "I" here is identical to an act of poetic making that, at the same time, has the further effect of making this "I" a simple replica of the author.

This textual transparency, emptied of all "content" other than the poetic making it displays, clearly recalls the discourse of worldly communication, the phatic salutation that "Tristesse en mer" gives as its model. The textual function of these two poems generates as their reading model the relation between a narrative addressor and addressee producing and receiving signs as social entities (exchanging greetings or producing/admiring the work of a craftsman), but within a contextual vacuum that is signified by the transparency of the window and the referential emptiness of the act of greeting.

We need not be taken in by this self-presentation of the text as contextually pure: the contexts (bad weather at sea, cannon blasts, and the beating of the hurricane) are indeed present in the texts themselves, and the simple fact of textual self-reflexivity prevents the reader from following the instruction to pay attention only to each poem's narrative function and to the "I" (the "Moi, je . . .") they so emphatically stage. What is symptomatic is the poems' production of this model itself, the act of repression that it implies, and especially the curiously retrograde nature of the focus on the author that results. "Impersonality" here is not a sign of modernism, but rather the anachronistic maintenance of a subject that can be textually set up only through the repression of the modern.

*

Emaux et camées is in this sense a *signed* collection and—for reasons that are diametrically opposed, and hence similar—one could make the same argument about Hugo's *Les Châtiments*. The "I" who speaks in this violently satirical discourse alludes just as directly to the persona of an author, who has taken refuge on his island just as Gautier has behind the "window" of art for art's sake, and the structure that tends to force the narrative and textual functions into a single mode of address exists in Hugo as well as in Gautier. For here, once more, melancholy is "bracketed out"—not because it is refused or denied (as in Gautier's case), but simply because (in Hugo's case) it does not arise, since in exile Hugo was free to fully express the anger that is vaporized as melancholy.

Thus, at one end of the poetic-political spectrum that encompasses the melancholic text—on the "right" if you will—is an impassiveness that amounts to a refusal of violence (and of the melancholy that is symptomatic of this repression), while at the other end of the spectrum—on the "left"—one finds an anger that unleashes itself verbally, constrained as it is only in the area of political action. Exiled from France, Hugo is marginalized and excluded from ordinary political practice just as much as Gautier, who is an "inner exile." On his island, Hugo consequently champs at the bit and, in poetry of vituperation and aggressive demands, pours out an anger that stands in for other, more immediately effective forms of pressure on the regime in power.

This is readable in a poem like "Au peuple" (VI, ix), in which the sea metaphor becomes the vehicle for a violence that has no need to hide behind a meteorological alibi, or to hide its explicitly and openly political meaning. It is not the subject of the poem who acts out this violence, however; he expects it instead from a people capable of "shattering" despots as the ocean shatters a ship, and this is the violence that is *wanting*. The subject, the "I" who addresses words of reproach to the people—and whose anger against the despot has thus been transmuted into this injured tone of disappointed expectations—figures himself as a marginalized character, standing alone on the "sacred shore" ("la grève sacrée"), pending a rising of the tide that he cannot himself bring about.

AU PEUPLE
Il te ressemble; il est terrible et pacifique.
Il est sous l'infini le niveau magnifique;
Il a le mouvement, il a l'immensité.
Apaisé d'un rayon et d'un souffle agité,
Tantôt c'est l'harmonie et tantôt le cri rauque.
Les monstres sont à l'aise en sa profondeur glauque;
La trombe y germe; il a des gouffres inconnus
D'où ceux qui l'ont bravé ne sont pas revenus;
Sur son énormité le colosse chavire;
Comme toi le despote, il brise le navire;
Le fanal est sur lui comme l'esprit sur toi;
Il foudroie, il caresse, et Dieu seul sait pourquoi;
Sa vague, où l'on entend comme des chocs d'armures,
Emplit la sombre nuit de monstrueux murmures,
Et l'on sent que ce flot, comme toi, gouffre humain,
Ayant rugi ce soir, dévorera demain.
Son onde est une lame aussi bien que la glaive;
Il chante un hymne immense à Vénus qui se lève;
Sa rondeur formidable, azur universel,
Accepte en son miroir tous les astres du ciel;
Il a la force rude et la grâce superbe;
Il déracine un roc, il épargne un brin d'herbe;
Il jette comme toi l'écume aux fiers sommets,
O Peuple; seulement, lui, ne trompe jamais
Quand, l'œil fixe, et debout sur sa grève sacrée,
Et pensif, on attend l'heure de sa marée.
                              Au bord de l'Océan, juillet 1853

[TO THE PEOPLE
It resembles you; pacific yet dread
A level under the Infinite spread;
It moves, 'tis immense, 'tis soothed by a ray,
And kindled to wrath by Zephyr at play;

'Tis music or discord: sweet is its song,
Or hoarse its shriek as complaining of wrong;
Monsters at ease sleep in its depths dark-green;
The water-spout germinates there unseen;
It has gulfs unknown, 'neath its surface plain,
And those who visit them come not again;
It lifts ships colossal and shatters them
As you shatter despots. Black is its frown;
The beacon above it shines like the light
You have from heaven, your steps to guide right;
It caresses and chides if soft its mood
Or angry, but by no man understood
Is its humour. Like the terrible shock
Of armour clangs its wave on the rock;
Night listens with awe to the portentous sound
As it feels that, like you, the depth profound
Having roared at eve, shall destroy at morn,
For the wave is a sword. Venus when born
It hails with a hymn, immense and sublime,
Which has resounded through eons of time:
Its universal blue, its wide, wide expanse
Shelters the stars that there tremble and dance;
It has a rude force, a mercy superb,
For it roots up a rock, and spares an herb;
Like you, it throws on proud summits its foam
O People, it loves round the world to roam;
Only—it never deceives when, with eye
Fixed on its surface, one watches it nigh
Standing on the sacred seashore, pensive, alone,
And, spellbound, one awaits the coming of its tide.
                          On the Atlantic shore, July 1853][22]

Although this "I" who waits becomes explicit in the poem only in the
vaguely anonymous form of *on* ("one"), as in lines 13 and 15 and the last
line, the text's apparatus of address works hard to establish an equivalence
between the subject of the discourse and the signer of the collection. Thus
the title "Au peuple" ("To the People") fuses into a single phrase (*énoncé*)
the narratee to whom "I" is addressing his description of the Atlantic's
"dread yet pacific" power and the addressee or reader the poem is addressing. Moreover, the notation "Au bord de l'Océan, juillet 1853" ["On the

Atlantic shore, July 1853"] allows us to identify the author who claims attention through this dating of the text (which is an implicit *fecit*) as the same enunciator as the narrative subject, who describes himself as a "pensive" and haunted figure, obsessively waiting—"l'œil fixe"—on the seashore. (It is here, incidentally, and notably in the word "pensif," that a thematics of melancholy can be discerned—one that is without impact, however, on the textual practice.)

The meaning of the poem lies in the fact that this "grève sacrée" ("sacred seashore") is *not* the place de la Grève so familiar to the people in their revolutionary role. But the paratextual framework of the poem has as its sole function to name the protagonists of a communicational situation— addressee-speaker-referent—which in the narrative function are generally referred to using pronouns, as in the opening and closing lines: "*Il te* ressemble" ["*It* resembles *you*"] and "*on* attend l'heure de *sa* marée" ["*one* awaits the coming of *its* tide"]. While it is true that the People-addressee is named in the third to last line of the poem, the Atlantic referent is specified only in the note at the end, which also reveals the coincidence of the pensive *on* ("one") of the poem and the author-signer of the text in his historical role as Exile.

This marginalization of a subject identified with the person of the poet is also to be read in the very frequent use of irony that characterizes the rhetoric of *Les Châtiments*. Irony, which is by definition a phenomenon of reading, is a manifestation of the textual function, since it implies that the narrative discourse of a text is to be read as a kind of quotation (or more generally mentioning) that can be surrounded by invisible quotation marks.[23] It is an *other* who is speaking in the text and who refuses to take responsibility for the words that are in this way attributed; that is why this device is so valuable for a text such as *Madame Bovary* (see chapter 7). Irony is therefore a particularly striking—and almost pedagogical—demonstration of the distinction it is necessary to make between the narrative and textual functions; it also shows how a text can serve as a dual form of address—to the narratee on the one hand and to the reader on the other. An empirical reader who puts himself or herself in the place of the narratee of an ironic text is a naive reader; in this sense *all* texts are ironic. An appropriate reading of such a text presupposes an *other* reading position.

For to grasp an effect of irony is, in a certain sense, to recognize an absence—the absence of "someone." Something is being hinted at or insinuated, but the insinuator eludes identification. Just as the quotation marks surrounding ironic discourse are invisible, so too the one who "cites" the discourse presented in the narrative function remains elusive. Yet, given these quotation marks, it is only natural to assume that there also exists a subject of the act of mentioning that produces them. In Flaubert's work, as we shall see, the insufficiency of the ironic "solution" is directly linked to the ironist's inability to distinguish himself from the structures of the discourse that he "ironizes." In contrast, it is this ambiguous presence-yet-absence of the ironist that Hugo exploits in order to figure textually his own absence/presence on the political scene in France. Although out of view, he was difficult to ignore. In like fashion, the ironic text stages the doings and sayings of the protagonists and bit players in the political drama that was being played out in France, while simultaneously reserving a position for the one who was offstage and out of view—the position of mute commentator and implicit judge, that is, of moral consciousness and *critical* intelligence. Reading an ironic poem by Hugo consequently amounts to discovering the presence within *oneself* of an instance of judgment corresponding to this ironic textual subject; for without the margin of consciousness that enables readers to distance themselves from the position of the narratee, an ironic reading of the text would simply not be possible.

As an example of the way irony functions in Hugo, I take the first canto of his poem "Nox," which in the 1853 edition served as the opening work of *Les Châtiments*.

Nox
C'est la date choisie au fond de ta pensée,
Prince, il faut en finir,— cette nuit est glacée.
Viens, lève-toi! flairant dans l'ombre les escrocs,
Le dogue Liberté gronde et montre ses crocs.
Quoique mis par Carlier à la chaîne, il aboie.
N'attends plus longtemps! c'est l'heure de la proie.
Vois, décembre épaissit son brouillard le plus noir!
Comme un baron voleur qui sort de son manoir,
Surprends, brusque assaillant, l'ennemi que tu cernes.
Debout! les régiments sont là dans les casernes,
Sac au dos, abrutis de vin et de fureur,
N'attendant qu'un bandit pour faire un empereur.
Mets ta main sur ta lampe et viens d'un pas oblique;
Prends ton couteau, l'instant est bon: La République,
Confiante, et sans voir tes yeux sombres briller,
Dort, avec ton serment, prince, pour oreiller.

Cavaliers, fantassins, sortez! dehors les hordes!
Sus aux représentants! soldats, liez de cordes
Vos généraux jetés dans la cage aux forçats!
Poussez, la crosse aux reins, l'Assemblée à Mazas!
Chassez la haute cour à coups de plat de sabre!
Changez-vous, preux de France, en brigands de Calabre!
Vous, bourgeois, regardez, vil troupeau, vil limon,
Comme un glaive rougi qu'agite un noir démon,
Le coup d'Etat qui sort flamboyant de la forge!
Les tribuns pour le droit luttent: qu'on les égorge.
Routiers, condottieri, vendus, prostitués,
Frappez! tuez Baudin! tuez Dussoubs! tuez!
Que fait hors des maisons ce peuple? Qu'il s'en aille!
Soldats, mitraillez-moi toute cette canaille!
Feu! Feu! Tu voteras ensuite, ô peuple-roi!
Sabrez le droit, sabrez l'honneur, sabrez la loi!
Que sur les boulevards le sang coule en rivières!
Du vin plein les bidons! des morts plein les civières!
Qui veut de l'eau-de-vie? En ce temps pluvieux
Il faut boire. Soldats, fusillez-moi ce vieux.
Tuez-moi cet enfant. Qu'est-ce que cette femme?
C'est la mère? tuez. Que tout ce peuple infâme
Tremble, et que les pavés rougissent ses talons!
Ce Paris odieux bouge et résiste. Allons!
Qu'il sente le mépris, sombre et plein de vengeance,
Que nous, la force, avons pour lui, l'intelligence!
L'étranger respecta Paris: soyons nouveaux!
Trainons-le dans la boue aux crins de nos chevaux!
Qu'il meure! qu'on le broie et l'écrase et l'efface!
Noirs canons, crachez-lui vos boulets à la face!

[NIGHT
This is the date chosen in the depths of your mind,
Prince, it's time to finish the job,— the night is bitter cold,
Come, arise! catching the scent of crooks in the shadow,
The mastiff Liberty is growling and flashing its sharp teeth.
Even though Carlier has chained him, the dog is barking
      fiercely.
Don't wait any longer! It's the hour to hunt prey.
See how December sends forth its thickest, blackest fog!
Like a robber baron leaving his manor,

Lead a surprise attack against the enemy you are besieging.
Arise! the regiments are waiting in the barracks,
Supplies ready, drunken with wine and furor,
Waiting only for a bandit to make an emperor of him.
Put your hand over your lamp and take a crooked path.
Take your knife, the time is ripe: the Republic,
Confident and without seeing your dark eyes shine,
Is sleeping, Prince, with your oath as its pillow.

Soldiers, go forth! Send the hordes into the streets!
Attack the representatives! Soldiers, throw
Your generals into convicts' cells and tie them up!
Force the Assembly to Mazas, with your rifle butts in their
    backs!
Drive out the high court with the flat of your swords!
Brave knights of France, transform yourselves into Calabrian
    brigands.
And you, bourgeois, filthy mob, vile dirt,
Look at the coup d'état that is coming out flaming from the
    forge,
Like a bloody sword brandished by a black demon!
The tribunes are fighting for justice, so slit their throats.
Mercenaries, stool pigeons, prostitutes,
Strike with your weapons! Kill Baudin! Kill Dussoubs! Kill!
What are the people doing outside their homes? Tell them to
    disperse!
Soldiers, gun down all this rabble for me!
Fire your guns! You'll vote later, O sovereign people!
Hack up law, honor, and justice!
Let the blood flow in rivers down the boulevards!
Let the wine flow from full barrels while the corpses pile high
    on stretchers!
Who wants some hard liquor? In this rainy weather
People need to drink. Soldiers, execute this old man.
Kill this child. Who is this woman?
It's the mother? Kill her. Let this whole vile populace tremble
And let the cobblestones bloody their heels!
This odious city is stirring and resisting! Arise!
Let Paris feel the dark and vengeful scorn
That we, brute force, have for it— for intelligence!
The foreigner respected Paris: let's take a fresh approach!

Let's drag it through the mud tied to our horses!
Let it die! let's crush it and wipe it out!
Black cannons, hurl your cannonballs headlong into its
    face!][24]

This piece is in two "movements." In the first an anonymous voice, that of a close adviser—the voice of conscience in the guise of evil counselor—addresses the Prince (Napoléon III was the "Prince-President" before December 1851) to recommend a coup d'état. It is the voice of a flatterer who says what the addressee wishes to hear and who suggests a furtive treachery, following the urgings of his own nature: "Mets ta main sur ta lampe et viens d'un pas oblique" ["Put your hand over your lamp and take a crooked path"]. In the second movement there emerges another anonymous voice that, in contrast to the insinuating flattery of the first voice, is distinguished by its authoritarian, commanding tone. This second voice addresses successively the various "allies" of the Prince—soldiers, bourgeois, and the common people—in order to incite them to revolt, to an illegitimate seizure of power, and to bloodshed.

This second voice is clearly that of the Prince, who is the addressee of the first. After listening to the urgings of the first voice, the Prince goes into overt action and orders the repression of the representatives, the generals, the tribunes, and finally the people. The people thus play a double role as addressee of the Prince's words—"Tu voteras ensuite, ô peuple-roi!" ["You'll vote later, O sovereign people!"]—and as the object of his repression—"Soldats, mitraillez-moi toute cette canaille!" ["Soldiers, gun down all this rabble for me!"]. The relaying of these narrative voices (that of the flatterer, then that of the Prince) therefore has the effect of characterizing the two narratees and demonstrating their affinity. The Prince appears at first as one who is ready to listen to the subversive urgings of the flatterer, and who then gives the order of repression. But at that point it is his accomplices who show themselves ready to listen to these same urgings, to obey these commands emanating from such a source: soldiers revolting against legitimate authority, bourgeois passively watching the coup d'état without intervening, and the common people who are both objects of flattery and victims of the mass slaughter.

Yet, at the moment when the poem reaches the climax of verbal violence it attributes to the Prince, a certain simplification occurs. The group of accomplices identifies itself as "nous, la force" ["we, brute force"]. The enemy to be destroyed, identified with Paris, is characterized no less ener-getically as "lui, l'intelligence." Thus the battle lines become clear:

Ce Paris odieux bouge et résiste. Allons!
Qu'il sente le mépris, sombre et plein de vengeance
Que nous, la force, avons pour lui, l'intelligence!
. . . .
Noirs canons, crachez-lui vos boulets à la face!

[This odious city is stirring and resisting! Arise!
Let Paris feel the dark and vengeful scorn
That we, brute force, have for it— for intelligence!
. . . .
Black cannons, hurl your cannonballs headlong into its face!]

If repression is a matter of force, resistance devolves on intelligence.

From this we can see that the poem is to be understood as perpetuating and pursuing the work of "intelligence," which, having been crushed in Paris, has taken refuge on the island of Jersey, from where it is sending out a poetic discourse of resistance against the usurper. Irony is the mark of intelligence and of its refusal to accept defeat. Like intelligence, irony is an absence that cannot be disposed of; despite its invisibility, it is *still there*, unyielding and indomitable. The "bloody sword" (*glaive rougi*) of the coup d'état is answered with words of hatred, while brute force's scorn for intelligence is answered with irony, and the cannonballs "spat" in the face of Paris by its enemies provoke in turn the verbal spitfire of *Les Châtiments* exploding in the emperor's face.

Yet if so, poetic irony—the sign of intelligence and resistance—enters into the sphere of struggle defined by the words attributed to the Prince, since it is modeled after what it resists: brute force. Spitting verbal cannon-fire in the face of the usurper, poetic irony exercises a vengeance equal to that called for by the Prince against Paris. The ironic textual subject is therefore scarcely distinguishable, in the end, from the narrative subjects of the text, and particularly from the main narrative subject: the Prince (who is first the addressee, then the speaker). This textual subject employs different means (those offered by ironic discourse), but nevertheless pits himself against those narrative subjects—violence for violence, intelligence against brute strength—taking on the resisting role that is defined and named ("intelligence") by their own reliance on oppression. It is a kind of return of the repressed, except that since what is repressed here has not *accepted* repression, it is not subjected to censorship and consequently cannot return in transformed guise. The textual subject fights on an equal footing with the ruling order that wishes to repress or even eliminate it but succeeds only in marginalizing it.

Given that the narrative subject of the poem is clearly Louis-Napoléon ("Prince"), it is easy for anyone possessing the minimum cultural background to put a name on the ironic subject: It is that refractory exile, Victor Hugo. Although irony is a phenomenon of reading and of textuality, in "Nox" it abdicates its "textual" powers and asks to be read as a political voice among others, a voice having a specifiable subject that acts, on the stage of history, *alongside*—even if in opposition to—other characters, whose voice is represented in the narrative function. Accordingly, "Nox" is *signed*, as one might expect, with the closing notation "Jersey, November 1852" and with a concluding invocation to the "Muse of Indignation" that constitutes (in the optative mode) a variant of the self-reflexive signature or *fecit*:

> Muse Indignation! Dressons sur cet empire heureux et
>   rayonnant,
> Et sur cette victoire au tonnerre échappée,
> Assez de piloris pour faire une épopée!

> [Muse of Indignation! In honor of this bright and joyous
>   empire,
> And this victory that the thunderbolt spared,
> Let us raise enough pillories to write an epic!]

Needless to say, the tone of irony here is particularly emphatic.

Thus, the anger that feeds the open resistance to the coup d'état, and that responds to its violence with a violence all its own, conceives its discourse as originating in a subject identifiable with an individual, even if this subject is set apart and marginalized by events.[25] The analogy with aestheticizing poetic discourse is striking: anxious as it is to exclude violence and hold it at bay, the impassibility of the "autonomous" text figures itself as a protective pane of glass through which can be seen an author-persona who, likewise, has withdrawn and taken refuge in his work in the face of events. It is, on the contrary, in the discourse of melancholy and of the repression of anger (of the same anger that this impassibility itself seeks in vain to repress) that a readable subject emerges—a subject that is problematized, dispersed, plural, in short, vaporized.

"De la vaporisation et de la centralisation du *moi*—Tout est là," Baudelaire wrote in a famous passage in his notebooks ["It all comes down to the vaporization and the centering of the self"].[26] In chapter 5, we will see why "vaporization" does not produce as its alternative the term one might expect: "condensation." Yet given the choice between a vaporization and a centering of identity, we can already note that in Second Empire literature the centered self appears to be necessarily *in collusion with the ruling order*, despite the fact that this same centered self may be marginalized (like the female figure in "Tristesse en mer" or the exiled subject of *Les Châtiments*), and even if it tries wholeheartedly (as in the second case) to resist that order. The anger of resistance has its seat (its *assise*) in a self that has the same structure as what it resists. Immobile on its couch, shielded behind its protective glass, the aesthetic self "takes no notice" of events that it objectively winds up supporting simply by failing to resist them.

Yet between these extremes of resistance and retreat, the decentered self of the melancholic subject—that vaporized, faltering, lacking subject of a new textuality—occupies a precarious middle ground of semiresistance and semiretreat, a ground neither of resistance nor of retreat, which is that of the oppositional and the "depolitified." Lacking both the power and the strength to resist, as well as a "seat" in which to stabilize itself, this oppositional subject is condemned to live out events in melancholy and the nausea of disgust, indeed to experience melancholy *in the form of* nausea and disgust. But as early as the Second Republic, Gérard de Nerval had declared: "Je ne voudrais pas ici faire de la politique. Je n'ai jamais voulu faire que de l'opposition." ["I do not wish to engage in politics here. I have never wanted to do anything but practice opposition."][27]

THREE

THE DUPLICITY OF POWER AND

THE POWER OF DUPLICITY

In 1835 Stendhal abandoned *Lucien Leuwen*, discouraged by the illiberal atmosphere prevailing in Rome as in Paris, and even more by the news he received in Civitavecchia of the reintroduction of censorship in France. A novel depicting the electoral practices of the July Monarchy now had little chance of being published; consequently Stendhal turned to *Henry Brulard* and soon after to *La Chartreuse de Parme*. Here the portrayal of political maneuvering takes cover under a representation of Restoration Italy, and the frenzy with which *La Chartreuse* was written suggests something of the return of the repressed. The strategy of displacing the fictive reference to another place or period so as to permit indirect commentary on the author's own society is, of course, a classical one. It had been demonstrated a little earlier, in 1834, by Musset's *Lorenzaccio*, a play that was judged unperformable and thus was not staged until the end of the century.

There is a crying need for a critical monograph on the political fiction of the 1830s, but I undertake here only to read another drama of the period that was in fact performed, in spite of its political thrust. After problems with the censorship apparatus, which have been documented by Jean Richer in his edition of the play, *Léo Burckart* was staged in 1839 at the Porte Saint-Martin. The play was written in collaboration with Alexandre Dumas, whose contribution is most evident in the firmly constructed plot. It is an excellent example of what was possible in the way of oppositional writing and, more specifically, of political theater (a traditional bête noire for censors) in the years of disenchantment that followed the July Revolution. Taking up the socially sensitive question of political assassination in the wake of *Lorenzaccio*, and especially after Fieschi's assassination plot, Nerval's play could not afford simply to dramatize, as it does, the phenomenon of political duplicity. It needed a duplicity of its own, a duplicity of writing. Thus, for example, it adopts the system of indirect references just mentioned, making allusion to the political realities of the July Monarchy in France through the representation of post-Napoleonic Germany in the year 1819.

The duplicitousness of *Léo Burckart* goes considerably further, however. The play provides us with an ideal case through which to examine the interconnection between the duplicity of power and the oppositional duplicity of artistic production, as well as the parallels (and differences) between oppositional writing in two periods of postrevolutionary disenchantment that at first sight seem very similar: the early years of the July Monarchy and those of the Second Empire. Following our effort in the preceding chapter to distinguish the oppositional writing of the 1850s from the two contemporary trends represented by Gautier and Hugo, our examination of *Léo Burckart* will serve as another means to probe the specific nature of the textual phenomenon that is the object of our study.

It is indeed curious that when Nerval applied in 1838 for the censor's permission to perform his play, this office was operating without legal status. The censorship law voted in 1835 was a provisional measure authorized for two years only; it was never renewed, so that the de facto censorship that existed throughout Louis-Philippe's reign had lost its de jure legitimacy as early as 1837. This is a striking example of the illegitimate exercise of power, the same inauthenticity that Musset, Stendhal, and Nerval exposed in their texts and that Nerval attempted to oppose more directly by a court challenge. Quite possibly, the sense of its own illegitimacy is what led the censor's office, in 1838, to pay particular attention to the climactic scenes of act 4 (or "day 5" in the 1839 text that Nerval reprinted in *Lorely* and that will be my point of reference here). Amid masks, disguises, betrayals, and counterbetrayals galore, we witness a gathering of secret societies, explicitly described as a replica of the diplomatic congresses of the period, in which a minister passes himself off as a student, students impersonate soldiers of the prince, and two other characters function in complementary fashion—Paulus as a double agent, Henri de Waldeck as a double-crosser. In this topsy-turvy universe, the genuine is indistinguishable from the theatrical, the parodic from the real. Given the ambiguity of its own conditions of operation, the censor's office may well have suspected an implicit commentary on the duplicitousness characterizing the methods of power in practice during the period.

Not surprisingly, the censor's office makes no mention of this in its official report and gives quite different reasons for its reservations concerning the play:

> Secret societies, with their foreign passwords and strange ritu-
> als, their somber practices, their tribunals whose sentences of
> death by rope or dagger lead to political assassinations—this
> sinister milieu, displayed so vividly and dramatically onstage,
> strongly affects the imagination and can produce the most dan-
> gerous impressions.[1]

Faithful to the reading habits of the period, the censor—consciously and
explicitly—took into account only the referential function of the text,
which is of course tied to its narrative function. Much like the future
judges of *Madame Bovary* and *Les Fleurs du mal*, the censor of *Léo Burckart*
subscribed to a strange ideology, according to which a fictive imitation of
evil can provoke other imitations, which will be realities. According to this
view, a vivid portrayal of German secret societies could foster the growth
of such societies in France.

Such an account fails to observe that the scenes it incriminates are also
those in which a very high level of generic self-reflexivity is concentrated.
By showing the theatricality characterizing both the methods of government and the methods of resistance adopted by the plotters, and more particularly by showing the intricate intermingling of the theatrical signs of
power and opposition, *Léo Burckart* raises the question of its own possible
duplicity. More disturbing still (especially in the eyes of a censor), it raises
the question of the political allegiance of the theatrical text: Is the play on
the side of power or on the side of the students and their secret societies?
Or can it be that, by showing the students and the representatives of power
engaged in similar techniques of duplicity, the play is refusing either allegiance and distinguishing itself from both? If so, by refusing to allow itself
to be classified as *for* or *against* either party, it is perhaps producing a certain undecidability as the form of duplicity most characteristic of itself.
This would be a duplicity that responds to the ambiguities inherent in the
exercise of power with an even greater ambivalence or, more accurately
perhaps, with a different kind of ambivalence and equivocation. These are
some of the questions I propose to examine in this chapter.

The play's level of ambiguity was likely to have disturbed—in an unconscious or barely conscious manner—a censor whose duty it was to classify
texts according to categories such as "for" or "against," "acceptable" or
"unacceptable." Subversiveness can reside elsewhere than in the category
of "against"; it can result from a certain way of confusing the categories so
as to be classifiable as both "for" and "against," and hence neither "for" nor
"against." In any case, there is a striking lapsus in the censor's report that

suggests the hesitation and uncertainty Nerval's text seems to have inspired, and can still inspire, in a reader anxious to classify it in simplistic political terms. A series of carefully nuanced, almost tangled clauses leads to a sentence of conclusion whose syntax seems to imply the censor's intention of *rejecting* the play; but instead we read: "La majorité a pensé que cet ouvrage est admissible à raison du sujet qu'il traite et des images qu'il présente" ["The majority felt that this work is acceptable, given the subject it treats and the images it presents"]. This leads Jean Richer to exclaim in his notes to the critical edition: "Faute probable pour *inadmissible!*" ["Probably an inadvertent substitution of *acceptable* for *unacceptable!*"].

Did the censor approve or reject *Léo Burckart*? The intention in 1838 was probably to ban the staging of Nerval's play. But what we know of its performance history leads to the conclusion that it was never either clearly authorized or really forbidden. The play was at first sent back to the author with instructions to rewrite certain episodes—instructions that (according to Jean Richer) Nerval probably made no real effort to follow. It was then accepted, but grudgingly, after the lawsuit initiated by Nerval had threatened to expose the illegality of the censorship procedure and had led the minister "soon afterward to remove the difficulties the play faced," to quote the careful phrasing of the official who later recalled the incident.[2] In Nerval's own version of the story, the minister is reported to have said: "Reprenez votre pièce, faites-la jouer, et si elle cause quelque désordre, on la suspendra." ["Take back your play and have it performed. If it causes any disturbances, we'll close it down."][3]

The play was therefore staged, without the questions it raised having been in any way resolved. Its challenge to the methods, categories, and assumptions of the censor was not taken up (and for good reason). Quite predictably, the government responded to the text's ambiguity by resorting to the same type of duplicity that the play itself describes and calls into question. Thus the whole affair took place in an atmosphere of extraordinary equivocation, with the institutions of power responding ambiguously to a play that was itself undecidable. One is reminded of the description in "Sylvie" of this same period as "une époque étrange." The case is a striking illustration of how governmental duplicity, wielding the arm of censorship, can give rise to a writerly or textual duplicity of such a kind that it baffles the powers of censorship itself.

*

Another *acte manqué* in the censorship report confirms the hesitation of the authorities. The following sentence was first written, then deleted:

> On pourrait y trouver, sauf la différence des dénouements, la
> tragique histoire de Kotzebue et de Karl Sand, mais rien n'y
> ressemble à ce qui se passe ou s'est passé chez nous et de notre
> temps. (p. xxxix)

> [Except for the difference in ending, the play might recall the
> tragic story of Kotzebue and Karl Sand, but nothing in it re-
> sembles present or past events in France or in our time.]

Does the play reproduce an occurrence that took place in Germany some
time back? Or does it "resemble" in some way "present or past events in
France or in our time"? In the end, the censor hesitated either to affirm
that the play was about Germany or to deny that it was about France; his
reticence is surprising, given the clarity of the references to French society
that can be perceived today. The troubles and agitations of the early years
of Louis-Philippe's reign are evoked quite clearly, and the allusions seem
almost as clear to the ambiguities of power and the *politique des intérêts* that
characterized the period, as well as to the widespread individual opportunism—"l'avide curée qui se faisait alors des positions et des honneurs" ["the
mad, greedy rush toward titles and honors"]—that Nerval describes in
"Sylvie." The audience at the premiere was certainly not deceived. Nerval
reports that Diégo's line—"Les rois s'en vont, je les pousse" ["Kings are
on their way out, and I'm pushing them"]—drew a storm of applause, to
the great embarrassment of the author and theater director. He adds that
the play would certainly have been banned as a result had it not been for a
salutary bungle: The black velvet *loups* (half-masks) ordered for the climactic and highly suspect scene of act 4 failed to arrive on time, and the actors
were forced to perform in silly Harlequin masks, which considerably di-
minished the scene's dramatic intensity and impact.

It would be difficult, therefore, to attribute the censor's hesitation to the
sheer cleverness of the authors and to their seemingly transparent strategy
of substituting a representation of Germany in 1819 for the France of the
1830s. The audience, in any case, was naive in applauding Diégo's contro-
versial line with such enthusiasm, since the rest of the play shows this character to be a bragging phrasemonger, intoxicated with words, yet weak
and ineffectual when it comes to deeds. The play's perspective on revolutionary action is therefore far more subtle than it first appears, and the
public's misreading of the text, viewing it as clearly pro-revolutionary, is
part and parcel of the same ambiguous history as the censor's hesitation
when confronted with the task of identifying its subject and political alle-

giance. For the duplicity of *Léo Burckart* is itself double: there is the "simple duplicity" of disguise (substituting Germany for France), but to this is added a form of duplicitousness that turns out, like that in *Lorenzaccio*, to be inscrutable because it conceals no level that might be thought "sincere" or nonduplicitous. In short, the play wears a mask beneath which there seems to be no true face.

Nevertheless, the spectator of 1839 could recognize in the play themes relating to the deepest preoccupations in France at the time—and not simply at the anecdotal level of political assassination. The characters are concerned with the political unification of the German-speaking states; but—following the great Revolution and its various sequels—French society was also divided politically, if not geographically, and stood in need of (re)unification. Léo's social dream, expressed in his reproachful speech to the unruly students (p. 139), envisages not only a wholly new Germany refashioned through intense intellectual labor ("une Allemagne à refaire, avec les longs travaux de la pensée et les dures veilles du génie"), but also a society in which *merit* would replaced privilege ("Toutes les carrières vous sont offertes! l'avenir n'a plus de barrières privilégiées"). Such a dream clearly echoes the great ambition of the French bourgeoisie in the first half of the century: to found a unified society based on bourgeois liberalism.

That was just the problem, however; for just as in the play Léo's liberalism and gradualism stand in opposition to the activism and immediacy of the students' aspirations, so too the disturbances that marked the early years of the July Monarchy were the sign not so much of radical division with respect to principles as of deep discord concerning the means of unifying French society—a discord that stood in the way of achieving the common goal that everyone seemed to desire. On the one hand, Léo is the spokesman for a certain liberalism that held power in the 1830s; but on the other, the rebellious students—with their recourse to any means of destabilizing power and provoking disorder through agitation, revolt, assassination, secret plots, and subversive songs—clearly represent the "idealism" of middle-class French youth that had been deeply disenchanted by the outcome of the July Revolution and by the political evolution of Louis-Philippe's monarchy from constitutionalism to authoritarianism. Finally, characters like Henri de Waldeck and Paulus stand for the *arriviste* opportunism of those who, discouraged by the political chaos of the period or else indifferent to the broad social questions it raised, sought merely to fish in the troubled waters in order to advance their personal fortunes.

Thus Louis-Philippe's France could easily identify itself in the mirror held up to it by *Léo Burckart*, and it is highly symptomatic that the crux of the play lies in the animosity, yet deep affinity, that exists between the characters of Léo and Frantz. They are linked not only by their mutual desire to bring about the unification of Germany, but also by their opposition to the opportunism and duplicity of the *politique des intérêts*, as practiced notably by the prince, who refers casually to these policies as "tous les moyens de gouvernement ordinaires" ["all the ordinary methods of government"] (p. 235). What divides them, and divides them radically, is the question of means: *How* to fight the duplicity of power? *How* to unify Germany? Frantz shares the scorn of his "brothers" for all "political and legal fictions" (p. 297) and dreams instead of direct action. Léo, on the other hand, accepts the role of diplomat but expresses his hatred for *words* ("les mots," p. 283) and, in their place, tries to invent a politics of verbal directness. In a moment of hubris, he proclaims: "J'avais toujours dit que celui qui de nos jours ferait de la diplomatie franche et loyale, tromperait tous les autres" ["I had always maintained that a person who practiced frank, honest diplomacy these days would deceive everyone else"]. This formulation ironically foreshadows his own fate of being co-opted by the duplicity of power. But the point is that each of these two characters, the agitator and the statesman, has developed an aversion for all forms of *mediation*. The main difference between them is that Frantz proposes to substitute direct action for the mediations of diplomacy, while Léo hopes to substitute a policy of openness and frankness for the political use of language as an agency of duplicity.

The sign of their common opposition to duplicity is, of course, the love they share for Marguerite, a character representing simplicity and, at the same time—as her name (a gallicization of Goethe's Gretchen) suggests—a symbol of the ideal Germany to which both men aspire. After Marguerite, Léo's loyal wife, is neglected by her husband when he is caught up in the insidious web of duplicitous politics, she seems tempted to give herself to Frantz, her childhood friend. And yet he is as inclined as Léo to sacrifice her (with equally symbolic significance) to the demands of his political activities. This dual love, doubly shared but doubly neglected, has clear implications. On the one hand, it shows that, despite the errors that lead them astray, Léo and Frantz possess authentic values, as well as aspirations that are essentially noble. On the other hand, their neglect of Marguerite reflects the perversity of a course of political action that draws them away from the ideal to which they nevertheless aspire.

Marguerite continually complains that she is cut off from political events she does not understand (because people do not bother to explain them to her), but that nevertheless involve her directly and have a strong impact on her life. She denounces the irresponsibility of social movements that refuse participation to certain people or else marginalize them to such an extent that they are reduced to the role of helpless spectators of a course of action that in no way takes account of their interests. Léo's Germany, like Frantz's, is a Germany for men, and therein lies the special irony of the fact that their common goal is symbolized by a woman whom they exclude from political activity of any kind. Léo goes so far as to instruct his wife in feminist analysis: "Il faut qu'un mari soit toute sa vie un amant, et qu'il songe sans cesse à divertir [sa femme] de cet ennui profond qui les accable toutes, depuis que la société leur a imposé le désœuvrement comme une convenance" ["A husband must be a lover to his wife all his life and must continually strive to distract her from the profound boredom from which women have suffered ever since idleness was imposed upon them as a social convention"] (p. 197). Yet Léo offers Marguerite these arguments without realizing the profoundly antifeminist character of his intention, which is to make her patiently accept her exclusion. Once again, as in the case of Gautier, and as we shall see with Baudelaire (in chapter 5), the differentiation of gender roles proves to be a blind spot in the spirit of opposition; although in Nerval's case this blindness resides in the characters and not in the text itself, which is a crucial distinction.

The Germany envisaged by both Léo and Frantz is, however, a Germany of the bourgeoisie. Unless we view Marguerite as the symbol of *all* the social exclusions entailed by the construction of that society, we must admit that—with the exception of one anticolonialist statement uttered in passing by Diégo—the play seems completely blind to working-class issues. In that sense *Léo Burckart* clearly reflects the bourgeois mentality of the July Monarchy. Its only excuse is perhaps that the play is set in Germany of the post-Napoleonic period, when the country was still in the earliest stages of industrialization. On this point it is therefore more difficult to exonerate Nerval's text, although Nerval would prove more sensitive to working-class realities after 1848.

In any case, despite their deep love for the same Germany and their shared aversion for the politics of mediation and duplicity, Léo and Frantz prove to be *frères ennemis* as soon as the question of *means* arises. Frantz, as I have said, favors direct action, while Léo favors open, honest diplomacy. For Léo the writer, who before his elevation to ministerial power was a political essayist, the duplicity of government is conceived of in terms of censorship. Censorship had forced him to express himself *à demi-mot* or in disguised terms, emblematized by the fact that honest Léo was known as a writer by his pseudonym, "Cornélius." Once he is in power, the battle he wages is against what amounts to censorship *within* the government. Léo's resistance to this internal censorship is reflected in his praise of openness in government, in his habit of preaching at people unmercifully (his wife, the students, and even the prince all bear the brunt), and especially in his refusal, criticized by Paulus, to employ intermediaries. Instead of leaving the students to a magistrate, he arrests them himself; instead of sending a delegate to a political congress, he attends it personally. Léo's refusal to mediate or veil his political actions in any way makes it impossible for him to go back on his decisions.

The veil of secrecy is essential, however, for the student groups to which Frantz belongs. Their project of direct political action implies that, for them, the repressive enemy is represented less by censorship than by the police, and particularly by police spies. The danger for them, as political conspirators, is that their plots could be uncovered; frankness and openness are therefore inimical to them. Their defense against the police attempt to penetrate their activities is a whole apparatus of passwords, masks, initiations, and general mystery. As a man of action, Frantz thus relates to words in a way that runs completely counter to Léo's desire for unmediated frankness; it involves hieroglyphics, cyphers, obscure initiatory formulas, and student slang (which, in French translation—*renards*, *pinsons*, *renomistes*, etc.—produces its own effect of incomprehensibility). Stendhal's fictional universe, obsessed as it is with pseudonymy and cyphers, confirms the general preoccupation in Europe with the issues of censorship and police power during the first half of the nineteenth century. Yet the specificity of Nerval's text lies in its insistence on the polarization of opposition provoked by the duplicitous methods of power: these "moyens de gouvernement ordinaires" produce, on the one hand, a desire for openness and, on the other, a counterattempt at impenetrability. Let us note, however, that Léo is in a position to try out his policy of sincerity because he has already achieved power, whereas Franz and the other students must resort to masks and mystery precisely because they are *excluded* from power.

The *frères ennemis* opposition that structures the play leads to multiple ironies. Instead of eliminating the duplicity of power, Frantz and Léo are led to eliminate each other from the political scene. Moreover, instead of opposing their common enemy, they wind up turning against each other weapons drawn from each other's arsenals: the apologist of openness disguises himself in order to spy on the students' secret gathering, while the man of secrecy openly (and quite easily) invades the minister's home with the aim of assassinating him—an action symbolically equivalent to censorship, given Léo's identity as a writer. Such is the force of governmental duplicity that it neutralizes its opponents by pitting them against each other. For it is precisely because of his campaign against the unruliness of the students that Léo becomes vulnerable to the *co-optation* of his oppositional strength by the government, and hence to the loss of his value as a leader. Once co-opted, once engaged in spite of himself in duplicitous methods, Léo becomes the agency of *infiltration* to which the students are vulnerable because of their cult of secrecy. This leads in turn to the failure of their plot and the disintegration of their organization.

Nerval's play therefore raises two main questions: How is it that openness can be co-opted by duplicity? And how is it that secrecy can be open to infiltration? To respond to these questions, let us take a closer look at the relationship between the prince and Léo (as exercisers of power) and between Frantz and Diégo (as representatives of the conspiracy).

It is striking—and I am not sure this point has been made—that the three key texts of political literature of the 1830s (*Léo Burckart, La Chartreuse de Parme*, and *Lorenzaccio*) all represent the exercise of political power by pairing a ruler (Nerval's prince, the prince of Parma, Alexandre de Médicis) with an associated instrumental figure, who as minister (Léo, Mosca) or favorite (Lorenzo) is mystified to varying degrees. The thematic focus is not so much on the corruptness of power as on the tendency of power to corrupt people of integrity who approach it. It is true that, compared with Musset's duke and Stendhal's prince, the prince in *Léo Burckart* seems almost a man of integrity and nobility. Similarly, Léo's fate—political defeat and humiliation with respect to his principles—appears less complex than Mosca's and less tragic than Lorenzo's. But Nerval's prince is nevertheless a man who practices duplicity without giving it a second thought. This is illustrated early in the play by the way he recruits Léo to his service by pretending to admire his principles, when he is merely satisfying the wishes of Diana, his mistress. Later, after Léo has succumbed to this ploy, the prince uses the revelation of this earlier duplicity as part of another manipulation, designed to induce Léo to adopt "les moyens de gouvernement ordinaires." Despite this, Léo still expresses naive faith in the integrity and success of his diplomatic policies: "Ma diplomatie est seulement de la franchise et du bon sens" ["My diplomacy consists merely of openness and good sense"], he maintains (p. 231). The prince's revelation shatters Léo's faith in his own integrity with a second, more humiliating revelation:

> Là-bas, vous croyez avoir réussi par votre éloquence, n'est-ce pas? eh bien! sur vos neuf voix, quatre ont été achetées à prix d'argent par l'Angleterre, dont l'intérêt se trouve être le nôtre, mais qui avilit notre cause.

> [You think you succeeded by your eloquence alone, don't you? Well, of the nine votes you claim to have won, four were bought by bribes from England, whose interest coincides with ours, but whose collusion dishonors our cause.] (p. 235)

This whole strategy is cleverly conceived to make Léo recognize that he has been involved from the start in duplicitous policies, and that therefore he might as well continue.

Indeed, Léo has no other choice, now that his pride and blindness have been exposed. After having bitterly reproached Paulus for using police methods to steal Diégo's incriminating papers, Léo is forced to contradict himself: he rewards Paulus generously and then uses the information obtained from him to infiltrate the students' gathering, where he draws upon himself the threat of assassination that had previously been directed at the prince. So it is the prince's game plan, not his own, that he ends up carrying out.

Nerval's text draws attention to the difference in tactics used by the old prince and by the new one in dealing with Léo. The former ruler had resorted to repression, and notably to censorship. The brother who succeeds him (a point that is not without relevance) prefers co-optation. The French spectators of the period would of course have recognized (tacitly at least) the obvious parallels with recent events in France, where the crown had been passed from the elder to the younger branch of the royal family in a monarchy characterized initially by flexibility, in contrast to the rigidity of the *Restauration*. The modern reader understands that if the crucial question posed by these texts of the 1830s concerns the possibility of participation in the political process, it is because this question could not have been raised openly under the Restoration, when the social hierarchy remained (or wished to remain) intact and the later, supposedly more liberal, methods of government were not yet in place. At the same time, Nerval's play illustrates quite lucidly the superior political effectiveness of co-optive tactics, since they are capable of neutralizing a man like Léo, whereas an authoritarian system could not prevent him from exercising considerable power and, even despite censorship, from influencing a wide audience with his political pamphlets. Paradoxically, under a regime of censorship, Léo retains his integrity by sacrificing openness (though the adoption of a pseudonym, for instance); by contrast, under a duplicitous government, such openness is sheer naïveté and, as such, proves to be the source of his own undoing. Thus, while the former regime tried in vain to muzzle free speech, the new government succeeds in neutralizing it through methods of co-optation.

It is the victory of the prince's duplicity over Léo's integrity that leads directly to the government's infiltration of the students' secret meeting and hence to the revelation of their plot and the destruction of their organization. Yet the vulnerability of secret societies to penetration of this kind stems from a certain complicity on their own part with power, which the text underlines through a series of unmistakable parallels. For example, the "king" of the students is seen administering justice (day 2, sc. 9). Similarly, the gathering at the Wartburg recalls the councils of the Holy Roman Empire, as well as post-Napoleonic diplomatic congresses. Another significant parallel is that, threatened by police espionage, the secret societies counter with espionage activities of their own and infiltrate the government by enforcing a regulation that their members must accept any position they might be offered. Thus Paulus attends and participates in the students' deliberations, but he also serves as secretary and adviser to Léo, the prince's minister. When Léo finally agrees to stoop to police methods, he easily penetrates the students' conspiracy, since Paulus knows their plans and is perfectly willing to reveal them. It becomes apparent that there is great permeability between the secret societies and the minister's office: each has easy access to the other. In that sense Diégo's role is superfluous, since Paulus is perfectly capable of revealing the plotters' secrets without him.

Diégo's role has thematic significance, however. By multiplying the links in the chain leading from the prince to the students—through Léo, who depends on Paulus, who spies on Diégo, who betrays his "brothers," and notably Franz—Nerval highlights the fact that mediation is the prime feature of a world in which Léo believes it is possible to act openly and Frantz thinks he can guard secrets. But Diégo's betrayal also demonstrates the operation, among the students, of what René Girard calls "mimetic desire."[4] Their vulnerability to police infiltration derives superficially from their own use of police methods, but more deeply from the complicity inherent in their mimetic ambitions. Diégo embodies the resentment and jealousy of those who are excluded from power, as well as the desire for luxury and elegant forms of dissipation that is reflected in the students' beer drinking and tavern sacking and that underlies their parody of the structures of royalty, as well as their imitation of police spy tactics. Although Diégo condemns exploitation, he does so in a glib, superficial manner; presented with a pineapple slice, he virtuously proclaims: "La sueur des malheureux noirs a arrosé ce fruit délicat" ["The sweat of miserable blacks watered this delicate fruit"]. He then proceeds to join the party: "Si nous allions jouer, maintenant que je suis présenté?" ["Can we go play cards, now that I've been introduced?"] (p. 187). Diégo's penetration into the prince's palace (disguised as a South American general) parallels Léo's surreptitious entrance (cloaked and masked) into the students' secret meeting, as well as Frantz's dual penetration into Léo's house (first as Marguerite's would-be lover and, the second time, as the minister's would-be assassin). These parallels illustrate the permeability of milieux as well as the close affinity between Diégo's political jealousy (with respect to the privileges and pleasures of the court) and Frantz and Léo's sexual jealousy (with respect to Marguerite). Needless to say, it is Diégo's desire to participate in the prince's fete that leads to his downfall, since his verbal intoxication is accompanied by a more debilitating physical drunkenness; Paulus is then able to exploit this weakness by taking from Diégo the papers that betray the students' cause.

Léo trusts in sincerity, just as Frantz trusts in secrecy; both stand out as characters who are both noble and naive because of their failure to take into account the reality of *opportunism*, which is nothing other than the exploitation or realization of the permeability characteristic of a mediated society. Opportunism makes Diégo leap at the chance of attending the prince's ball, to the detriment of his comrades; opportunism also leads the prince to walk into a bourgeois living room to recruit Léo, just as it later causes him to make a diplomatic marriage, despite his love for Diana. But the truly opportunistic characters of the play are the chevalier Paulus and the aristocratic Henri de Waldeck; it is no coincidence, but in fact is quite symptomatic of this ambiguous text, that the first is a rather sympathetic character, while the second is an undiluted villain of melodramatic stamp. The function of these two double-crossers is to embody duplicity as the theme of the play and to remind the French audience of the swift changes in political allegiance that had occurred at every change of regime since the Revolution; they are also agents of mediation who exploit the permeability among the various political forces that are vying for power. The archaeologist turned policeman (drawing on his talents as a decipherer of signs) and the aristocrat turned conspirator (out of hatred for a society that admits a bourgeoise like Marguerite to its balls) link the the world of taverns, where power is coveted, with the world of palaces, where power is exercised.

Yet just as the noble characters in the play appear both admirable and ingenuous, so the opportunists appear both realistic (i.e., *not* ingenuous) and ignoble, although the play expresses a certain ambivalence toward opportunism through a clear division of roles. Henri de Waldeck is unmasked as a villain in an episode of pure melodrama. (As Peter Brooks has shown, this genre emerged about 1800 and strongly influenced both romantic drama and Balzac's novels. Brooks has pointed to the cultural significance of melodrama as a manifestation of a nostalgic desire for ethical clarity in a political and moral universe rendered opaque and ambiguous in the aftermath of the Revolution.[5] Melodrama is therefore both a reflection of and a reaction to the duplicity of the modern world.)

On the other hand, Paulus—who lucidly shows Léo his political errors (particularly his failure to make use of mediatory screens) and no less lucidly predicts his fall—appears less as a traitor than as a clear-sighted individual who acknowledges realities. Paulus's double game does not prevent him from demonstrating a certain loyalty and even friendship for Léo, as well as affection for his student comrades; yet he makes no secret of the fact that his own interests always come first. So he has a kind of integrity; in his own way, he can be relied on. When Léo finally becomes suspicious and asks him: "Et maintenant, monsieur, qui me répond de vous?" ["And now, sir, what will assure me of your loyalty?"], Paulus candidly replies: "Mon intérêt" ["My self-interest"] (p. 247). Similarly, when Paulus warns Léo that he will fall from power and the minister asks him: "Mais, dans cette prévision, comment pouvez-vous me servir?" ["But in that case why are you acting as my assistant?"], once again Paulus replies quite unhypocritically: "Parce que, plus je vous aurai été utile, plus je serai nécessaire à votre successeur" ["Because if I will have served you well, I will be all the more necessary to your successor"] (p. 249).

This is opportunism without hypocrisy: Paulus's paradoxical *francparler*, his reliability (if not his loyalty), and his lucidity combine to make him one of the most sympathetic characters of Nerval's play. When Frantz and Léo, the two noble characters of the play, have confirmed their powerlessness to act in the world of duplicity and mediation (Frantz by his suicide, Léo by his retirement), it becomes clear that the future belongs to Paulus, who has now become indispensable to the prince. How will he use his power? To foster freedom? To support the police? All we know, in his case, is that any such decision will depend above all on a careful analysis of his own interests.

In his preface, Nerval reports that contemporary critics viewed the play's ending as "une conclusion empreinte de scepticisme" ["a conclusion marked by skepticism"]. To this, he makes the cogent reply: "Le même reproche pourrait être adressé aux drames historiques de Shakespeare, à *Wallenstein* ou à *Goetz von Berlichingen*" ["The same criticism could be made of Shakespeare's historical dramas, of *Wallenstein*, or of *Goetz von Berlichingen*"] (preface, p. 2). But it is less the skepticism of the conclusion than the openness of the denouement that is striking. For by refusing to judge Paulus, the play simultaneously refuses to commit itself, to take a position "for" or "against" the world of duplicity in which Paulus is so comfortable. *Léo Burckart* can be seen as a play marked by disenchantment, condemning any opposition to power as unrealistic, since power is duplicity and as such occupies the whole terrain between the purely ideal positions occupied by Léo and Frantz: sincerity that is vulnerable to co-optation, on the one hand, and secrecy that is vulnerable to infiltration, on the other. Or else one can see it as a play that condemns the practice of power as destructive of those who, like Léo and Frantz, genuinely care about the fate of their country and wish to serve the general welfare.

The play reflects—and encourages in the spectator—sympathetic feelings toward Léo and Frantz that conflict with its *judgments*, and notably with its refusal to condemn a society that destroys people of integrity and rewards opportunists like Paulus. Clearly, there is a fundamental and significant ideological contradiction here. But this ambivalence also suggests that the text is *itself* opportunistic, responding to the duplicity of the world it portrays with an undecidability that is a kind of *double jeu* and exploiting, in a world of mediations, the first characteristic of discourse, which is to be opaque. However, this textual opportunism does differ in its political posture from that of the characters; for if the play cannot afford to practice either Léo's brand of frankness (it would be banned) or Frantz's cultivation of secrecy (it would become hermetic), it is not, like the opportunistic characters, self-interested in its practice of ambiguity. It has nothing to gain; or rather, the only thing it has to gain is the right to speak. What *Léo Burckart* demonstrates is that, under the political conditions of France in the 1830s, access to public discourse is obtained not by openness or secrecy, but by a mode of enunciation that manages to be both open and secretive, affirmative and reticent, thereby baffling the standard categories of judgment. In the face of the duplicity of power, *Léo Burckart* demonstrates the power of duplicity.

*

Frantz, pronounced in the French manner, is a well-named character, not because he "stands for" France (which is, in fact, represented by the play as a whole), but because he is associated with Nerval's Ile-de-France. Long after the performances of *Léo Burckart*, the protagonist of "Sylvie," who in many ways resembles Frantz (notably through his role as a melancholic, unrequited lover and as an initiate associated with theatricality), will, like Frantz, represent the "unrealistic hero." Such a figure is heroic not in spite of, but *because* of, his unrealistic attitudes; it is his refusals, in the midst of a materialist society with its *avide curée*, that make him a sympathetic figure, although they simultaneously condemn him to impotence. As in *Léo Burckart*, the "point of view" of the text is extremely difficult, indeed impossible, to grasp; but in the case of "Sylvie" this ambiguity stems from an extraordinarily complex narrative discourse that is both ambivalent and filled with multiple ironies (see chapter 4). Moreover, in "Sylvie," written in 1853, not only has opportunism become a minor theme, but there is no figure or perspective that recalls the role of Léo. By that date it seems to have become impossible, even in a retrospective text set largely in the 1830s, to portray a writer whose duties might associate him with the practice of power.

But it is precisely this dream of the writer called to participate in government that is expressed in *Léo Burckart*, even if the play ultimately demonstrates the difficulty, even the impossibility, of achieving such a dream in a world given over to the duplicities of power and co-optation. Moreover, if one substitutes the term "intellectual" (which at the time did not yet exist) for "writer," Lorenzo and Mosca clearly represent this same dream, which still seemed imaginable in a period and under a regime in which Lamartine was a *député* and Hugo was to become a *pair de France*. Yet Lamartine's role in the "gouvernement provisoire" of 1848 and Hugo's exile in 1851 would only confirm the pessimistic speculations of the 1830s concerning the inevitable corruption of the writer-intellectual through contact with power and, consequently, the need to separate art from politics. In this

way, through both its resemblances and its differences from *Léo Burckart*,
"Sylvie" serves to measure the distance traversed by literature between the
1830s and the 1850s. It is surely not coincidental that it was in the same
year (1850), and in response to a new censorship law (*l'amendement Rian-
cey*), that Nerval would develop his new "Valois" style with "Les Faux-
Saulniers" (the same style in which "Sylvie" was later written) and that he
was led to recall *Léo Burckart* and the circumstances of its performance.
Moreover, two years later, in 1852, he would reprint the 1839 version of
the play in *Lorely*.

Yet "Sylvie" is a "writerly" text; its undecidability derives from its "writerliness" and notably from the duality of narrative and textual functions
that I see as characteristic of the new writing of the 1850s.[6] *Léo Burckart*,
as a play, derives its undecidability from a characteristic of drama that has
been noted since Aristotle: the absence of a discourse attributable to a narrator, and thus of a narrative "point of view." (This is not the same, of
course, as saying that a play is not a narration.) With hindsight, however,
one can nevertheless discern in the play some interesting foreshadowings
of the writerly techniques that later developed, and notably the effacement
of the narrative function. It is significant, for example, that *Léo Burckart* is
the product of a collaborative effort, so that no one can be sure what is
Nerval's work and what is Dumas's. It is not that Nerval's authorial responsibility was ever really in doubt; he never denied that responsibility, and in
any case it was as easy for the authorities to condemn two authors as to
condemn one. However, this practice of collaborative writing anticipates—and perhaps even lays the groundwork for—the "dialogic" writing
practice that Nerval was to develop in "Angélique," a textual blending of
multiple voices into which the narrator, as a representation of the discursive subject, tends to merge.

Let us take a closer look at one of the self-reflexive moments in the play
that calls attention quite clearly to the duplicity of writing. Diégo is about
to be arrested for scratching graffiti on a statue in the prince's gardens with
his dagger—or perhaps, in a more bourgeois manner, with his pipestem:

> L'Officier. — Qu'a-t-il écrit?
> Premier Soldat. — Rien: des mots sans suite. Il a gâté le
>   marbre, voilà tout; d'ailleurs, je ne sais pas lire.
> Officier (*à l'autre*).— Qu'a-t-il écrit?
> Deuxième Soldat. — Il a écrit: "*Tu dors, Brute.*"
> Premier Soldat. — Voyez-vous? mon commandant, des in-

jures à un factionnaire! Oh! que non, je ne dormais pas, bourgeois.

Diégo. — Ignorant! qui prend pour lui un souvenir de l'anti-quité, une citation latine...Mais vous connaissez cela, vous, commandant?

Officier. — Je ne connais que mon service, monsieur; et tout ceci commence à me devenir suspect.

[Officer. — What did he write?

First Soldier. — Nothing: a string of meaningless words. He simply scratched up the marble; anyway, I don't know how to read.

Officer *(to the other soldier)*.— What did he write?

Second Soldier. — He wrote: "*You're sleeping, Brute.*"

First Soldier. — You see, sir? Insults to a sentinel! Oh, I certainly was *not* sleeping, bourgeois.

Diégo. — Ignoramus! You think I'm referring to you with an allusion to antiquity, a quotation from Latin. . . . But you are certainly familiar with it, sir?

Officer. — All I know is my duty, monsieur; and this whole business is beginning to look suspicious to me.] (p. 155)

What are we to make of this "glyphic" (if not strictly "hieroglyphic") in-scription? For Diégo, it is a quotation from Latin, *une citation latine,* whereas the language of the text is half French, half Latin (much as the subject of *Léo Burckart* is half French, half German): because the Latin vocative of "Brutus" is indistinguishable from the French word "brute," it is as if two voices are speaking here. Through the character of Diégo, Nerval mocks the students' love for classical allusions and their self-inflating nostalgia for antiquity. Even Frantz knows that "les époques ne sont jamais semblables et les moyens différents aussi," and he states firmly: "Je ne suis pas Romain, mais Allemand." ["Historical periods are always different, as are the methods used in them. . . . I am not Roman, but German."] (p. 149). In this way the text is suggesting its own modernity with respect to the classically minded revolutionary tradition (which it nevertheless incor-porates even in the act of distancing itself from it): it is pointing to a cer-tain originality with respect to methods, an originality that is partly figured by the ambiguity of the modern pipe and the old-fashioned dagger as writ-ing tools, and partly by the (con)fusion of languages, producing a scram-bled message.

Yet the general oppositional thrust of Diégo's message remains clear, as does that of the play as a whole. Although doubly ciphered—through the allusion to Roman history, which the soldiers fail to understand, and through the fact that it imitates the messages historically addressed to Brutus by his friends (messages that were not themselves straightforward)— the inscription constitutes a call for resistance and revolt. It is important that the message should be so unambiguous for the textual addressee (reader or spectator), but so opaque to the representatives of authority: the first soldier does not know how to read, while the officer only knows his duty; indeed, his professional suspiciousness is so generalized that he misses the specific point completely. In similar fashion, Nerval's dramatic writing seems to rely on a certain opacity to the eyes of its official readership, and it is easy to imagine the author of the censor's report grumbling discontentedly, like the officer in the play, that "this whole business is beginning to look suspicious to me." At the same time, the text presents itself as readable in the eyes of a different readership that is more perspicacious, more complicitous, better informed, perhaps, but also more intuitive; in fact it presents its illegibility in official eyes as an object of reading for these other, more "privileged" readers. Encapsulated here are the problematics of reading characteristic of oppositional texts, which need to calculate and adjust their readability or unreadability according to their potential audiences, present or future, hostile or sympathetic.

At the same time, the patent reference to *Lorenzaccio* (the mutilated statue, the obsession with Roman history and its problematic connection with modernity, etc.) introduces an important intertextual dimension; for Musset's play develops the thematics of language more extensively and explicitly than Nerval's. Diégo's love of words and ineffectiveness in action, his nostalgia for antiquity, together with his easy corruptibility and drunkenness, make him a rather superficial caricature of Lorenzo. Perhaps Diégo serves in this way to divert attention from the deeper resemblances between Frantz and Musset's figure, who are both victims of a certain "historical melancholy" resulting from an awareness of their modernity, combined with a sense of their political powerlessness. Similarly, the play's treatment of the incompatibility between scholarly study and action (represented by Léo and Frantz) derives partly from *Lorenzaccio* and partly from their common ancestor, Goethe's *Torquato Tasso*.

Above all, it is the theme of duplicity—of the mask that sticks to the face in a world of mediations in which neither absolute frankness nor absolute secrecy is possible—that is common to the two texts, although Nerval is more interested in the duplicitousness of a whole society, while Musset prefers to trace its psychological and existential effects in an individual case, delineating the anguish of a character whose identity disintegrates in a society in which the preeminence of words has paralyzed action. Clearly the two texts are closely related. However, whereas *Lorenzaccio* anticipates the writing of the 1850s through its illustration of the melancholy caused by masked identity (which it relates to the problematics of language), *Léo Burckart* anticipates the 1850s through its exploration of the relation between sociopolitical duplicity and the enunciatory duplicity characteristic of oppositional art. The effect of Nerval's intertextual reference to *Lorenzaccio* is therefore to acknowledge the relevance and modernity of Musset's themes, but also to underline the difference between Musset's text and his own.

It is precisely on the level of self-reflexivity—that is, of textual enunciation—that Nerval's play shows itself to be more radical than Musset's. The undecidability of *Lorenzaccio* is clearly linked to its thematics of duplicity, but it also stems from the play's status as a "tableau" of a particular society; consequently it is concerned with the function of representation and with the moral categories of good and evil. The self-reflexivity of the text is especially clear in the story of the young painter Tebaldeo, the idealist and ethicist in art who nevertheless allows himself to be recruited by Lorenzo to paint the duke's portrait. Through the equivalence set up between the portrait of the duke, the debauched tyrant, and the "tableau" of Florence, his whore, the play raises questions about the aesthetic legitimacy of representing vice. The representation of evil can to a certain degree serve the cause of good, since by posing for his portrait, Duke Alexandre enables Lorenzo to steal his coat of mail, thus furthering the latter's antiauthoritarian project (doomed to inadequacy as it is). Yet at the same time, it removes art from its vocation as the manifestation of an ideal beauty and a world of dreams. In short, the ambiguity of Musset's text arises from the conventions of an aesthetics of representation and the traditional identification of the beautiful with the good; it hopes to do a little good (a little more good, perhaps, than Lorenzo?) through the representation of evil. Any censor would be perfectly at ease with such categories, which relate to the play essentially in its referential and narrative dimension.

It is not in terms of representation and referentiality, however, that Nerval's play situates its ambiguity, but as a function of the undecidable place from which it is speaking. In this respect it seems to claim for itself a certain autonomy with respect to the political world it portrays, the world in which it is the categories of good and evil, for and against, that matter; for it is precisely such dichotomies that its own enunciatory position contests. Through the inscrutable duplicity of this enunciation, Nerval's play also signals the possibility of a different kind of discourse, *un discours autre*, with powers of intervention of its own in the social world, powers that it owes solely to its "autonomization" with respect to conventional categories and the undecidability that results. In this sense literary discourse is anything but "cut off" from the social discourse of its time: it defines itself instead as a specific form of discourse in competition with the others, citing them in order to distance itself from them more effectively. In other words, literary discourse competes by "opting out"; but at the same time it joins in the general social discourse by adopting an equivocal enunciation of its own. More than the moral ambiguity with which *Lorenzaccio* is largely concerned, it is this enunciatory undecidability of *Léo Burckart* that opens the way for the writing of the 1850s. This writing was to emerge as a melancholic, uncentered mode of discourse "defined" by an absence—the absence (or at least the very considerable effacement) of the subject as an instance of judgment. Lacking a judging subject, the texts become proportionately difficult to judge. Yet through the "opportunism" of its discursive method, in a social and political world that it defines as both manipulative and opportunistic, Nerval's play—much like *Lorenzaccio*—also anticipates the identity problem that would characterize the melancholic genre as a whole: the problem of differentiation posed by a textual discourse that necessarily participates in the social conditions it denounces, such as the hypocrisy portrayed in Baudelaire's writing or the stupidity (*la bêtise*) portrayed in Flaubert's.

At one point in *Léo Burckart*, one of the students in the conspiracy exclaims: "Ah! moi, je n'aime pas les masques. Masque d'ami, visage de traître, voilà mon opinion!" ["How I detest masks! A friendly mask goes with a traitor's face, if you want my opinion!"] (p. 277). The message is clear: Hermann dislikes the duplicity of hiding some genuine verifiable intention behind a misleading appearance (for example, speaking of France in order to portray Germany)—what one might call "simple duplicity." The unmasking of the traitor Henri de Waldeck soon proves that Hermann was in fact justified in mistrusting the mask of friendship. The duplicity one finds in both *Lorenzaccio* and *Léo Burckart* is never simple, however, and the formula "masque d'ami, visage de traître" is a curious one, particularly if one considers that it attributes duplicity not simply to misleading appearances, but also to the real intention underlying them. There is ambiguity everywhere, since beneath the mask of friendship lurks the duplicity of treachery. The face hidden beneath the mask is in the long run only another mask: Hermann lives in a world of generalized duplicity, of *complex* duplicity, that threatens the distinction between truth and falsehood, just as men of secrecy (like Frantz) and men of openness (like Léo) are threatened, indeed destroyed, in a society that practices the "ordinary methods of government."

It was from a duplicitous world that Nerval's play learned its lessons, since it breaks down the categories of political complicity and resistance—of "for" and "against." Whether it is from the government's point of view or from that of the resistance, *Léo Burckart* presents a mask of friendship that is difficult to distinguish from the face—or rather the mask—of treachery. The play is both for the government and against the resistance, for the resistance and against the government; it articulates an enunciatory position that makes a mockery of all such questions. This is a strategy that would be adopted in turn by the literature of the 1850s.

But the literature of that decade could no longer directly target political life, as had the literature of the 1830s, with only a slight veiling of the facts. The literature of the Second Empire was not so much depoliticized (*dépoliticisée*) as it was "depolitified" (*dépolitiquée*), to borrow Baudelaire's key term—that is to say, disenchanted with the "ordinary methods of government," whose co-optive and corruptive influence had already been underlined in the literature of the 1830s. These duplicitous government tactics had, moreover, crushed the revolution that was attempted with such enthusiasm in 1848. Literature became *dépolitiquée* ("depolitified"), just as people who lose their virginity are *dépucelés* and those who get deloused are *épouillés*—that is, disengaged from politics in the way that others are relieved of their innocence or their parasites. The dream of the writer exercising political power was indeed dead! Literature, as a result, became "privatized." Nerval was politically active in the 1830s in ways that Baudelaire and Flaubert (both born in 1821) could not possibly be; consequently, he is the modernist writer in whose career it is perhaps easiest to trace this gradual process of privatization. After the *Voyage en Orient*, written during the 1840s and still clearly reflecting political preoccupations, Nerval went on to develop a new autobiographical style in "Aurélia" and in the so-called Valois texts (of which I shall take "Sylvie" to be characteristic, since its theme of symbolic suicide offers a telling parallel with the suicide of Frantz in *Léo Burckart*).

This depoliticized literature was to lead to forms of "suicidal" writing distinctly different from the style and techniques of *Léo Burckart*, despite its undecidable enunciatory position and its thematic and self-reflexive interest in the duplicity of signs. The "narrative function" is alive and well in most texts of the 1830s; in order to neutralize it and to avoid direct expression of a narrative point of view, it is not surprising that Nerval chose the theater as his medium in *Léo Burckart*. In prose and poetry, the means of producing a decentered, indeterminate enunciatory position had not yet been developed; to achieve this, Nerval would go on to develop a "melancholic" textuality that sought to circumvent and even explode the constraints of narrativity. It is on this type of writing that we will now focus our attention.

FOUR

SUICIDE WITHOUT PISTOLS

"Sylvie" is in many ways a story about disengagement, or "letting go": it asks us to reflect about what it means to disengage, and on whether disengagement can be a positive act. Whereas Frantz and Leo, in *Léo Burckart*, involve themselves in a society—that of Restoration Germany—that indirectly represents the years of the Bourgeois Monarchy in France, the outcome of their involvement being respectively suicide and retirement, those same years following the July revolution are described in "Sylvie" (published in 1853) as the period when the novella's protagonist makes a crucial choice, the choice *not to be involved*; and this choice in turn determines the nature of the literary production he will turn to, as narrator of the same novella, in a period that is left undated but can be assumed (in view of the date of publication) to coincide with the period following the revolution of 1848 and the coup d'état of December 1851. Since the disengaging gesture in each period can be described as a kind of suicide—an amorous suicide in the 1830s and a writerly suicide in the 1850s—it seems that a resemblance, continuity, or overlay between two postrevolutionary periods is again being hinted at; and since the suicide in each case is an oddly passive one, a suicide by inertia—by an unwillingness, refusal, or inability to choose—one is tempted to read "Sylvie" as both a comment on and an enactment of the forms of oppositionality that will be characteristic of the writing of the 1850s. We can describe them summarily as constituting a *significant* act of letting go, a refusal to become involved, that invites reading and reflection as to its whys and wherefores. For such disengagement, like all suicidal gestures, is clearly symptomatic; and as such it is necessary to view it as inevitably forming part of exactly that of which it seems not to be a part.[1]

The novella consists in large part of a series of memories, overlaid one on the other, in which the narrator of the 1850s recalls his early manhood in the Paris of the 1830s, and through his memory of that period an earlier

series of memories of his childhood in the Valois and his subsequent returns to that region, the last forming the crucial action of the 1830s. There
is in addition a "dernier feuillet" (chap. 14) or final leaf of the album whose
pages he is thus metaphorically turning, which brings us up to date with
the protagonist's existence in what has become, twenty years later, a kind
of extended afterlife or *survie*. At the same time, drawing attention (by
apologizing for it) to his "outmoded style" ("style vieilli") and thus intro-
ducing himself as a writer, he now steps forward in a new guise, as narrator
of his story; so that it is partly as protagonist and partly as narrator that he
describes his continued visits to the Valois as bittersweet experiences in
which, having lost his beloved Sylvie to a pastry cook, he now plays the
role of friend to her family. The happiness she represented is out of reach,
yet he has a position, so to speak, at its edge; he has opted out, but that
very fact gives him a place, however limited, in her world and in her affec-
tions. Indeed, she shares his literary taste for the outmoded, since the two
read together "a few poems, or a few pages of those short books hardly
anyone writes these days."[2]

They are, it seems, an inverted Paolo and Francesca, for whom reading
together is not a prelude to passion but a sign that passion is spent, and
who read not the sexually arousing story of Guinevere and Lancelot but
. . . What *are* those "short books hardly anyone writes these days"? One
thinks of the Renés, Obermans, and Adolphes of the early part of the century, stories of weak heroes whose love is a form of failure; and metafic-
tionally, therefore, one is led to think of "Sylvie" itself as another short
novella in the same series and in similar ("outmoded") style, a story that
the protagonist and Sylvie might enjoy reading together. But the characters themselves are conscious in a half-joking way of their own resemblance
to the key figures of an earlier short novel, a novel of male weakness and
suicide that stands at the beginning of the tradition of "short books," once
so popular and now so neglected: Goethe's *Werther (Die Leiden des jungen
Werthers*, 1774). "I sometimes call her Lolotte, and she thinks I slightly
resemble Werther, minus the pistols, which are no longer in style." Ironically, the only way this generally out-of-date protagonist is in step with his
own age is in the *lack* he displays, let us say the lack of determination that
makes him incapable of the resolute behavior (the pistol shot) that would
irreparably and definitively sever him from his age. It is this lack of determination that condemns him instead to what can be exactly described,
therefore, as a "modern" form of suicide: suicide as a modus vivendi and a
way of surviving.

Sylvie's friendly diagnosis of her friend as a suicide by irresolution is an accurate one. If suicide is a form of reproach and rejection, it was as a mute reproach and an unnoticed rejection of the ambition and egoism of July Monarchy society that in the 1830s the protagonist, with a few soulmates, had opted for a form of disengagement and inertia: "the ivory tower of poets." "Ambition was not for us at our age, and the eager scramble for positions and honors that was going on at that time turned us away from the possible spheres of action" (chap. 1). Instead, at the topmost point of the poets' tower, "we breathed the pure air of solitude, we imbibed oblivion in the golden goblet of legend, we intoxicated ourselves on poetry and love." This ivory tower describes the rarefied, mystic atmosphere, entirely cut off from any awareness of reality, of the young man's idealist love, an *amor de lonh* for the actress Aurélie, whom he comes to imagine, in the flash of insight on which the novella's crisis turns, as none other than the aristocratic Adrienne of his childhood in the Valois, a tall, moonlit figure whom he had crowned with a laurel wreath before she disappeared into her castle and, becoming in due course a nun, eluded him forever. "To love a nun in the shape of an actress! . . . and supposing they were one and the same!—That way madness lies!" (chap. 3). Drawing back from these fascinating but also frightening implications of what represents one possible alternative to the *avide curée*, the eager scramble for advancement going on around him, the protagonist is impelled, therefore, in another direction, a direction that is specifically mediated by the memory of Adrienne that accounts for his love for Aurélie. He recalls the simple reality of his rural childhood, figured however, not by the inaccessible Adrienne, but by the comradeship and affection of a peasant girl; and he undertakes a spur of the moment trip back to see his half-forgotten friend Sylvie.

Whereas the fabulous resemblance of Aurélie and Adrienne had seemed, alluringly, to deny time, the problem with Sylvie lies, symmetrically, in the way the attractiveness of country reality is inseparable from an inescapable acknowledgment of the power of time, forgetfulness, and change, which introduce difference into the former intimacy of the two friends. As he travels, the protagonist already recalls how each time he met Sylvie, it was to discover them drifting apart because each was subject to differing historical forces, figured by "Paris" and the "Valois" respectively; and the present trip will only confirm this difficulty. He has become a Parisian and acquired a sophisticated education, leaving behind him the peasant girl. But this selfsame peasant girl, who now seems to him a figure of salutary innocence, has herself gradually changed in the intervening time, following the

historical transformations of the region. She no longer pursues the traditional craft of lace making but is employed in the new cottage industry of
making gloves; instead of singing the old folk songs she warbles operati-
cally; she reads novels and—as if she were Emma Bovary—exclaims: "It's
a landscape straight out of Walter Scott, isn't it?" The final blow will be the
protagonist's discovery that she has a lover, *le grand frisé* ("Big Curly"): he
is a pastry cook whom she plans to marry and with whom she will set up
shop in Dammartin, thus completing the process of *embourgeoisement* that
simultaneously puts her out of the protagonist's reach and makes her part
of the social order to which he seeks an alternative. Hearing the news of
her impending marriage from a third party, he simply fails to press, or even
to make explicit, his own suit, but again lets go. "I asked no more questions. The Nanteuil-le-Hardouin coach returned me to Paris the next day"
(chap. 12). His only remaining option is to set about seriously courting
Aurélie, the actress, who understandably rejects him on the sensible
grounds that he is not in love with her but loves an image—he seeks a
"drama," she says—and who settles comfortably for a fellow member of
her troupe. The protagonist is quite alone.

What is tantalizing about all this is a certain indeterminacy that is inherent in his irresolution—his failure to engage entails the poignancy of
"what might have been." Sylvie might have accepted the protagonist instead of *le grand frisé* had he but asked; and there are signs that the changes
he so dislikes in her are superficial—that the lively, innocent peasant girl
survives in the pert modern miss. Aurélie too might have accepted him
instead of the wrinkled *jeune premier* had he been willing to approach her
earlier instead of loving her mystically and from afar. These were possible
forms of happiness, although they could never, it seems, have been more
than partial ones. He would not have turned to Sylvie had not the "presence" of the unattainable Adrienne in the figure of Aurélie redirected his
attention back to the Valois; conversely, he would not have courted Aurélie
had not Sylvie first seemed to reject him for the pastry cook. Neither of the
two alternatives to the "eager scramble" for success offers complete satisfaction, for each requires renunciation of the other, theatrical illusion excluding natural beauty and vice versa. Adrienne, the mediating figure,
being unavailable, they are the two halves of a "single love," like Aldebaran,
which displays only one "side" at a time; and the split between artifice (the
"drama" of art) and the natural (the beauty of the "folk song") cannot be
healed. Neither "side," in short, offers a fully acceptable alternative to what,
because it denies them both, must itself be rejected—the world of Parisian

society and the "scramble" for success. Yet this Parisian world is at the same time the only sphere of possible *action*, the only world in which it is possible to make a success of one's life, which is why it defines its split alternative(s) as sphere(s) of inaction and site(s) of failure. The protagonist, in short, has no option but to fail, whether by withdrawing from the sphere of success or by hesitating between the split alternatives that remain: a maddening illusion detached from reality, and a reality itself hopelessly contaminated by "Paris."

That is the significance of his suicide by irresolution and of the indeterminate survival to which it condemns him, as the friend now living on the fringes of the petit-bourgeois happiness represented by Sylvie and her family. But as Gabrielle Malandain[3] has pointed out, such a "failure," lonely and nostalgic as it leaves the protagonist, is unmistakably to be understood as preferable to the only forms of success contemporary society offers; and the option the protagonist has exercised in favor of failing has a clearly condemnatory sense with respect to the society he disdains. Less a failure, then, than a victim of alienating historical circumstances, he is entitled to judge those circumstances from a moral standpoint that justifies his "suicide" not as the pitiful response of a misfit, but as an honorable disengagement that is the only way to survive in a world that offers no better option. Renunciation—or more accurately, perhaps, the Faustian "Sollst entbehren!" ["Thou shalt go without!"]—is the only form of heroism, and the only form of expression, that is available when all "possible spheres of action" are closed. It is also a path of wisdom, the wisdom of "experience" that the final leaf celebrates in its "outmoded style," as the protagonist's sole justification for the existence of privation he has led.

But experience is also a mediating element that effects a shift in the narrative emphasis in this "final leaf." After a reading of "Sylvie" focused on the protagonist's story, a rereading is foreshadowed that will be attentive to the significance of his experience, and hence to the narrative act of which he has become the subject; and this means that, having witnessed the protagonist's suicide by irresolution, we become aware of a second suicide committed by the narrator, a suicide through *writing* that will be a suicide by indeterminacy complementing the protagonist's suicide by irresolution. For on the one hand, experience is the "fruit" of the protagonist's history of indecision, a matter of "lost illusions":

Illusions fall one after the other like the layers of rind on a piece
of fruit, and the fruit is experience. It has a bitter taste, but

> there is something acrid in it that is strengthening—may I be
> forgiven this outmoded style. (chap. 14)

But on the other hand it is also produced as what prompts the narration of
"Sylvie," conceived as an attempt to share that experience and to communicate the sense in which the protagonist's story of failure has nevertheless
been fruitful and strengthening. As such, "experience" is the site of transformation in which the man who has survived his own suicide becomes a
writer. And it is this writer, I submit, whose writing, as it is instantiated in
"Sylvie," is the site of another suicide and the vehicle of another mode of
survival, themselves predicated—like the protagonist's own suicide and
survival—on another mode of disengagement, another form of letting go.

For to be a "Werther minus the pistols" means, in one instance, to commit suicide without killing oneself, which is what the protagonist, in his
irresolution, has done. But it can also mean to commit suicide *by some other
means* than firearms—for instance, by means of the pen ("style," after all—
as in "outmoded style"—puns etymologically with stiletto). For such will
indeed be the narrator's mode of suicide, inasmuch as his writing stages
the "death" of the narrator *as an instance in control of the meaning of the text*,
a disengagement from the exercise of his narrative options that reproduces
the protagonist's irresolution by producing the text as a site of indeterminacy.

The form of renunciation involved here is that of a certain concept of
selfhood; but through it another form of survival will also be achieved, in
the sense that the death of the narrator in his own writing produces a readable text, a site in which "he" will live on as the object of the interpretive
readings that the text, by its elusiveness, actively solicits. Readability is the
mode of survival of texts, and it is conditioned precisely on textual indeterminacy as the failure to specify or control the meaning of what is given to
be read. In more technical terms, its condition is the subordination of the
"narrative function" (as a relation to the narratee that is controlled by a
narrator) to a "textual function" that is a site of mutual interaction between
a writing and a reading. For needless to say the sense in which the bitter
taste of the protagonist's experience contains something acrid and
strengthening is never specified in "Sylvie": the responsibility for determining that sense is abdicated by the narrator and passed on to the reader,
the protagonist's conviction that he *has* acquired worthwhile experience
serving only as a signal to the reader, on the narrator's part, that there is in
the novella a certain meaning, a certain wisdom that is worth seeking out.

This "something acrid and strengthening" is, in short, the name the text gives to the *lack* within it, not the protagonist's lack of resolution so much as a failure of meaning that is produced by the narrative suicide of which it is the site, a lack that makes it the object of a potentially endless reading. And the curious image by which it is the falling away of illusions, one by one, like "les écorces d'un fruit," the rinds of a fruit, that produces experience, is one that simultaneously exemplifies the hesitancy induced in the reader by the indeterminacy of the narrator's style (for what fruit has several rinds? is the "fruit" all rinds?) and strongly suggests that the fruit of experience is a negative quantity—it has, so to speak, no pulp—and is describable only obliquely, in terms of the illusions whose loss constitutes it. It cannot be directly said, but must instead be read.

I want to make the claim that, by thus superimposing on the story of a suicide an appeal to learn from that suicide which is itself the site of another suicide, "Sylvie" situates itself generically as a version of the form of writing that is known as the "suicide note" (even though some such "notes" are as long as "short books"). In doing this, it simultaneously identifies the tradition of short books that it belongs to as a tradition of suicidal writing—writing *about* suicide (a form of "suicide note") that is, as in the case of the narrator of "Sylvie," a suicide *through* writing. Let me try to specify somewhat, in what follows, the content of this claim.

*

If by "discourse" one understands the set of signifying practices that constitute a culture, any act of suicide is a discursive event. But as a discursive enunciation in this sense, suicide has the specific characteristic of being particularly strong on the rhetorical side but fundamentally weak on the signifying side. It has a discursive authority that is, at least potentially, immense: it is hard to think of a more effective way of gaining attention for one's statement than to kill oneself. But in the very act that produces such authority, the person who commits suicide simultaneously and irrevocably loses the possibility of specifying the meaning of that enunciatory act, let alone of controlling the interpretations that may be put on it after the event (or even of contributing to determining them). The gain of authority is accompanied by—indeed predicated on—a proportionate loss of the power to control the reception of the message, whose significance is thereby reduced, at best, to a generally oppositional one. The most one can conclude is that the suicide, as enunciating subject, had "something to say" that was not being heard, or was passing unnoticed, or was being misinterpreted.

The remedy habitually sought for this semantic weakness of the act of suicide as discursive enunciation is the suicide note, in which recourse to the supposed specificity of verbal expression seeks to make up for the inadequacies of discursive enunciation while continuing to profit from the authority procured by taking one's own life. Foreseeing his or her own future inability to control the interpretation of that discursive statement, the suicide seeks to "survive" the act—to counter the effect of death as an abdication of discursive control—by continuing to exist in the world as the subject of a linguistic enunciation whose words will ensure that the meaning of the suicide's act will be understood as it should. As a genre, therefore, the suicide note has a double function: As its authority ploy it announces the self-inflicted death of an individual and hence the disappearance of a cultural (discursive) subject (in the standard incipit, "I shall be dead when you read this"). Yet it seeks to contextualize the disappearance and to give it its proper significance, for example, by distributing blame or claiming responsibility, accusing society as a whole or some individual of what amounts to the murder of a victim, or alternatively assuming the heroism or saintliness of a willed act of renunciation. In short, since there can be no such thing as a suicide by accident, and every act of suicide therefore implies the *significance* of some individual's death, the function of the suicide note, whether brief ("Farewell, cruel world!") or extensive, is to manifest that signification. It means, "I did not die by accident."

Such an assertion ("my death is not arbitrary"), however, amounts to a negative attribution of significance in the way that "I have lost my illusions" is a negative statement of the value of experience. And try as it may, a suicide note cannot specify, beyond all possibility of contestation or reinterpretation, the actual, positive significance that attaches to the act of suicide: the only *assured* meaning a note can produce is that this death *was* a suicide—that is, a culturally (discursively) significant act. Beyond that, as an interpretation itself, it is subject to interpretive reading, as the key formula, "I shall be dead when you *read* this," ironically insists. A note laying claim to an act of heroic self-abnegation is open, for example, to the deflating reinterpretation of self-aggrandizement (the person was a "loser" from the start and did not have the courage or insight to admit it). An accusation of "cruelty" directed at the world or at some person or persons is readable as a manifestation of egoistic blindness and self-pity, a failure to recognize the rights of others. Thus Emma's note, in *Madame Bovary*—of which we learn only that it begins: "Qu'on n'accuse personne . . . ," ["No one is to blame . . . "]—is clearly to be read, in the novel's context, partly as a piece of melodramatic rhetorical posturing on Emma's part and partly as a textual indicator that her death *is* in some sense and in some degree blamable on other people and hence as an invitation for the reader not to interpret Emma's world as she herself sees it; in either case, the note fails as an attempt by Emma to impart her view of the significance of her suicide.

This means that the suicide note repeats, in the sphere of verbal enunciation, the discursive indeterminacy, the inability to control meaning, that characterizes the act of suicide itself, an indeterminacy whose effects the note was supposed to countermand or at least to limit. Which is to say that the suicide note begins to look like a place where something like a "substitute" suicide can take place, a suicide without pistols in which a verbal enunciation about suicide proves to have a cultural value—that of the "death" of the enunciating subject—equivalent to an act of suicide "proper." More particularly, the suicide note enacts the phenomenon Jacques Derrida has identified as supplementation, in which any attempt to assign meaning to an enunciation functions not to determine the meaning of that enunciation, but to indicate its interpretability. Hence it is an invitation to assign other meanings, whether to the "original" enunciation (in the case of "Sylvie," the protagonist's suicide) or to the interpretative enunciation (the narrative as a second suicide) that supplements it. The note supplements the suicide and repeats it by calling forth further supplementation.

What "Sylvie" did in 1853, then, was to define "writing," in discursive terms, as a site of cultural suicide—that is, as an oppositional act whose rhetorical force is predicated on a proportionate degree of semantic indeterminacy—and to define it verbally as an act of supplementation, like the suicide note, that produces further supplementation (as in the claim that the protagonist's suicide by irresolution has been productive of [a supplement of] "experience" that justifies the writing of his story—an "experience," however, that it is not for the text but for [the supplement that is] the reader to understand and specify). Here, then, literature first (?) defined itself as the cultural equivalent of suicide and as part of the linguistic genre of the suicide note. But in doing so it immediately made it clear, as always happens, that other literary texts had preceded it in so defining themselves, and by implication, in paradigmatically defining literary discourse itself as a site of cultural suicide. These other texts are, of course, the "short books" that we see Sylvie and the protagonist poring over in the scene of reading that inverts the Paolo and Francesca episode in Dante—a scene of reading in which we can now see an expression of the suicide's characteristically utopian hope, as the author of a suicide note, that the death of the subject (the protagonist's renunciation) will authorize a text capable of producing a state of harmony and communicative understanding (figured by the two heads bent over a single text) that will repair the disharmony (the protagonist's alienation from the bourgeois world, and the split between the artificial and the natural that reduces him to irresolution) that brought the subject to suicide in the first place.[4] I would venture the assertion that the reading theory implicit in any suicide note, "Sylvie" included, is utopian in kind. But the characteristic tonality of "Sylvie" derives from its espousal of such a utopian model combined with the ironic knowledge it enacts in its own mode of narration—that the death of the narrator into writing is not so much a condition for producing communication as unmediated communion as it is productive of "textuality," in the sense of a site of semantic indeterminacy that activates reading as a process of endless supplementation.

The short books "Sylvie" refers to can be seen to fall into two narrative categories. There are those that are confessional in mode (*René, Oberman, Adolphe*, etc.): here a narrator who is supposedly identical with the protagonist gives what might be called the authorized account of the weakness or deficiency in love that functions in such texts as a symbolic suicide on the male hero's part (a suicide that is indeed necessarily symbolic, in the sense of nonliteral, since the existence of the text is predicated—as in "Sylvie"—on the hero's surviving his own "death" in order to become the narrative subject). In these texts the protagonist's "suicide" is the condition of an act of writing that *cannot* be described as writerly suicide, however, because, although the text functions like a suicide note in giving an explanatory account of the circumstances of the protagonist's "suicide," it remains firmly under the control of a narrative subject whose version of the events—usually a self-pitying one—is not understood to be open to challenge. There is no abdication of semantic determinacy of the kind that occurs in "Sylvie," and such texts consequently bathe in a certain pathos of identification that precludes irony: the narrator espouses the perspective of the protagonist, while little space is left for readerly interpretation. Such pathos is antipathetic to modern readers and invites resistant readings like those of Margaret Waller.[5]

On the other hand, if *Werther*, as a novel, is a "suicide note," it corresponds to an act of suicide on the protagonist's part that, however "symbolic" it may be (in the sense of generally meaningful), nevertheless produces an actual death (this is "Werther *with* pistols"). This is technically feasible because in *Werther* there is distance between the protagonist and a narrative instance that, whatever its degree of sympathy with the protagonist, has renounced any claim to an authorized understanding of the significance of his death. The text's formal alternation between reproduction of Werther's first-person letters and passages of more distanced third-person narration corresponds to a degree of interpretive wavering, on the part of the narrating instance, between identification with the protagonist's self-serving (or at least not self-critical) asseverations and a perspective that seems to espouse, or at least not to reject, more commonsense, "bourgeois" views of the young man as misguided, emotionally unstable, and a social misfit. The narrative perspective, in other words, is an ironic one in the sense that, without precluding sympathetic identification with young Werther's woes or sufferings (the *Leiden* of the book's full title), it simultaneously fosters a cooler, less identificatory assessment of their meaning and importance. In this it renounces for itself the privilege of interpretive confidence and produces a kind of hesitation that is suggestive of a "narrative suicide" on the text's own part and that, historically, lies behind the ironic writing of "Sylvie" and later of *Madame Bovary*.

Madame Bovary is not a "short book," but it is easy to see the sense in which it belongs to the same ironic subgenre of the literary suicide note as *Werther*. Here it is the device of free indirect style that enables the text to balance the "pathos" of readerly identification with the perspectives of a suicide against the "irony" of a distanced reading. But *Madame Bovary* is more like "Sylvie" than it is like *Werther* in that it does not just renounce responsibility for deciding whether identification or distance is the appropriate perspective to bring to bear on the suicidal character, as *Werther* does; it also withholds from the reader its guidance as to what the content of such a distanced interpretation should be, contenting itself in this respect with purely negative indications in the form of clear signals that the views of bourgeois common sense, which *Werther* was willing to entertain, are certainly inadequate, and indeed inoperative. But *Madame Bovary* is third-person narrative, whereas the radical originality of "Sylvie" lies in its combining "open" narrative irony, of a kind that foreshadows Flaubert, although it does not technically involve free indirect style, with a confessional narrative mode that is reminiscent of the "short books" of first-generation French romanticism.

Joining the confessional, identificatory narrative of a suicidal protagonist turned authorized narrator and the ironic, distanced narrative that renounces interpretive authority with respect to the significance of that protagonist's "experience," "Sylvie" is situated, then, at a rather delicate point of intersection that makes it, more than any of the texts it might be compared to, the site of a *joint* "suicide pact" between its protagonist and its narrator. As in the confessional tradition, it adopts the conventions of first-person, autobiographical treatment of the events, assuming and implying therefore a continuity both of existential experience and of moral judgment between its protagonist and its narrator; but as an interpreter of the significance of that experience and the value of that judgment, this narrator is singularly elusive and, so, radically suicidal in his turn, throwing the responsibility for such interpretation and judgment onto a necessarily distanced reader (distanced by definition, since unable to identify with this elusive narrator), while making available to the reader no perspective on the events that is not the subjective perspective of the first-person narrative. We are placed in an inevitably ironic reading position, while sharing a first-person restriction of vision that prohibits the text (as does free indirect style in *Madame Bovary*) from suggesting the positive content an ironic interpretation might have. We know only, again as in *Madame Bovary* but because of the confessional identification with the protagonist's viewpoint, that neither protagonist nor narrator should be judged in terms of the conventional, "Parisian" definitions of what constitutes success.

Such "contentless" irony—as a pure negativity with respect to the positive identifications we are simultaneously encouraged to make—produces the text as indubitably oppositional (we know whom it stands with and against what). And yet it is oppositional in a purely negative sense—one for which no positive content is supplied (we do not know why, or in the name of what, we should stand with its identifications and oppositions) and that consequently becomes a matter of pure readability. The specification of oppositional content is projected onto the potentially limitless future of the text's encountering—somewhere, sometime—an "appropriate" reading, the character of whose appropriateness it does not, however, and presumably cannot, specify. To the extent that a distinction between oppositionality and resistance, such as I posit in *Room for Maneuver*,[6] can be made to hold, it depends on the distinction I am making here between the "negative" and the "positive" content of an ironic stance, and as a consequence it makes readability the critical marker of oppositionality.

In "Sylvie" such readability occurs most prominently in the "final leaf," where the largely narrative mode of the earlier chapters is succeeded by what is expressly introduced as a reflection on the "experience" derived from the story that has just been related. The device by which the suicidal disappearance of the narrator as a source of interpretive control is secured and the responsibility for interpretation thrown onto the reader is what Friedrich Schlegel, discussing romantic irony, called permanent parabasis, or "endless digressiveness."[7] The significant feature of permanent parabasis in the context of narrative suicide is that it does not bring about an absolute disappearance of the narrative instance, which is present from moment to moment in the text, but discontinuously so, so that it cannot be constructed as the site of a coherent subjective perspective or argumentative intention. For the reader there is a sense of textual drift as the "controlling" narrative subject becomes a kind of blur; but this effect is produced not by a Derridean "free play" of signifiers (to which narrative control would be *irrelevant*), but by the ceaseless coming into focus, and then into a new focus, of a subject that seems incapable of ever coinciding with any of its other states of momentary presence. That is why it is not contradictory to say that the "final leaf" is the place where a narrator figure appears as a successor to the story's protagonist, and the place where the narrator as controlling subject most perceptibly abdicates his privilege of interpretive control. He appears, only to perform a kind of disappearing act.

Thus, for example, having discussed his "experience" in the passage I have quoted, with its curious fruit imagery, the narrator turns immediately, with an apparent non sequitur, to Rousseau: "Rousseau says that the sight of nature consoles one for everything. I sometimes try to rediscover my own groves of Clarens lost to the north of Paris, in the mist. Everything has completely changed there!" What exactly is being said here? Is Rousseau's maxim introduced in order to be confirmed, or disconfirmed, by the comments that follow? Does the narrator find consolation in the sight of nature? Can groves "lost to the north of Paris, in the mist" be "[his] own groves of Clarens" (given that, as every reader of Rousseau knows, Clarens is in Switzerland)? What does it mean to "try to rediscover" them in circumstances where "everything has completely changed"? Is the narrator identifying with or disassociating himself from Rousseau in this passage? Questions like these flicker in the reader's mind, a part of which is still occupied, perhaps with attempting to grasp the sequitur, if there is one, that links the comments about "experience" and those about Rousseau and returning to the Valois. And so it goes to the end: no stable judgment about the sense of the story—and particularly about whether the Valois is a place of comfort because of its continuity with the past or a disconsoling place because "everything has completely changed"—ever emerges.

All of this, furthermore, is deadpan. Nothing suggests that the narrative is not in the charge of a controlling consciousness that is ordering the discourse, and yet that consciousness, as a controlling instance, remains elusive. We have the sensation that someone is speaking, but we cannot identify the intentionality that would give subjective coherence to the discourse. The subject position is not vacant, but it is occupied by a profoundly attenuated subjectivity that comes into and out of focus like the twinkling of a star or the "deceptive planetary body of Aldebaran" (chap. 14), in which—like the protagonist's loves—one aspect cannot come into view without obscuring another that will come into view in turn. The narrative enunciation, in short, stages a certain "fading" of the subject, which makes the abdication of narrative control readable and significant, like an act of suicide, without however specifying—again as in the case of suicide—the significance it might have.

Much later, in "Crise de vers" (1886–96), Mallarmé was to refer, famously, to the "elocutionary disappearance of the poet, yielding the initiative to words . . . [which replace] the breathing perceptible in lyric inspiration of former times or the enthusiastic personal guidance of the sentence."[8] It is exactly this "enthusiastic personal guidance of the sentence" that the reader of "Sylvie" becomes aware of as *missing*—I mean that its absence is interpreted as a sign not so much of nonexistent subjectivity as of a subjectivity that is "missing" in the sense that an engine is said to "miss," and so also in the sense in which to be missing is to manifest a lack. The suicide of the narrative subject in Nerval's text is not a fait accompli; it is enacted as an ongoing process, an "elocutionary" disappearance in that a performed disappearing act is made readable by rhetorical means. In this way we witness a suicide occurring before our very eyes, a suicide through renunciation of the "enthusiastic guidance" given to the sentence—and indeed to the set of sentences that constitute the text—by a controlling narrator.

And if the resulting "initiative yielded to words" passes on the responsibility for interpreting the events being recounted to the reader, it also makes the reader responsible for understanding, explaining, and interpreting this abandonment of narrative control itself, this yielding of initiative or letting go of narrative privilege about which the only thing that is clear is that, as a kind of suicide, it is an oppositionally significant act. The suicidal gesture that blurs the "narrative function" and consequently brings to the fore the "textual function" as a writing that requires interpretive reading suffices to identify the text as oppositional; but it simultaneously shifts onto the reader the responsibility for constructing *the terms of its oppositionality*, that is, for understanding what is at stake in the suicidal act it stages and for interpreting it appropriately.

*

Anger vaporized? The writing of "Sylvie" is clearly melancholic in that sense; but in order to begin constructing the oppositional sense of the narrative suicide it stages, one needs to note also the many indications that the diffuseness of identity and the indeterminacy of meaning that suicide produces—in short, the attenuation of difference that occurs in the novella— are associated with a certain sense of happiness. Whereas the protagonist's suicide by irresolution makes him a man of solitude and nostalgia, though with access to the fringes of happiness on the occasions of his visits to Sylvie and her family, I will suggest that the narrator's suicidal abandonment of narrative control is a way of producing, for him, less a marginal form of happiness than the happiness of a certain marginality. Better yet, he attains a certain *liminality*—specifically the bliss of approaching release from the conditions of individual identity, which include the logic of the "excluded middle" and of the separateness of categories, themselves associated with the order of time. As a child, the protagonist narrowly escaped drowning in one of the ponds of Valois; and he is reminded (chap. 12) that the major outcome of his accident was the stopping of time, the "drownding" of the *beast* ("La *bête* est *nayée*," he is remembered to have wailed on discovering that his watch had stopped ticking). "Big Curly" pulled him out that time and restored him to the world of individual identity and history—but predisposed from then on, it seems, to become a man ill at ease in temporality and nostalgically inclined to seek, as Bachelard would have put it,[9] "une mort heureuse" in the dissolution of difference. Such a man would be inclined to a certain in-difference that forecloses the making of choices by making distinctions unclear; and for such a man, to let go, to disengage, might feel less like failure or even renunciation, and more like a departure in the direction of happiness itself.

As it happens, there is, not only in "Sylvie" but in all of Nerval's Valois writing, a loose set of attenuated phenomena—misty or moonlit landscapes, husky women's voices, the hazy diction of folk song—that are coded as deeply pleasurable and that function at the same time as objective correlatives (or figures *en abyme*) for the weakened narrative control that produces writing as a site of indeterminacy. A certain old-fashioned climate theory links the landscape and the women's voices (Adrienne, for instance, has a voice that is "clear and penetrating" but "slightly veiled, like the voice of the girls in our misty region [*pays*]" [chap. 2]), while a theory of nation and race derived from German romanticism associates folk culture with an essential spirit of the people: as early as 1842, in "Les Vieilles Ballades françaises," Nerval spoke of folk songs as the fragmented remnants that survive as evidence of "la vraie langue," the true French language of "our old provinces." These theories are never more than hinted at in passing, with the result that the diffuseness characteristic of misty landscape, husky voices, and fragmented folk song also results from the vague, offhand way such phenomena are themselves associated. They form a fuzzy set—a fuzzy set of fuzzy entities—and the fuzziness emblematizes textual uncertainty, in the way that the description of Adrienne's voice, for example—for how is a voice at once "clear and penetrating" and "veiled" or husky?—itself figures the textual enunciation, at every moment crystal clear and yet, through permanent parabasis, elusive, shifting, and diffuse when taken as a whole.

Nerval's insistence on origins and authenticity in his discussion of folk song is symptomatic, however. If some lost original purity—"la vraie langue"—is still somehow accessible to us through scattered and fragmented remnants of song, with their uncertain grammar, their assonances and half-rhymes, their archaisms and dialectal forms, it is probable that in Nerval's writing not just folklore but all the phenomena of indifferentiation (or more accurately of attenuated differentiation) hold a similar secret and attract fascinated attention. Like folk song, they hint at a possible return to an origin, that is, to a state imagined as preceding the emergence of categories of difference and the fall into time. They appear, in any case, as the agents of a threshold experience, in which the observer or listener has the pleasure of approaching, without ever quite attaining—as in a slow, suicidal swoon—such a prelapsarian state of absolute indifferentiation, an experience that is both like and radically different from the marginal happiness the protagonist achieves on his visits to Sylvie and her family. (The relation of these two figures, in other words, is itself fuzzy.)

A perceptive study by Jeanne Bem has pointed out how characteristic it is of Nerval that his "original" essay on folk song itself disseminated, or vaporized, through his Valois writing, as if in imitation of the history he imagines (that is, the myth) of an original language degenerating into a scatter of texts. The ontogeny of Nervalian writing repeats in this way the phylogeny of the language, producing in each case an unstable text, characterized as Bem says by "variability" and "fleetingness" and having an enunciatory subject that is, in each case, "anonymous, both collective and single, present and absent, interchangeable and elusive." [10] But it might be stressed that if history is responsible for the scattering of the folk text as well as for the diffuseness of Nerval's writing, this writerly diffuseness is in one sense historically determined but in another *chosen* as a negative response, a reaction to the world of history, as it is represented by Paris and its *avide curée*, or eager scramble. It corresponds to a suicide—that is, to what is by definition a voluntary and so a signifying act even when it is a suicide by irresolution and an option in favor of indeterminacy; and as an attempted *return* to the aesthetic of folk culture in opposition to the social formation of modernity, it is a nostalgic attempt to reverse the entropic direction of history. "Vaporized," misty writing attempts to rejoin the originary, prelapsarian moment that folk song, like mist-enveloped landscapes and the husky voices of women, also hints at; and it is in that sense that writing, employing a language of differentiation but in such a way as to attenuate, reduce, or even deny difference, can be for Nerval—as in Stendhal's famous definition of beauty, later taken up by Baudelaire—a promise of happiness, "une promesse de bonheur."

If suicidal narrative has the character of a departure for happiness, it is no surprise, then, to learn in "Les Faux-Saulniers" that Watteau's famous canvas *The Departure for Cythera* "was conceived among the transparent, colored mists" [11]—"transparent" mists? "transparent" *and* "colored"?—of the Valois. Painterly sfumato functions like writerly indeterminacy. But in "Sylvie" a more thematic and compositional feature of the painting, its *theoria* (the chain of young people with linked hands heading for the point of embarkation), is associated with the dream of reversing time's direction, as if a scatter of people, and the attenuation of individuality figured by the linked group, was an alternative manifestation of the happiness of indifferentiation. [12] In both the archery festival, the memory of which provokes the protagonist's crucial return to the Valois, and the festival that was conceived as a reconstruction of the Watteau canvas there is a joyous procession, "renouvelée des jours antiques" (chap. 4)—note the word "renouvelée," it might be translated as "refreshed" or "rejuvenated from ancient times." But such a linked chain was also present in an even more remote and apparently originary memory, where, however, it is significantly *closed* into an unbroken circle that is itself *centered* on the image of a united couple, as opposed to the open-ended linearity of the *theoria*, so that it is suggestive of a unity preceding the dispersions of history. On the lawn in front of Adrienne's château (chap. 2), the protagonist was the only boy in a circle of girls, who danced and sang "ancient airs learned from their mothers, and in such naturally pure French that one really felt we existed in the old *pays* of the Valois, where for more than a thousand years the heartbeat of France was felt." "Suddenly, in conformity with the rules of the dance, Adrienne and I found ourselves standing side by side in the center of the circle," and still following the prescribed ritual of the ring dance, the protagonist kisses her. It is a hieratic moment, a kind of hiero-gamy—"From that moment an unknown disturbance took hold of me"—and it will be necessary for us to return in due course to this kiss, which is the prototype of the scene of reading with Sylvie at the end of the novella, and to the singularity of the one privileged boy in the circle of girls.

But it is now that Adrienne begins to sing:

> The fair Adrienne had to sing in order to be allowed back into the ring: . . . in her clear, penetrating voice, slightly veiled like that of the girls of this misty region, she sang one of the old romances filled with melancholy and love. . . . The melody ended at each stanza on one of those quavering trills that are so effective when a young voice imitates in a modulating shake the trembling voice of ancient crones.

Thus the voice that is simultaneously clear and husky is also capable of a tremolo effect that is "effective" precisely because it produces an illusion of equivalence between a voice known to be young and a querulousness associated with age, as if the instability of the note was capable of miraculously blurring the difference due to the dimensionality of time. And this effect is simultaneously natural (in accordance with the view that folk song is the "natural" mode of expression of the people) and artificial, a product of artful technique (the singer is "imitating" the shaky voices of old women). Given the split between nature and artifice, in the persons of Sylvie and Aurélie, that reduced the protagonist to his suicide of irresolution, there is a first hint here that the narrator's suicide in the indeterminacy of writing is compensatory, a way of repairing, or of partially repairing, that split by recourse to an artistic technique that in his case "imitates" artificially the natural disjointedness and diffuseness, the parabasis of relaxed, spontaneous non literary or "popular" speech. For it is a stylistic "tremolo" similar to Adrienne's that the narrator brings off, in his characteristic dead-pan way, in the "final leaf" of the novella, in which the Valois he revisits in the 1850s is alternately described, in two matched paragraphs, as desolate and abandoned—"The ponds . . . lie vainly offering their stagnant sur-faces, disdained by the swan"—and as the cheerful rural landscape he knew in his youth: "In the morning when I open the window festooned with creeper and roses, a green horizon ten leagues long meets my delighted gaze" (chap. 14). (And there is, incidentally, a second model for this tech-nique of alternation in the "chants alternés," the response songs that Syl-vie's old aunt recalls from her youth as part of the traditional wedding festivities, the aunt herself reminding the protagonist of the wrinkled old fairies of pantomime who reveal their true, youthful faces at the end of the play; cf. chap. 7.)

Meanwhile, as Adrienne sings—and to turn now to landscape—falling darkness and the rising moon produce a dappled or chiaroscuro effect, but one that isolates the singer in a pool of light; and in the silence that follows her singing, the mist rises: "The lawn was covered with a soft condensation of vapor that spread in white droplets at the tips of the leaves of grass. We thought we were in paradise." The protagonist runs and fetches two laurel branches to form a silvery wreath that glistens on Adrienne's hair in the moonlight. "She resembled Dante's Beatrice smiling at the edge of the holy dwelling place." And indeed, this *is* a liminal moment, since she now runs back into the castle, leaving "the poet" alone on the edge of paradise—where Sylvie awaits him. The whole episode is deeply ambiguous, as if it were a memory of prelapsarian happiness (the circle, the couple at the cen-ter, the kiss) that, because it is a memory, is already marked by the charac-teristics of the postlapsarian (Adrienne's husky voice, the tremolo, the mist). The scene is liminal, so to speak, in two directions: it records the moment of exclusion from happiness, but it also represents the moment of closest approach to an absolute of bliss.

That is why, when the reader reaches the "final leaf" of the novella and learns of the protagonist's visits to Sylvie and her family and of the mar-ginal happiness he enjoys there, it will be possible to recognize these later scenes as a replica, but a downgraded one, in the realist register, of the mystic threshold experience on the lawn. They are marked by exclusion in the world of time more than by liminality as an approach to absolute bliss. Sylvie and the protagonist do not kiss, but bend their heads together in quiet absorption over a book; they do not dance under the elms and lindens of a splendid château "of Henri IV's time," but there *are* the ruins of a tower, also built of red brick, around which, under the lindens, they sedately walk. If the narrator's writing, the writing of a "short book" such as those the protagonist reads with such pleasure in Sylvie's company, seeks to reproduce the bliss of the liminal moment experienced on the lawn with Adrienne, it has also much in common—as the writing of "experience"—with the type of happiness the protagonist enjoys at Dammartin, in the domestic tranquility he marginally shares. For on the one hand, it has the power to produce effects of indeterminacy that recall the magic moment with Adrienne on the lawn—the mist, the husky voice, the folk song—but on the other this liminality with respect to the "saintes demeures" of the originary, prelapsarian, mystical state constitutes a marginality, like the protagonist's marginality in Sylvie's bourgeois family, in the world of history and with respect to the "possible spheres of action." This is the marginality chosen by the protagonist in the 1830s by his refusal of the eager scramble, and now necessarily shared by the narrator even as he reproduces the liminality that compensates for it. In this ambiguous status of liminality-marginality, his writing is like the Valois region itself, geographically close to Paris but remote from the capital in terms of travel time, and so culturally remote as well and still close to the old ways. "To reach Ermenonville these days, there is no direct road. Sometimes I go via Creil and Senlis, at other times via Dammartin" (chap. 14). And Sylvie, as a figure, is similarly ambiguous: within the up-to-date lower middle-class *commerçante* (close to Paris), a "jeune fille du Valois" survives with her "Athenian smile" that makes her worthy to stand, like Adrienne, at the threshold of paradise smiling like Beatrice at "the poet."

It is this combination of liminality and marginality—in the Valois, in Sylvie, in the narrator's writing—the commonality of "experience" between the narrator and the protagonist, that signals an unrecoverable distance between nostalgic techniques of recovery through writing and the lost originary moment. Indeed, that moment was itself already lost, perhaps, and so not truly originary at all. For the immediate marker of exclusion, after Adrienne's disappearance into the château where she became inaccessible to the protagonist, was the split he then experienced between Adrienne and Sylvie, herself angry at having been forgotten, which can only mean that the split was already latent in the moment of the round dance and the kiss, since the protagonist's friendship with Sylvie thus turns out to have predated his fascination with Adrienne. This original fissure will become the split between the natural and the artificial figured by the protagonist's later hesitation between Sylvie and Aurélie (who recalls Adrienne); and it is the same split that the narrator's writerly suicide is assigned the function of healing, on the model of the singing heard in the Valois.

Let us look more closely, therefore, at this singing. Aurélie is an actress who does not sing; but if Sylvie once liked to hum the old songs as she made lace (chap. 3), she will herself have become, by the time of the protagonist's fascination with Aurélie and his return to the Valois in the 1830s, a much more ambiguous figure—anticipating her later ambiguity as the wife of "Big Curly"—from the point of view of her musicianship. For where the theatrical world of the artificial has the power to counter the effects of time, the sphere of the natural is subject to those effects, in the form of an inability to escape the forces of history; and the effect of history will be to deprive the natural of its spontaneity by bringing it into an uneasy relation with artifice, like the relation of the Valois to Paris. The sign of this relation in the case of Sylvie's singing will be the training of her voice—and the training of the voices of the Valois functions in turn, I submit, as a figure of the inevitable artistry of writing that, like the narrator's, can only "imitate" the fuzzy spontaneity of naturally occurring phenomena such as misty landscapes, husky voices and folk song (the last, again, ideologically "naturalized" as a spontaneous expression of the people). Because it is a rhetorical achievement (the practice of parabasis), such writing can neither be nor become natural, under pain of ceasing to have cultural *significance* as the site of a "suicide." But the attachment to rhetoric means in turn that such a suicide cannot achieve its goal, if that goal is the return to an originary moment of fusion, *before* the splitting of the natural and the artificial. It can only be a performance of suicide, turned as much toward the world in which it is marginalized as toward the conditions of blissful liminality that it seeks to reproduce.

Adrienne's voice, we recall, was already capable of artful imitation on the lawn. And on the only later occasion when the protagonist was to see her again, she was an actress (prefiguring Aurélie), but singing—as is appropriate for a nun—in a religious allegory or mystery play, a cosmic drama (one imagines a kind of staged oratorio) in which she sang the part of a "spirit" rising from the abyss with a message of consolation and hope. "Her voice had increased in strength and range, and the endless coloratura of the Italian style embroidered with birdsong the austere phrases of a pompous recitative" (chap. 7). In what now reads like an oddly accurate description of baroque performance style, Adrienne's voice, which seems at this point to have been trained and indeed to be almost operatic in its mastery of coloratura ("les fioritures infinies du chant italien"), nevertheless retains its power to combine the artificial and the natural, so that this singing, as a kind of virtuoso version of the tremolo of folk song, functions as an important model for what will be, in due course, the narrator's own style. The model is significant in particular, however, for its emphasis on training and artistry.

By contrast, it will be deeply disappointing to the protagonist of the 1830s to learn that Sylvie has learned to sing like an operatic soprano, for she now rejects folk song as out of date. "Sylvie modulated a few notes of an aria from a modern grand opera. . . . She was *phrasing!*" (chap. 11; emphasis in the original). Sylvie's phrasing seems to refer tantalizingly back to Adrienne's own control of the "austere phrases" she embroiders with birdsong; but the protagonist's horror signals that both singers have in fact fallen into a style of musicianship that substitutes clearly outlined enunciatory segmentation for the indefinite diction of folk song, and so associates artistry with differentiation and distinction. His shock is followed in this case by further disappointment when, in spite of her new skill, Sylvie refuses to sing like Adrienne, as the protagonist—seeking to establish or produce an affinity between the two women—attempts to lead her though Adrienne's part in the oratorio (now attributed to "Porpora, on verses of the sixteenth century"). His bafflement increases, finally, when her response to his preoccupation with Adrienne (and more covertly, in his thoughts, with Aurélie) is finally to hum a snatch of folk song, with the characteristic indistinction of diction he loves so much, thereby demonstrating—but by way of insisting on the difference between herself and Adrienne(-Aurélie)—that she has not, after all, forgotten the old ways:

> A Dammartin l'y a trois belles filles,
> L'y en a z'une plus belle que le jour . . .

To which she adds the deflating and dismissive comment: "mais il faut songer au solide," we must keep our feet on the ground. It is, in short, her unwillingness to be confused with Adrienne that makes her keep the two styles—the operatic and the folk, the artificial and the natural—separate; and that, from the protagonist's viewpoint, is the most discouraging attitude of all, for Sylvie has by now, thanks to her new artistry, the potential to heal the split (the split between the natural and the artificial, the split between herself and Adrienne), but in her insistence on modernity and up-to-dateness, on individuality, difference, and the "solid," she refuses the possibility of such healing.

We are thus invited to understand, I think, that:

1. As the "originary" figure, Adrienne contains within her, as a latency, both of the poles of attraction, represented by Sylvie and Aurélie, between which the protagonist will hesitate (which is why, in the 1830s, it is the memory of Adrienne that mediates the Aurélie-Sylvie relation).

2. In this text (as opposed to "Aurélia"),[13] it is the Sylvie-Valois side, not the Aurélie-Paris side of the split that is understood to offer the best possibility of healing—not a full realization of happiness, but the marginalized form of liminality that is the best the narrator can hope to achieve.

3. But Sylvie, who stands for the ambiguity of the Valois and for the possibility of this form of happiness, is also a figure for the separateness of categories, for the distinctness of the differences—between herself and Adrienne, herself and Aurélie, the present and the past, the natural and the artificial—that the narrator must learn to combine and to blur in the suicidal writing of indeterminacy.

4. By contrast with Sylvie, it is the theatrical figure of Aurélie whose resemblance with Adrienne stands both for the reconciliation of the artificial and the natural and for the denial of history and time. In spite of its affinity with folk song and the Valois, the narrator's writing has therefore something to learn from the theatrical world of Aurélie (whom precisely we see visiting the Valois in chapter 13).

How, then, are we to understand this?

As we have seen, the suicide of the narrative instance through parabasis produces writing in which words are vaporized, distinctions are attenuated, sense becomes hazy, and fragments of story scatter while referring strangely to one another, like album leaves or fragments of folk song preserving the remnants of a lost unity. From folk song also, such writing has learned the effectiveness of tremolo as a device that jumbles the order of time, confusing youth and old age (by using the word "jumble," I am seeking to translate the French *brouiller*, which shares a radical with *brouillard*, "fog"); and already in folk song such an effect is simultaneously natural and a product of art. But another jumbling of time occurs, as we have also seen, as a result of the narrator's "style vieilli," or outmoded style, which, paradoxically, is simultaneously his most up-to-date feature, since it makes him a Werther, but "minus the pistols, which are no longer in style" (chap. 1). Such writing is, historically, the first to define the writerliness of French modernism as "modern" precisely by virtue of its refusal of the world of modernity.

Among the figures of the novella's indecisive status in the order of time are the buildings of the Valois that it describes with deadpan effects of temporal ambiguity: "this modern ruin has been rejuvenated" (chap. 4), "this unfinished edifice is already nothing more than a ruin" (chap. 11). And on these monuments, verses and maxims are inscribed that remind the protagonist/narrator in the "final leaf" of his own complicity with an era (that of the rococo) in which, as he says, "le naturel lui-même était apprêté" ["naturalness itself was affected"]. If folk song is a model of naturalness subject to artistry, here—in this "outmoded style" the narrator once found "sublime"—is another, high cultural model of indistinctness between the two but produced now through artifice; and it is hard not to draw a connection between this style in which "naturalness itself was affected" and the "outmoded style" the narrator has attributed to himself less than a page earlier. But an "outmoded style" in the 1850s cannot be exactly the same as the style that was *prevalent* in the age of Boucher pastels, Watteau sfumato, and the verse of Roucher, just as a "short book," now that they are hardly ever written any more, is not quite the same as its models in Goethe, Chateaubriand, Senancour, or Constant. Its naturalness, already a product of artifice, is necessarily further compromised because it has become a matter of "imitation"—of belated pastiche, not of spontaneous production, as the narrator's self-consciousness about his "style vieilli" clearly indicates.

The figure in the novella for this complex situation is the "jeune premier ridé," the wrinkled fellow who plays the matinee idol parts in Aurélie's troupe. "His latest success had been in the role of the lover in the play imitated from Schiller, in which my opera glass had detected that he was so wrinkled. Up close, he looked younger" (chap. 13). This figure, who onstage looks older than he actually is even as artistry rejuvenates him, instructs us that a pastiche such as "Sylvie" is ("imitated" from its rococo and early romantic models as the play, here, is "imitated from Schiller") is necessarily at a *double* remove from its object, if that object is defined as an ideal or an absolute predating the fall into difference and time. What it imitates (whether rococo style or folk song) is itself already a combination of the natural and the artificial—categories whose separation is consequently acknowledged even as their difference is artfully overcome. But it is itself an imitation of its models, and so belated and artificial (like Aurélie with respect to Adrienne) in relation to them. Like the "jeune premier ridé," such writing is younger than it seems (i.e., it is modern), but its artistry produces a jumbling of time (it confuses the order of the youthful and the aged, like the wrinkly old fellow playing the young lover) that in point of fact *ages* it (like the actor seen through an opera glass), by emphasizing and making *significant* the "wrinkles" of its "style *vieilli*." (Although English cannot capture the pun—"[artificially] aged"/"out of date"—in *vieilli*, "wrinkles"—meaning tricks of the trade as well as signs of age—offers a nice compensatory one, translating the connection the text implies between the belatedness inherent in its reliance on artistry, as a pastiche, and its necessary distance from the youthfulness the pastiche seeks to reproduce, or indeed to create.) The "jeune premier ridé," however, is the figure Aurélie judges worthy to marry her: "Celui qui m'aime, le voilà!"— *he* is the one who loves me, she says (chap. 13).

The writing of "Sylvie," then, has a "Big Curly" (or Valois) side and a "Young Wrinkly" (or Parisian) side, and the rhyme—really an assonance— between the two names ("le grand frisé," "le jeune premier ridé") is significant. To the extent that this writing resolves the split between the natural and the artificial (and so succeeds in jumbling the order of time), it realizes a potential inherent in Sylvie's Valois; but it does so finally through devices of pastiche that relate it to the theater, the Parisian domain of Aurélie, thereby confirming the split that it sought to heal, and with it rediscovering the order of time. In simplified terms, the protagonist returns to the Valois to share marginally in the happiness of Sylvie's family, yet the narrator, who shares the protagonist's "experience" but whose text makes him an indeterminate figure and a figure of indeterminacy like the "jeune premier ridé," also becomes a lover worthy of Aurélie. Consequently, the blending or blurring of the difference between protagonist and narrator, arising in a novella that tells the life of the one (a suicide by irresolution) in the style of the other (a suicide by indeterminacy)—a style that combines what the other had hesitated between—functions as a final attenuation of differences, the final healing of the split that makes the text worthy of Adrienne herself, the figure in whom Sylvie and Aurélie are themselves blended. With the "lover" of Sylvie it shares marginality with respect to the modern world (a marginality due, however, to the narrator's preference for the "vieilli"); with the "lover" of Aurélie it shares liminality—the liminality of jumbled time, *le temps brouillé*—with respect to "paradise" (a liminality made possible, however, by the ambiguity of the Valois). But both the marginality and the liminality of the text are a function, in the end, of *narrative* suicide—and as the last line of "Sylvie" establishes, if the protagonist is separated from both Sylvie and Aurélie by their marriages, it is not by marriage but by death that, jointly, protagonist and narrator are separated from Adrienne. "Poor Adrienne," sighs Sylvie, "she died in the convent of St. S . . . , in 1832 or thereabouts."

It is this gulf of death that narrative suicide seeks to overcome, transcending the privation with respect to marriage that is the protagonist's lot. But it is its inability to transcend death and restore the lost, originary moment of absolute fusion that keeps it, with the protagonist, on this side of the gulf: liminal with respect to the mystic goal, and socially marginal. It remains therefore a mere performance of suicide, an "elocutionary disappearance" that is compromised with artifice and thus indelibly marked by the fatal split and subject to the reality of time, whose effects it can mitigate but not abolish, or even repair.

*

One important question remains. Marginal with respect to the world of social success, and liminal with respect to a more mystic form of bliss, the text is in each case engaged, with a degree of self-consciousness that is difficult to ascertain, in a politics of gender. For in 1830 an "eager scramble" for honors and positions is implicitly coded as male, and it is therefore a world of masculine competition the protagonist rejects in casting his lot with the two forms of the feminine—the natural and the artificial, Sylvie and Aurélie—which prove incompatible and reduce him to the suicide of irresolution. Male rivalry is still present here, however, in the persons of the two successful suitors, "Big Curly" and "Young Wrinkly," each an alter ego of the protagonist, and each of whom, in marrying Sylvie or Aurélie, confirms the separateness of the two women, as well as of the subject and the other. Each marriage, moreover, implies that "Werther minus pistols" is a figure for sexual impotence (that of the protagonist) before it figures the suicidal writing through which the narrator will attempt to attenuate the damaging differences and restore the conditions of mystic marriage with Adrienne: the kiss amid the rising mist on the lawn.

These conditions, however, are such as, very strikingly, to abolish competition between males for the possession of a woman. Privileged as the only boy in the circle of girls, the protagonist is further singled out in being selected (no doubt inevitably if the rules of the dance decreed a mixed-gender couple) to occupy the center of the ring with Adrienne and receive her kiss. "From that moment, an unknown disturbance took hold of me." It is—to extrapolate—as if, in gendered terms, writing was the narrator's *revanche* for the rejection of the protagonist as suitor: the successful husbands are now eliminated, and in the misty subjectivity of the suicidal narrator the nebula of women, whose dispersion was confirmed by their marriages, becomes available once again and reconstitutes, in his mind, something equivalent to the round dance on the lawn, in which each identity is "linked," as by joined hands, to the others.

It is hard to miss the implication that this hazy but privileged male identity at the center of, and in a sense in control of, a group of interchangeable, or partly interchangeable, women is the personage Freud liked to refer to as His Majesty the Baby. The symptomatic phrase, as Jeanne Bem points out,[14] is not in "Sylvie" but recurs elsewhere like a refrain: "Encore un air avec lequel j'ai été bercé" ["Yet another song I remember from the cradle"]. The power and attraction of folk song, and by extension of the associated phenomena of indeterminacy (misty landscape, husky voices, human chains, textual indeterminacy), lies for Nerval in its regressive ability to transport him back, through memory, to the bliss of the cradle and to an identity simultaneously indeterminate and frontierless, but central. Biographically, Gérard de Labrunie, who "never saw [his] mother"[15] because she accompanied his father, an army surgeon, on the Napoleonic campaigns and died of a fever in Silesia, was tended in the cradle by a number of affectionate young women, presumably of the peasant class, in the house of his maternal uncle in the Valois hamlet of Mortefontaine. It is intuitively easy to imagine the impact of this early experience on the child's identity formation and to see why the adult who never *saw* his mother should associate identity with collectivity—the chain or circle of young people—and particularly with the voices of girls, while reserving a privileged place, representing the "blank" of his mother's absence, for an inaccessible, unitary origin beyond the grave—a place of privilege, represented by the solitary figure of Adrienne, that he himself (in the couple at the center of the circle) is uniquely privileged to share. In later taking as his professional name the pseudonym Nerval, Labrunie made a clear option, *as a subject of writing*, in favor of the maternal Valois (the reference is thought to be to a certain "champ de Nerva") and, refusing the law of the father (held responsible for the death of the mother), situated writing, and its subject's identity, under a feminine and motherly, if not strictly maternal, aegis.[16]

But Felicia Miller, the author of an extremely suggestive study of male fascination with female voice in the French nineteenth century,[17] has made it possible to push the analysis further and simultaneously to generalize it beyond the specificity of merely biographical particulars. Miller draws attention to recent (post-Lacanian) psychoanalytic hypotheses concerning an "acoustic mirror stage," primarily constituted by the mother's voice, that is thought to precede the visual mirror stage identified by Lacan. In light of this new idea, we can understand that the Nervalian Imaginary, while functioning, in the way that Lacan posits, as the site of an illusion of autonomous personal identity, would be more than usually traversed by a sense of the grounding of such identity in alterity, as a result of its having been constituted as the place where the male child's identity is indissolubly bound up with the figure of a group of interchangeable women whose "presence," in the first place, was the presence of their collective voice, the women themselves being, so to speak, disembodied. Male autobiographical writing, as Miller brilliantly shows for Rousseau and Proust (but one might think also of Leiris as well as of Nerval), tends to be the place where the subject seeks to reproduce the maternal voice that holds the secret of identity and simultaneously to wrest that function from the female so as to reconstitute it as a male prerogative. One might conclude that, if Nerval was to become an early modernist experimenter in the writing of indeterminacy, it was by virtue of the biographical accident of an identity formation that predisposed him to an intuitive understanding of identity's constitution in alterity and multiplicity; and the oppositional character of this writing, the refusal of a certain social formation that gives it its meaning as a form of cultural suicide, has, in psychoanalytic terms, the character of an unresolved Oedipus.

But there is a more political point as well. Male writing, so viewed, is a site of desire in which, as Miller points out, the female voice is fetishized by being "disembodied": that is, it becomes available in the role of Echo to a male Narcissus. In "Sylvie" this disembodiment occurs as a result of the transformation of the protagonist, rejected by flesh-and-blood women who exercise independence of judgment and of action, into a narrator in whose memory they become available again—but in a way that is no longer subject to realistic constraint—and undergo the effects of indeterminacy produced by suicidal writing. They lose the ability to define themselves in terms of individuality and difference and become, to a degree, interchangeable as the narrator's subjectivity reconverts them into the kind of fuzzy set that gives him pleasure. If the practice of writing in Nerval is feminized, in the sense that in it a disempowering suicide of the male subject occurs in such a way as to produce effects of indeterminacy bordering on fusion with a feminine "principle," this option in favor of marginalization and femininization on the part of the narrator cannot therefore be interpreted in any straightforward sense as an abdication of male gender privilege. Rather, gender difference, and with it the privileging of masculinity, is maintained even as, along with other category distinctions, it is diffused and rendered indeterminate through narrative suicide; and this is because such indeterminacy is itself being used here as an instrument of masculinist *revanche*. For it is not only that writing feminizes its male subject and produces, among the many indeterminacies for which it is responsible, a certain blurring of gender difference; a male subject also stands to gain from this blurring, and it is this survival of a politically masculinist project in writing that seems in other ways oppositional with respect to social dominants that it is important to try to clarify.

In "Les Faux-Saulniers" (and so, later, in "Angélique"), the characteristic throatiness of women's voices in the Valois is said to give them a "contralto" quality: a certain innkeeper's daughter is said to have "the characteristically charming *manner of speaking* of foggy regions, which gives *contralto* intonations to the youngest girls."[18] This term, as Gautier's poem "Contralto" (*Emaux et camées*) makes clear, was available at the time as a euphemistic signifier of sexual ambiguity:

> Que tu me plais, ô timbre étrange!
> Son double, homme et femme à la fois,
> Contralto, bizarre mélange,
> Hermaphrodite de la voix!

> [Strange vocal register, how I love thee!
> A double sound, man and woman at once,
> Contralto, strange blend,
> The hermaphrodite of voice!]

The question for us, then, is whether, with respect to the categories of male and female, or feminine and masculine, the contralto quality Nerval attributes to the female voice that figures his own suicidal writing signifies a *neither/nor* consequent on the attenuation of gender difference, or whether it means rather, as Gautier's poem certainly suggests (speaking of a voice that "mingles the mistress's signs / With the more masculine accents of a male friend"), a *both/and* that maintains and enforces gender difference by grounding it in the supposed biological givens of sexual differentiation. Does the hermaphroditic quality of the contralto voice affirm the fungibility of gender difference or assert and maintain that difference by affirming a sexual *coincidentia oppositorum*?

The historical part of Felicia Miller's study is helpful here. She shows that in nineteenth-century opera—the musical genre par excellence, at least among the literati—it was soprano and, to a lesser degree, tenor voices that substituted for the increasingly rare castrato voice that had dominated eighteenth-century opera. Consequently it was a certain sexless quality that was appreciated in these voices, a neither/nor "purity" that came to be associated with the vocal range that gave the tenor voice a feminine quality in its upper register (especially the "head tones") and made the soprano voice particularly prized when—to use Nerval's technically inaccurate but suggestive word—it "modulated" between the "angelic" clarity of the highest notes and the throaty tones of the contralto register. Thanks to this versatility of register, such voices could be said, like Adrienne's, to be simultaneously "clear and penetrating" and "veiled"; and it was this ambiguous coloring of the trained operatic voice and the sexual indeterminacy it suggested that so captivated male listeners. In the case of Nerval, it seems possible to propose, then, that it is the dissociation of the "modulating" female voice from sexuality (what Miller describes as a function of its disembodiment) that makes it possible to imagine such a voice as a site of *gender* indeterminacy, such that it figures the possibility of a man and a woman being joined in a kind of transcendency of sublimation, as in the children's pure kiss on the lawn, but also in the asexual couple formed when the protagonist and Sylvie read together at Dammartin. The price for this gain is evidently paid by the woman, who undergoes disembodiment as the condition of the happiness enjoyed, through regression to infancy, by the male subject. She is, like Adrienne, fetishized into a state of angelic purity or, like Sylvie, idealized into the virginal status of maternal sister (the implications of Sylvie's marriage to "Big Curly" are denied in the comparison with Goethe's Charlotte, who was "maternal" only in the sense that she had the duty of caring for her younger siblings).

Conversely, however, *sexual* difference is maintained, as in Gautier's interpretation of the contralto, and with it—by virtue of the sex-gender system—gender distinctions as well, to the extent that the suicidal narrator's writing of indeterminacy is understood as a turning toward the *mundus muliebris* as an alternative to the competitive male social world, an embracing of the lost mother as a rejection of the law of the father, and a feminization of the male subject productive of a hermaphroditic *coincidentia oppositorum* that does not deny him his maleness. Women lose out again in this case, through being relegated to a marginalized position; but now the narrator can be said to join them, paying the price of feminization—the renunciation of power and success, the impotency of a "Werther minus pistols," social marginalization—both for himself and for his writing. It is the "sexual" feminization of the male in this sense that the "contralto" quality of Valois voices signifies, at the same time as it figures the attenuation of gender difference (along with other categorical differences) in the achievement of "desexualized" purity.

In this process women are on the one hand marginalized, by virtue of the gender system, and on the other sublimated into sexlessness, losing twice so as to permit, in the latter case, the blissful dream of gender indeterminacy that bolsters narcissistic male identity and gives the narrator his *revanche* while, in the former case, bearing the brunt of the social system that confers significance on the male subject's rejection of the *mundus virilis* and makes it, not just a death, but a suicide—a meaningful renunciation. Where the women lose twice, however, the male subject is playing a gain against a loss: his suicidal *marginalization* as a feminized and disempowered subject is the condition of an identity gain through suicide, and of the form of happiness that becomes available to him in the near bliss of his return, through the writing of indeterminacy, to the *liminality* of one who approaches the edge of paradise. Where the protagonist loses, the narrator gains; what the narrator loses through social marginalization, he regains through the production of a desired identity.

The novella itself both constructs a relation of continuity between protagonist and narrator (as oppositional figures and social "losers") and affirms an important difference between them (in the discontinuity between a suicide by irresolution that produces marginality and a suicide by indeterminacy that produces liminality). And it is in the complex "modulation" it sets up between these two positions—the position in which the text is, like its protagonist and its narrator, feminized and consequently socially marginalized and the position in which it is, like the narrator, liminal and so aesthetically and emotionally revalorized—that gives "Sylvie" its specific character as a delicately, even intricately, but also very precisely self-situated piece of writing. But the same modulation also gives this text a certain paradigmatic status with respect to the writing of early French modernism, as writing that also plays off the "loss" represented by its social marginalization against a "gain" that is a gain in *readability*—a readability that is conditional on forms of indeterminacy and hence on what "Sylvie" defines as a narrative suicide. Such readability, we learn, has its compensations: those that are figured here by the two gendered heads—the head of

the protagonist as "Werther minus pistols" and the head of Sylvie as maternal sister figure—bent sexlessly over a single text that unites them in a
certain abstraction from the world that recalls, although it cannot reconstitute, the magical moment with Adrienne on the lawn. And it is this *gain in*
readability consequent on social marginalization that we can see being pursued, albeit in rather different terms, by writers like Baudelaire and Flaubert.

No other male-authored text of this period, known to me, displays anything comparable to Nerval's attraction to gender indeterminacy as a condition of bliss; nor do any lay claim so openly to feminized status, although
they make much of their social marginalization. Critics who read Nerval as
a protofeminist[19] are not mistaken; but it is important to stress that this
protofeminism has its limits, depending specifically as it does on the maintenance of strictly enforced gender differences as defined by the gynopho-
bic nineteenth century (a period particularly uncritical of its own misogyny). And it is this uncritical acceptance of patriarchal and essentialist
understandings of gender, not its willingness to blur gendered categories,
that "Sylvie" shares with other texts of the period, including those that,
like Baudelaire's and Flaubert's, are in other respects, and by virtue of the
authors' sense of their own social marginalization, so suspiciously critical
of their age and so lucid in their analysis of its blindnesses and contradictions. Textual indeterminacy, the "fog" of words, is a condition of the readability in which these authors, in different ways, seek oppositional advantage. But indeterminacy can never be allowed, even by Nerval, to extend
completely to matters of gender difference, the maintenance of which thus
often appears, as in "Sylvie," to provide a necessary framework of unchal-
lengeable categories, a kind of bedrock of unassailable certainty that makes
it possible for this male-authored writing to proceed with some assurance
in its invention and exploration of subversive forms of textuality. These
texts, in other words—like all forms of oppositionality—draw their power
to oppose from the very structure of the power they oppose.[20]

Unlike suicide with pistols, then, narrative suicide approaches limits that
it does not cross: "elocutionary disappearance" is the name of a readable
process, not that of an accomplished fact, and if narrative suicide courts
death, it does so not with a view to putting an end to living, but as a modus
vivendi. The modulations of marginality and liminality such an option presupposes also imply compromises and calculations of loss and gain with
respect to the conditions of life such a suicide seeks to withdraw or disengage from, as is tellingly illustrated by Nerval's flirtation with a critique of

the system of gender difference that nevertheless maintains masculine privilege. As we saw in chapter 2, Gautier's poetic persona draws back from suicide itself, "saved" by a woman's smile. Nerval chooses suicide, but a suicide of writing that has its own limits (his own death in 1855 does seem to have been an actual suicide, it is true). In Flaubert, too, the suicidal career of a woman character is distinguished, along lines that imply distinctions of gender and class, from writing that imitates and even identifies with such a suicide, but in the interests of its own survival through readability (see chapter 7). And then there is Baudelaire.

*

There is evidence that, as in the case of Nerval and, in a certain sense and to a certain degree, of Flaubert and Gautier, Baudelaire's was a suicidal personality.[21] But for the Baudelairean poetic persona, suicide is not an option, for here the oppositional modus vivendi takes a more polemical form, that of struggle. In the poems of *Les Fleurs du mal*, death is most often and most dramatically displayed as not a solution, but a perhaps illusory and probably disappointing "end" to life, implying the need to survive and to engage with the alienating social world. And death by drowning, which in Nerval or Hubert Aquin[22] is a preferred figure for writerly suicide as an oppositional option, is represented in Baudelaire as the threat of shipwreck;

> Vainement ma raison voulait prendre la barre;
> La tempête en jouant déroutait ses efforts,
> Et mon âme dansait, dansait, vieille gabarre
> Sans mâts, sur une mer monstrueuse et sans bords!

Or, in Richard Howard's version:

> Vainly my reason sought to take the helm—
> the gale made light of purpose, and my soul
> went dancing on, an old and mastless scow
> dancing across a black and shoreless sea.[23]

The reason is that indeterminacy, as this poem ("Les Sept Vieillards") establishes, is not for Baudelaire a way of softening the inhibiting distinctions and unreconcilable categories of the world but is itself the danger that threatens the boundaries of the individual, and particularly of the poetic self. Unlike the dreamy, misty, rural landscapes of Nerval's Valois, Baudelaire's urban, often industrialized, street is invaded by yellow fog— "smog" would be the word were it not anachronistic—and the invasion

("Un brouillard sale et jaune inondait tout l'espace" ["A dirty yellow fog engulfed the whole space"]) is so threatening to the individual subject's own identity and produces such a claustrophobic sense of the impossibility of escape that it requires all the heroism the subject is capable of ("roidissant mes nerfs comme un héros" ["steeling myself like a hero"]) to resist it. Thus the series of identical old men who emerge from the fog form not a blissful Nervalian chain but a hellish funeral procession, a "cortège infernal." The encounter with them wounds ("Blessé par le mystère et l'absurdité") the poet's soul.

Two associated reasons make this Baudelairean heroism so desperate. One is that indeterminacy is now on the side of the social formation and therefore threatens to swamp the poet, who cannot deny his social involvement, in a leveling wash of indifferentiation, the universal in-difference that he names ennui. But the other is that, poetry being itself a form of discourse that depends for the production of beauty on the reduction of difference through the resemblances it discovers in words and the metaphors and analogies it produces between elements of the world, it becomes difficult to distinguish the invasive world of in-difference from the also indifferentiating poetization of that world—in rhythmic melancholy or lyric exaltation, "spleen" or "ideal"—that seeks to oppose it. Instead of a suicide through indeterminacy, there thus arises in Baudelaire a drama of distinction that corresponds somewhat to the tension between social imbecility or *bêtise* and textual idiocy we have already glimpsed in Flaubert (chapter 1). "Les Sept Vieillards" clearly enacts this problem, readable as the poem is, on the one hand as the horrific depiction of an eerie, threatening world of dangerous "mystery and absurdity" and, on the other— and interchangeably—as an allegory for poetic practice itself as a specter plucking the sleeve of the passer-by and sending him home, reeling from the encounter, "blessé" like the hero in his encounter with the old men: "malade et morfondu, l'esprit fiévreux et trouble" ["sickened and chilled, my mind feverish and disturbed"].[24]

Emma Bovary's "fever" will similarly be described as resulting from an invasion of "vapors," and the hysteria we find in Baudelaire is symptomatic, like Emma's, of the crisis of distinction that besets modernism and defines its historical melancholy. The need for this distinction energizes "Sylvie" throughout and accounts paradoxically for its cultivation of an aesthetic of indeterminacy as well as for its reliance, in the final analysis, on a politics of gender difference. But in Baudelaire and Flaubert this crisis derives from the frightening sense that since, as the authors of *The Communist Manifesto* put it, "*alles* Ständige und Stehende verdampft," *all* that is upright and substantial turns to a fog (my emphasis), vaporization is universal. The degraded world and the artistic production that seeks to distinguish itself from it, as a condition of being able to exercise a critical function, have in common the fogginess and insubstantiality, the indifferentiation figured by Baudelaire's procession of identical, hostile old men. It is to the threat posed by such a perception, and to Baudelaire's response as a poet, that we now turn.

FIVE

POETRY IN THE
ASIATIC MODE

In his essay on British rule in India, Karl Marx described "Oriental despotism" as the "Asiatic mode of production"—in which vast expanses of arid and semiarid territory and scattered populations meant that only the state could undertake public works. Marx's point was that such regimes are frozen in a kind of immobility and that only incursions from the outside (such as the arrival of British capitalism in India) could set up the conditions necessary for change.[1] Baudelaire was probably unfamiliar with Marx's analysis; his Oriental sources are more likely to have been Nerval's *Voyage en Orient* (1851), as well as two earlier works: Hugo's *Orientales* (1829) and Goethe's *West-Östlicher Diwan* (1819), which had been translated into French in 1835 and to which Gautier alludes in "Préface," the opening poem of *Emaux et camées*, as we have seen (chapter 2).

Gautier's own Orientalist reverie—that of a pasha surrounded by the luxury of the seraglio and reveling in the pleasures of hashish—is so recurrent that it is not far-fetched to see an allusion or even a tribute to it in the figure of *l'Ennui* "[qui] rêve d'échafauds en fumant son hookah" ["who dreams of the gallows as he smokes his hookah"], that Baudelaire strategically placed in the opening poem of *Les Fleurs du mal*, immediately following the famous dedication to Gautier: "Au poète impeccable. . . ." It is clear that Baudelaire had thought carefully about Gautier's "Préface" and that he tried in his own liminary poems to respond to Gautier's aesthetics. This is especially apparent in "Paysage" (the opening piece in the section titled "Tableaux parisiens"), which I see as an ironic reply[2] to Gautier's text:

Et l'Emeute, tempêtant vainement à ma vitre,
Ne fera pas lever mon front de mon pupitre . . .

[And the riot in the street, storming vainly against my
   window,
Will not make me lift my head from my desk . . .][3]

For unlike Gautier's Oriental reverie, Baudelaire's does not have an es-
capist dimension, at least in the texts of "spleen." (The Orientalism characterizing the poems devoted to "ideal" will be discussed later.) For Baudelaire, Oriental despotism is a mode of production for Western art. Its
structure is made clear in the prose poem "Une Mort héroïque," which is
not a specifically Orientalist text but in which Fancioulle's fate as a mime
artist performing under sentence of death for political subversion is described, with accurate irony, as a *favor* due to the Prince's rigor (see chapter
1). In this chapter I will argue that Oriental despotism is a Baudelairean
figure for the repressive and authoritarian social regime of the Second Empire (a regime dominated by ennui); and that, consequently, the liminary
poem of *Les Fleurs du mal* presents the volume itself as the product of a
"favor" similar to the one Fancioulle enjoys. In short, Baudelaire's collection is a response to a politically and morally repressive bourgeois society
that was not (like the India described by Marx) static and precapitalist, but
an expansionist, high capitalist, *modern* society.[4] The proper framework for
an analysis of Baudelaire's poem is therefore "the age of high capitalism"
(to echo the title of Walter Benjamin's study)[5]—a framework evoked in
the poem itself by the figure of Ennui. The image of the Oriental despot
who dreams of the gallows, "l'œil chargé d'un pleur involontaire" ["his
eyes brimming with an uncontrolled tear"] refers to a hypocritical and repressive society, as well as to the "return of the repressed" to which such a
society is vulnerable.[6] My point is that, although the figure of the hookah
smoker is self-reflexive with respect to the poem, it simultaneously evokes
the poem's social context. More particularly, it situates the remarkable violence of the poem's own tone of address as a violent response to social
cruelty:

Hypocrite lecteur,— mon semblable,— mon frère!

[Hypocrite reader,—my alias,—my twin!]

By its brutal portrait of hypocrisy and by the sheer violence of its tone, the
poem seeks to avenge the hypocritical cruelty of the gallows dream, which
is otherwise masked by the indifference of Ennui. Whereas texts like Ner-

val's "Aurélia" struggle against social alienation (conceived of in terms of madness) through an effort to reconcile conflicting discourses,[7] the collection *Les Fleurs du mal* establishes a mood of provocation and polemic from the start through its liminary address "Au lecteur" ["To the Reader"].

What Baudelaire calls "hypocrisy" corresponds to the phenomenon we would refer to today—whether in psychoanalytic or political terms—as repression. Hypocritical and repressed, Ennui makes neither *grands gestes* nor *grands cris*, but "would gladly bring the earth to ruin and swallow all creation in a yawn." In response to the violence of "hypocritical" repression, poetic violence therefore functions as a return of the repressed. But since repression and the return of the repressed are so closely intertwined and so difficult to distinguish from each other (our only evidence of repression being the signs of its "return"), it is appropriate that in speaking of its addressee as "hypocrite lecteur," "semblable," and "frère," the poem should imply that the poetic subject is hypocritical as well. It is just that the poetic subject is hypocritical in a different way, or rather in *two* ways, the second of which sets him apart from the reader: In order to denounce the hypocrisy of the reader, who stands for the society that will receive the collection and that consequently furnishes its enunciatory context, the "I" of the poem must of course himself be sufficiently acquainted (as is the reader) with "ce monstre délicat," Ennui, to be able to analyze it effectively. That is a first point.

But poetic violence is a transmuted and purely symbolic violence that responds to the brutal (and real) violence of a hypocritical society in a disguised manner of its own. When it "returns," as Freud demonstrated, the repressed is transformed; it takes on a duplicitous guise that must be deciphered. Thus in its textual function (or more precisely in the relation between its textual and narrative functions), the poem enacts a hypocrisy of its own, since in a repressive society it is forced to counter censorship by producing a discourse that harbors knowledge it does not dare to express or even to acknowledge. Whereas the poetic subject, the narrative "I" of the poem, is the reader's "frère" and "semblable" because of his acquaintance with the same social reality of ennui, the textual subject of enunciation both contains and is "cannier" than the poetic subject. For it "recognizes" that it is (or produces itself as) a site of repressed drives and impulses that are in fact disguised expressions of those same *grands gestes* and *grands cris* that the repressed and hypocritical Ennui is unable to express.

Poetry is duplicitously cruel, in short, because social duplicity is cruelly but hypocritically repressive. In "Au lecteur," the deceptively calm figure of the Oriental despot, who "dreams of the gallows as he smokes his hookah," is as relevant to the poetic subject ("je") as he is to the reader ("tu"), who represents the poem's social context—those *semblables* or "twins" who are both so intimately acquainted with Ennui as a repression of latent cruelty. But it is important to realize that the despot fulfills a double function, not only as a metaphoric representation of the "I" who speaks in the poem and the "you" he addresses, but also as a self-reflexive figure of the poem as text with its own duplicitous structure—as a site of repression, but also as a site of the vengeful return of the repressed.

In "Au lecteur," however, ennui is merely the social symptom of a deeper and more pervasive metaphysical tyranny: the reign of evil. The figure of Ennui (which dominates the second part of the poem) echoes and amplifies the figure of Satan, which dominates the poem's beginning:

C'est le Diable qui tient les fils qui nous remuent.

[The Devil's hand directs our every move.]

According to the ethnographical research of Michael Taussig,[8] societies that experience a brutal transition from a precapitalist to a capitalist way of life (such as South American peasants who were suddenly forced to conform to the demands of a new industrialized agriculture) tend to view themselves as subjugated to the reign of the Devil. Baudelaire—whose life span (1821–67) corresponds to the rise in France of a bourgeois, capitalist, and industrialized society—bears witness to this experience. In "Au lecteur" everyone is damned, everyone is guilty, and the poet himself is no exception (the speaker of the poem says "nous" until the final lines), since all of them know Ennui, which is the sign of the Devil's dominion.

On the one hand, however, there is the hypocrisy of society that *submits* to the power of Satan Trismegistos, by whom "le riche métal de notre volonté est tout vaporisé" ["the precious metal of our will is completely vaporized"]. On the other hand, there is the hypocrisy of the poetic voice that *denounces* the Devil's repressive and "vaporizing" force, whose principal manifestation is the void of ennui. The vaporization that is the consequence of Satan's power therefore functions in a dual manner: by undermining the will, it produces the vice(s) of social hypocrisy, of which Ennui is "[le] plus laid, [le] plus méchant, [le] plus immonde" ["even uglier and fouler than the rest"] (p. 6). At the same time, it provides cover for poetic hypocrisy as a counterviolence to the violence of repression, which (given its diabolic origin) can itself operate only in a duplicitous manner. If the poetic subject ("I") is under the sway of vices shared by everyone else, but that he (unlike the others) fully recognizes, then the poem itself—despite its oppositional will, despite even the lucidity and vigor of its denunciation—functions like a verbal smoke screen. It is a vapor of words in which can be deciphered an anger that is both dissembled and dissembling, and capable (in Vallès's metaphor) of "firing without being seen to take aim." Hidden behind the vaporous smoke of Ennui's hookah lies the monstrous dream of the gallows—an image of the cruelty of a repressive society, *or* an image of the counterviolence that responds to it in *Les Fleurs du mal*, for example. "Au lecteur" calls for both readings; but that is why its main strategy is to distinguish between social and poetic violence. The whole thrust of the last two lines—where an accusatory *je-tu* distinction suddenly replaces the inclusive subject *nous*—is to provoke a violent split or disjunction within that identity, whose very violence calls attention to the urgency and importance of the distinction being made.

The question then is, Who is the real despot? The image of the hookah-smoking dreamer of gallows is first and foremost a political figure who recalls the social tyranny exerted, especially after 1851, by a victorious bourgeoisie whose boredom-producing order rested, both historically and continuously in the present, on the bloody repression of the working class. Yet in a poem where what is true of the reader is also true of the poet—and in a volume expressly dedicated to Gautier, that arch hookah smoker—Oriental languor and voluptuousness are also the sign of the poet, who is no less a victim of hookah-smoking Ennui than his fellow citizens, and no less duplicitous than they in harboring daydreams of violence. The primary duplicity of the poem is therefore that its apparently moral denunciation itself has a *political* dimension and that it is engaged in an oppositional struggle fueled by repressed anger. In this sense, the daydream of the gallows corresponds not to bloody repression of the common people, but to a no less bloody revenge of the people against their oppressors (irrespective of class) in an event such as the Terror.

The paradox is obvious: the same word *échafauds* (scaffolds or gallows) connotes both revolution and the repression of revolution. This ambivalence is the root of the text's "hypocrisy," its duplicitous evasion of censorship (in the institutional as well as psychoanalytic sense of the term). The text suggests that ennui is a symptom of repression not only in the psychological sense, but also in the political sense, since the bourgeois order is based on oppression. This analysis can also be applied to the poem itself, which conceals a dream of vengeance beneath its poetic smoke screen. To make this analysis, however, the reader must first recognize the political implications of the word *échafauds* in a text that, on the surface, appears to deal primarily with moral issues; second, one must recognize that the hookah-smoking figure of Ennui represents the poetic subject *je* as well as the more explicitly denounced reader ("Tu le connais, lecteur"). Finally, the reader must be aware of the equivocation produced by the dual role of scaffolds in recent French history as a symbol of the oppression of the people, as well as a means for revolutionaries' elimination of their oppressors. The duplicitousness of the word *échafauds* is what permits the poem's denunciation of Ennui as a manifestation of a repressive bourgeois order to cover for its enunciatory function as a vengeful manifestation of the return of the repressed. "Au lecteur" illustrates in this way the complexity of the rhetorical strategies available for use in poetic discourse as a linguistic assemblage functioning in an oppositional role. True, these strategies are more easily recognized by the twentieth-century reader, who has become well accustomed to the subtle twists and turns of texts produced in the context of authoritarian regimes, but they could certainly have been deciphered without difficulty in Baudelaire's time, provided the reader was in a relation of some complicity, political and intellectual, with the text.

In 1857, however, a text such as *Les Fleurs du mal*, which displayed a certain degree of moral frankness—even without any explicit political implications—was already viewed as oppositional. The collection was, after all, persecuted and partially censored because of its alleged outrage to public morals. Following an ideology of imitation that has already been mentioned, the indictment of the work rested on the alleged danger posed to society by such an explicit representation of moral degradation. The hypocrisy of this accusation—which amounts to criticizing the text for its *lack* of hypocrisy—is clear. But what exactly did this hypocrisy signify at the time? Baudelaire did not hesitate to recognize the duplicitous political motives behind the accusations of immorality.[9] The government seems to have utilized the pretext of moral outrage as a means of persecuting a publisher (Poulet-Malassis), a poet (Baudelaire), and a text (*Les Fleurs du mal*) that were already politically suspect. Such is the duplicity of power. But neither can one rule out the hypothesis suggested by Dominick LaCapra[10] in connection with *Madame Bovary*, that it was the novelty of the writing in *Les Fleurs du mal*—the power of duplicity—that attracted the uncomprehending but suspicious attention of the censor's office. Recent studies by Richard Sieburth and Nathaniel Wing support this interpretation.[11]

In either case, the complex mirroring of social and textual duplicity is highly ironic, since the hypocrisy of the text, sheltering its political cruelty behind moral recriminations, was not to prevent society from attempting—in its own typically hypocritical manner denounced in "Au lecteur" (i.e., unconscious of its own duplicity)—to suppress a text perceived as dangerous by making moral accusations where political matters were in fact at stake. It is as if the latent violence with which the poem responds to the hypocrisy of Ennui was perceived—in an unformulated and no doubt unformulable manner—by the dreamers of scaffolds in power who thus unwittingly confirmed the analyses proposed in the text by their attempts to repress it. For it is the nature of social duplicity to be unconscious of itself, not to "know" itself, and hence to need to be *denounced*: "Tu le connais, lecteur" ["Reader, you know it well"]. On the other hand, textual duplicity is null and void and its denunciation is powerless unless it is *penetrated* by an act of reading. Thus there is mutual vulnerability, produced in each case by the constitutive dynamics of duplicity. Society's blindness to its own moral and political hypocrisy makes it vulnerable to the counterviolence of exposure by denunciation. At the same time, the *knowing*, even self-conscious duplicity of the accusatory text is ineffectual so long as it remains unperceived, so that, because of its very readability, such duplicity is vulnerable to an ill-intentioned reading.

Yet whoever tries to penetrate a text such as "Au lecteur" will still run up against a smoke screen, a fog of words, since the structure of its duplicity is shaped by the "play" between its narrative and textual functions, which I see as the characteristic feature of the new writing of the 1850s. The figure of Ennui links the "I" of the poem to the "tu" that is the reader and to the society whose hypocritical and repressive structure it denounces. In the narrative function, the poetic discourse is centered, then, on a subject who recognizes his "brother" and "alter ego" in the social addressee. Taken as a self-reflexive figure of the text, however, the image of the hookah-smoking dreamer of gallows calls for a more suspicious reading of the poem—a reading attentive both to the calm outer surface of the hookah smoker and to the inner dream of gallows he invites us to look for in it. Such a reading would consequently perceive the text as *decentered*—decentered because split (neither the impassive smoker nor the cruel dreamer, but indissolubly both at the same time), but also because it is diffuse and scattered like a billow of smoke or a cloud of vapor. Such a text, despite its smooth surface and its absence of "grands gestes" and "grands cris," is entirely capable of swallowing up the world in a single cataclysmic yawn—a yawning, bottomless emptiness.

But finally, through the dual figure of the Oriental despot, the text affirms an affinity (or kinship) between the narrative subject *je* (which denounces its own hypocrisy in denouncing that of its *tu*-addressee and "brother") and a textuality that also presents itself through self-figuration as hypocritical, albeit hypocritical in a different manner. All the differences and dualities the poem enforces and depends on—its own inner split between narrative and textual functions, as well as its own "knowing" hypocrisy in relation to the unconscious hypocrisy it denounces in the reader— are undermined by insidious resemblances. It is not surprising, then, that this liminary text is filled (as we shall see) with anxiety concerning lines, barriers, and boundaries: Where does one draw the line between text and context, poetic discourse and social discourse? How does one distinguish between knowing and unconscious duplicity, between textual and social hypocrisy, between narrative subject and textual functioning?

The invasive presence of Satan is marked above all by his power to "vaporize," and the prime effect of this power is to obscure lines of separation and to blur distinctions. The modernity of "Au lecteur" and its tremendous *critical* power stem in large part from the fact that, at the outset of *Les Fleurs du mal*, it poses the question of duplicity but also that of *sameness*— sameness that vaporizes the very distinctions the poem works with and without which criticism likewise is disarmed. For this reason, although my study attends in the first instance to the already complex problematics of duplicity, it will not be complete without a discussion of the related thematics of sameness, kinship, resemblance, and metaphor. In *Les Fleurs du mal*, this constellation of themes forms the core of an aesthetics of the ideal, which "Au lecteur" represses, but that it produces also as the return of the repressed of all forms of duplicity. One cannot denounce one's reader without acknowledging his brotherhood, or produce the exotic image of the Oriental despot without admitting that he is well known to the *frères ennemis* and part of their own close acquaintance. If the poem brings such violence to the act of (d)enunciation that establishes its own duplicity as different from social hypocrisy, might it not be because it feels *itself* secretly threatened by that power of indifferentiation, that invasive "indifference" that it calls Ennui?

AU LECTEUR
La sottise, l'erreur, le péché, la lésine,
Occupent nos esprits et travaillent nos corps
Et nous alimentons nos aimables remords,
Comme les mendiants nourrissent leur vermine.

Nos péchés sont têtus, nos repentirs sont lâches;
Nous nous faisons payer grassement nos aveux,
Et nous rentrons gaiement dans le chemin bourbeux,
Croyant par de vils pleurs laver toutes nos taches.

Sur l'oreiller du mal c'est Satan Trismégiste
Qui berce longuement notre esprit enchanté,
Et le riche métal de notre volonté
Est tout vaporisé par ce savant chimiste.

C'est le Diable qui tient les fils qui nous remuent!
Aux objets répugnants nous trouvons des appas;
Chaque jour vers l'Enfer nous descendons d'un pas,
Sans horreur, à travers des ténèbres qui puent.

Ainsi qu'un débauché pauvre qui baise et mange
Le sein martyrisé d'une antique catin,
Nous volons au passage un plaisir clandestin
Que nous pressons bien fort comme une vieille orange.

Serré, fourmillant, comme un million d'helminthes,
Dans nos cerveaux ribote un peuple de Démons,
Et, quand nous respirons, la Mort dans nos poumons
Descend, fleuve invisible, avec de sourdes plaintes.

Si le viol, le poison, le poignard, l'incendie,
N'ont pas encor brodé de leurs plaisants dessins
Le canevas banal de nos piteux destins,
C'est que notre âme, hélas! n'est pas assez hardie.

Mais parmi les chacals, les panthères, les lices,
Les singes, les scorpions, les vautours, les serpents,
Les monstres glapissants, hurlants, grognants, rampants,
Dans la ménagerie infâme de nos vices,

Il en est un plus laid, plus méchant, plus immonde!
Quoiqu'il ne pousse ni grands gestes ni grands cris,
Il ferait volontiers de la terre un débris
Et dans un bâillement avalerait le monde;

C'est l'Ennui! — l'œil chargé d'un pleur involontaire,
Il rêve d'échafauds en fumant son houka.
Tu le connais, lecteur, ce monstre délicat,
— Hypocrite lecteur, — mon semblable, — mon frère!

[To the Reader
Stupidity, delusion, sin, and avarice,
torment our bodies and possess our minds,
and we sustain our affable remorse
the way a beggar nourishes his lice.

Our sins are stubborn, our contrition lame;
we want our scruples to be worth our while—
how cheerfully we crawl back to the mire;
a few cheap tears will wash all our stains away!

Satan Trismegistos subtly rocks
our ravished spirits on cushions of evil
until the precious metal of our will
is completely vaporized by this cunning alchemist;

the Devil's hand directs our every move—
the things we loathed become the things we love;
day by day we drop through stinking shades
quite undeterred on our descent to Hell.

Like a poor profligate who sucks and bites
the martyred breast of an ancient whore,
we snatch in passing at clandestine joys
That we squeeze hard like an old orange.

Wriggling in our brains like a million worms,
a demon demos holds its revels there,
and when we breathe, the Lethe in our lungs
trickles sighing on its secret course.

If rape, poison, the knife, and arson
have not yet stitched their ludicrous designs
onto the banal canvas of our pitiful destinies,
it is because our soul, alas, is not bold enough!

But here among the scorpions and the hounds,
the jackals, apes and vultures, snakes and wolves,
monsters that howl and growl and squeal and crawl,
in all the squalid zoo of vices, one

is even uglier and fouler than the rest,
although the least flamboyant of the lot;
this beast would gladly bring the earth to ruin
and swallow all creation in a yawn;

I speak of Boredom which—his eyes brimming with an
    involuntary tear
dreams of hangings as it puffs its pipe.
Reader, you know it well,
— hypocrite reader, — my alias, — my twin.]

In marking the line that separates the autonomous text ("inside" the
volume) from the social context ("outside" the volume), the *liminary* or
threshold text subverts such distinctions. The first dividing line it blurs is
the line separating inner from outer. Situated on the threshold of *Les Fleurs
du mal*, "Au lecteur" is an integral part of the volume's "architecture" (as
Barbey d'Aurévilly called it);[12] but through its address to the reader, the
poem *actualizes* the social relationships and historical context that determine its own readability and that of the collection as a whole. (An empirical reader of Baudelaire's time or our own who was ignorant of the phenomenon of ennui would not make much headway with the poem.) We
know that Baudelaire toyed with the title "Préface" (which would have
recalled Gautier but suggested a purely introductory function in relation
to the volume) before adopting the definitive title "Au lecteur." This title
has the advantage of specifying its function as one of address—a turning
outward that links the whole collection to its readers and social context and
gives us to read the text-context relation as *constitutive*.

Claude Pichois is unnecessarily troubled, then, when he writes in his
notes to the Pléiade edition of *Les Fleurs du mal*: "Not all the major themes
of the 1857 collection . . . are represented here. In the first section, 'Spleen
et Idéal,' it is obviously 'Spleen' that is insistently privileged."[13] Later I will
suggest that there is a relation of complementarity rather than one of incompatibility or mutual exclusion between "spleen" (as the mode of poetic
address) and "idéal" (as the mode of poetic structuring). For the moment,
let me simply point out that the function of "Au lecteur" is only secondar-
ily to serve as a thematic preface to *Les Fleurs du mal* by defining, summa-
rizing, or synthesizing its "content." Its primary role is to set up a relationship between text and reader that will be valid for the collection as a whole.
It is by outlining from the start the conditions of its readability that the
liminary poem is representative; and its value as an introduction or preface
lies in the way it presents the collection as a social discourse, participating
in the interactions of the polis. The relationship in question, as I have already suggested, is best described in terms of reciprocal cruelty—the cru-

elty of repression and the cruelty of the return of the repressed. The poem's discourse, as has been mentioned (but it is time now to move into a closer analysis), presents itself as similar to social discourse yet simultaneously and crucially different, the violence of textual duplicity responding to the repressive violence of social hypocrisy. And the "reader" who is named in the narrative function as the object of textual violence is therefore not necessarily the reader whose role according to the textual function is to gauge these relations of mutual violence and to grasp the poem as a product of two inseparable phenomena: repression and the return of the repressed.

The crucial moment in "Au lecteur" is therefore the rhetorical move, in the final lines, away from the all-inclusive *nous* that has until then dominated the poem, to a *je-tu* relationship that very subtly both confirms and disrupts the community implied by *nous*. The address to the reader as "mon semblable,—mon frère!" implies a relation of close similarity—but not of absolute identity—between the subject of the poem and his addressee. (That the personages are masculine and their gender is pertinent is a point to which I will return.) This sudden shift in mode of address distances the speaker from the reader and establishes a relation between them that is that between the subject and object of a discursive act. Building upon the commonality of their experience, this distancing strategy enables the speaker to *denounce* the reader for the very knowledge—and hypocrisy—they share. Their nonidentity grounds the act of denunciation that is itself motivated by their resemblance; and "I" affirms his difference in the very act that acknowledges the community of experience that makes his discourse meaningful.

For to say "hypocrite lecteur" is not in itself the same as saying one is hypocritical oneself. As intimately familiar as the speaker may be with hypocrisy, his denunciative act is itself the opposite of a hypocritical mode of speech. As a denunciatory act, it seeks to strip the other's hypocrisy from him. The accusation that unveils the reader's hypocrisy does at the same time have the effect of laying bare the speaker's *own* aggressivity and denunciatory cruelty, which until then had been hidden, hypocritically, behind the *nous* of community. In other words, the poetic "I" abandons his duplicity (which consequently is not quite the same as what the poem describes as hypocrisy) in the discursive act of denouncing the hypocritical duplicity of the other. For the prime condition of hypocrisy is its failure to acknowledge itself, and the poem clearly defines hypocrisy as duplicity unaware of itself—as the result of complacency, pusillanimity, and "vaporization" of the will. The words "Tu le connais, lecteur" ["Reader, you know him/it well"] and "hypocrite lecteur" (which follow as a natural conclusion, since in the logic of the poem, knowledge of Ennui is the same as acknowledging its hypocritical structure) are cruel because they brutally unveil what the reader had *not* known and had *not* acknowledged. But this very cruelty unmasks the text's own rhetorical "hypocrisy" by showing that it was, if not exactly as matter of fully "conscious" duplicity, at least an affair of discursive skill or strategy. The poem has been lulling the "reader" into complacency by addressing him with a complicitous *nous* in order to surprise him more effectively with the final denunciation of hypocrisy.

Textual hypocrisy and social hypocrisy are therefore not the same, since the text acknowledges its own duplicity, or at least makes it readable, whereas society remains unconscious of its duplicity and lays itself open to denunciation; yet text and society both share an element of repressed cruelty. In the final analysis, what binds them together is at the level of what is unacknowledged by the reader but laid bare by the text both in the reader and in itself. There is an Oriental despot in the reader, and the text makes the reader the object of an Oriental despotism of its own. In a sense it is the same despotism, the same hookah-smoking dreamer of gallows, the same figure of Ennui. But the despot in the text lays claim to being stronger and crueller, since by his denunciation he forces the discovery of despotism in the reader ("Tu le connais, lecteur!"), while retaining to a certain extent the advantage of his own rhetorical smoke screen or cover, the advantage of the poem's own duplicity.

There are, in fact, two logically linked accusations in the poem's last two lines, of which the second (reader, you are a hypocrite) generalizes and makes explicit the implication of the first (reader, you are acquainted with Ennui). The reader's hypocrisy, therefore, is twofold: it consists of failing to acknowledge his acquaintance with Ennui, but also and consequently of failing to recognize the hypocritical nature of Ennui itself:

> Quoiqu'il ne pousse ni grands gestes ni grands cris,
> Il ferait volontiers de la terre un débris. . . . (p. 6)

> [Although he makes no wild gestures or loud cries,
> He would bring the earth to ruin. . . .] [14]

In its last two lines, the poem therefore denounces a whole web of hypocrisies. The full implication of this ending is that what the reader's hypocrisy conceals is ennui, which itself is a mask for the reader's (and society's) latent destructiveness and cruelty. Yet the subject ("I") can know all this only from his own experience, from having himself been a victim of Ennui (as his admission of resemblance with the reader implies). An empirical reader needs to reflect that this is the case before being able to see that the poem functions as a masked denunciation of the speaker himself, as well as a direct denunciation of the reader. The poem's self-denunciation, revealing that it exercises hypocrisy like (but of a different order from) the hypocrisy it attributes to the reader, becomes readable only as a second-order realization, especially given the surprise effect of the sudden energetic denunciation of the "reader." But readable it is: indeed, readability is its characteristic; it is a masked self-denunciation.

In fact, the poem might take as its motto the Cartesian dictum *Larvatus prodeo*, which translates either as "I advance in disguise" or as "I step forward [and show myself] as a masked man." But to *say* "Larvatus prodeo" necessarily invites the second interpretation. The poem wears a mask and acknowledges it in its very manner of denouncing those who do not acknowledge their masks (either to themselves or to others); but this self-denunciation therefore remains a masked one. Consequently, two analyses of the poem suggest themselves, focusing either on its description of social hypocrisy as a refusal to acknowledge what one secretly knows or on its rhetorical deployment of "hypocritical" tactics, which it makes available to reading even as it deploys them. It is relatively easy to analyze the poem's description of social hypocrisy, and I shall do so in the next section; here I am beginning the task of analyzing its rhetorical duplicity, which makes possible the act of denunciation and is at the same time revealed through that act. But it should be understood that this is only a first or "cover" duplicity—something like a "simple" duplicity—that does not exhaust the endless duplicities of the text, to which it will be necessary to return in due course. For *Larvatus prodeo*, as an acknowledgment of duplicity, is a discursive act that must itself of necessity "advance in disguise," and it may well be masked in ways that it does not or cannot itself acknowledge.

The text's rhetorical "cover" or "simple" duplicity therefore amounts to this: that it is possible to read "Au lecteur" in terms of the *nous*-relationship that prevails in the greater part of the poem, as implicating the poetic subject (*je*) in the social ills that it diagnoses. We are all damned, since under the universal rule of Satan, everyone is guilty of hypocrisy. In this reading, which is that proposed by Felix Leakey,[15] the accusatory lines at the end appear as a relatively secondary addition, a defensive *tu quoque* (as Leakey maintains), reminding the reader that he too, as the subject's *semblable* and *frère*, is implied in the universal *nous*. This is a perfectly plausible reading, but one that is based solely on the narrative function of the poem, without taking into account the admission of hypocrisy that is made readable by the text's self-reflexive apparatus. It is only when one becomes attentive to the duplicity of the text itself that a more "suspicious" reading emerges—the reading I am proposing. Specifically, since the reader can be reached only by a potentially damaging admission on the text's part, that of its commonality with the reader, that situation can be turned to advantage by advertising it so overtly that this resemblance becomes a kind of mask or disguise, a disarming *captatio* that serves as a rhetorical smoke screen behind which can be carefully prepared the final violent blow that is ultimately dealt the "hypocritical reader." *In cauda venenum*, the venom is in the tail, therefore: the deployment of the pronoun *nous* serves both as logical justification and as rhetorical cover, lulling the reader's attention until the text's cruelty is unleashed at the end. In this reading the last line appears as an *ego quoque* that is secondary, but at the same time indispensable, since it is essential to the aggression.

An analysis of this kind also influences the thematic reading of the poem, in a way that brings to light another aspect of its duplicity. For the allegation of universality implied by the choice of *nous* serves as cover for a rhetorical coup (denunciation of the reader) that is nothing other than a political and social act distinguishing the discourse of the poem—and that of *Les Fleurs du mal* as a whole—from the prevailing social discourse of hypocrisy. Within this frame of ideas, the universalism of the metaphysical and moral language of the text—its description of a latter-day *theatrum mundi* that has become a puppet theater from which God is absent but in which "the Devil holds the strings that move us" and vaporizes the "precious metal" of our will—may appear as the "cover" for the text's relatively precise political implications, even on a thematic level. Indeed, in his comparison between "Au lecteur" and another liminary text, the dedication "Aux bourgeois" of the *Salon de 1846*, Dolf Oehler has persuasively demonstrated the political dimension of the poem's subject matter. "In both dedicatory texts," writes Oehler, "Baudelaire recalls the misery of bourgeois existence, its emptiness, lack of fulfillment, and the impossibility of its fulfillment." Later Oehler points to ennui as the visible sign and the unavoidable consequence of "bourgeois order." [16]

A political reading of "Au lecteur" is therefore perfectly plausible and has already been done by others. If it is correct to argue that hidden—but perceptible—behind the metaphysical vision projected by the poem is a political denunciation, then it is evident that the moral vocabulary abounding in the text—which has led Leakey and others to read it as a kind of sermon—serves to mediate the transition from the metaphysical order (Satan's rule) to the political order (bourgeois rule). The moral deficiencies of human society (the result of Satan's rule) provide the grounds on which political discourse can make the crucial distinction between "social" hypocrisy and "textual" duplicity—a distinction its own social identity depends on.

One could argue, of course, that the strength of the poem lies precisely in its failure to make clear distinctions or recognize boundaries between the metaphysical, the moral, and the political. Social concerns are couched in moralistic language and given a metaphysical dimension in the triumph of Satan, a figure who is not only the world's puppet master (which is a political image in the final analysis because of his absolute wielding of power), but also the reverse alchemist responsible for "vaporizing" the gold of our will into base elements (which is essentially a moral image). But the intertwining of themes is such that one could easily see it as a way of "scrambling" the reading of the text (and hence as another form of textual duplicity), especially since of all the different levels of thematic readability that the poet proposes, the political dimension of the poem is the most understated, the most dependent on hint and allusion, on "firing without being seen to take aim."

The moral and metaphysical picture is one of despotic power exerted by Satan over subjects too complacent, too pusillanimous, too addicted to the daydreams of Ennui to resist. By its denunciatory act, the poem seeks to stir these subjects against the master who has "vaporized" their will. Under conditions of political censorship, the explicit political relevance of such a picture of individual dereliction and universal submission as an implicit allusion to the post–1851 order of things could not, of course, have been stated; but it would have been visible without difficulty to the readers of the time, sensitized as they surely were by the institution of censorship and accustomed as they must have been to reading allusive and indirect texts. As modern readers, we must therefore try to recognize the signals to "follow my gaze" in a text that, in so many ways, makes it clear that it knows much more than it says. More than it *knows how* to say, no doubt; but also more than it *dares* to say.

What emerges, then, is this: the poem's *nous* activates on a thematic level, but rhetorically shelters, a denunciatory attack on bourgeois hypocrisy personified by the reader. But behind the moral failings it inventories under the designation of "hypocrisy" (and these we have yet to study), the poem points to a metaphysical source (Satan) that can be seen as its ultimate target. *Behind* this denunciation of Satan's power, however, one senses a political thrust, an implied attack on the social order maintained by the authoritarian regime of Napoléon III. Just as the reader knows Ennui without recognizing it, the poem harbors a meaning that it refuses to *acknowledge*, but that it makes readable to those who know how to penetrate its duplicity. Moreover, this is a possibility of reading that the text itself opens up when, in the final lines, it uncovers its strategy and, at the same time, claims a duplicity all its own.

*

Social hypocrisy, that of the reader, consists of failing to acknowledge what one *knows*. The implication of the first two stanzas—with their nominative and somewhat incongruous list of moral failings ("la sottise, l'erreur, le péché, la lésine") ["stupidity, delusion, sin, and avarice"] and their long periphrastic definition of complacency without naming it—is that some sins are recognized (i.e., *named*), while other sins remain unacknowledged (*unnamed*), and that the latter are more serious. Complacency—"nourishing" one's remorse as a beggar nourishes his vermin, believing that repentance and remorse can "wash all our stains away"—appears as the first example of what the poem will identify as hypocrisy. For in the Baudelairean universe, strongly influenced as it is by Joseph de Maistre's *Les Soirées de Saint-Pétersbourg*, there is no expiation of sin, no redemption: the fallen state of mankind is irredeemable, sin is ineradicable, and human "progress" is a lie or an illusion. In a provocative manner, the poem assumes that we know this but perversely prefer to believe otherwise: we simply do not want to acknowledge what we intimately *know* to be the case.

The question that quite naturally is raised by the poem is therefore this: How is such perversity possible? The answer is a metaphysical one, partly implied (God is dead), partly explicit: Satan rules the world, and his power consists of "vaporizing" the will. The alchemical image used here to describe Satan's power returns in the "Epilogue"—the liminary closing piece that Baudelaire projected for the 1861 edition of *Les Fleurs du mal*; but there *poetic* alchemy functions as a counterchemistry to the Devil's entropic work against the city: "Tu m'a donné ta boue et j'en ai fait de l'or" ["You gave me your mire and I transformed it into gold"]. This confirms that in "Au lecteur" the ultimate target of poetic attack, beyond the reader to whom the collection is addressed, is the Devil himself, that elusive enemy who, in "L'Ennemi," "eats away at our heart" ("nous ronge le cœur"), as here he vaporizes our will. Satan presides over a world subject to time (which "eats away life") and to dispersion; yet people are fully responsible for their fate, since their moral complacency is what makes Satan's rule possible. As Joseph de Maistre famously put it, "Toute nation a le gouvernement qu'elle mérite" ["Every nation has the government it deserves"]. In the poem itself, we read: "Sur l'oreiller du mal c'est Satan . . . Qui berce longuement notre esprit enchanté" ["Satan . . . subtly rocks our ravished spirits on cushions of evil"]; we are "enchanted," yet it is our own complacency that allows us to be bewitched and corrupted.

Vaporization is a key term in the Baudelairean universe, and not simply in the moral sphere. Here Satan's vaporizing power over human will clearly anticipates the image of the hookah-smoking dreamer that appears at the end of the poem and suggests that demoralization is a form of addiction. At the same time, this vaporization leads from the moral inertia denounced in the poem, through Ennui, to the complex realm of *spleen*—that poetic atmosphere so characteristic of the Baudelairean universe and whose signs are misty air ("air brumeux"), freezing rain, the untraversable barrier ("muraille immense") of the fog of exile, streams of black, sooty smoke rising to the firmament, the lowering sky forming a cover ("le ciel bas et lourd pèse comme un couvercle"). The landscape of spleen maps out the boundaries of exile, separating God from man, heaven from earth, desire from its object (a point to which it will be necessary to return in discussing "Le Cygne" in the following chapter). Spleen is therefore a melancholy domain of separation and division, but with boundaries that are both marked and blurred—and hence rendered problematic—by the penetrating fog that fills every nook and cranny ("tout l'espace"), as in "Les Sept Vieillards." And this invasion, this "meteorological" vaporization, functions in the subject as the sign of a moral vaporization of being, a torpor and impotence in the face of evil—in short, of the victory of ennui, "fruit de la morne incuriosité" ["fruit of gloomy indifference and lack of curiosity"].

One trait distinguishes Baudelairean spleen from the unconscious and hypocritical ennui of the "reader," however. In spleen, the inertia, helplessness, torpor, and addiction are something from which the subject *suffers*. And just as spleen makes the world into a prison and a place of exile—that is, of separation—so the suffering identity of the splenetic subject is *divided*. Knowing that he is morally *responsible* and yet at the same time a *victim* of Satan Trismegistos, the subject is divided against himself. He resembles the poet in "La Pipe," who is simultaneously the *smoker* of his pipe (which declares itself to be "his") and *smoked* by it:[17]

Je suis la pipe d'un auteur;

. . . .

J'enlace et je berce son âme
Dans le réseau mobile et bleu
Qui monte de ma bouche en feu.

[I am the writer's pipe;

. . . .

I wrap his soul in mine and cradle it
within a blue and fluctuating thread
that rises out of my rekindled lips.][18]

In "La Pipe," the poet is a "grand fumeur" ["a great smoker"], an active subject who is at the same time in the thrall of a "puissant dictame"—a powerful but soothing drug. In "Au lecteur," the same thematics of addiction clearly underlies the description of "Satan Trismégiste / Qui berce longuement notre esprit enchanté." Even though it is divided in this way between active smoker and passive smoked, the splenetic identity is still *aware* of its subjugation to a soothing spell, a subtle bewitchment, to a vaporizing invasion that tends to blur distinctions, including the distinction between splenetic subject and victim of Ennui.

The poem of course reproaches the hypocritical reader above all for his *submission* to Satan's power, a reproach that shows that—despite his subjection to the addictions of ennui—the splenetic subject still has a margin of consciousness that distinguishes him from the other victims of Satan. But spleen itself still tends in the direction of the same sinister blurring of distinctions that signals Satan's total victory and the absence of any resistance to his reign. The foggy boundaries that make the universe of spleen into a place of exile and separation become imprecise and expand, so that fog fills all space, as in "Les Sept Vieillards," and distinctions between exterior and interior, "actor" and "scenery," are obscured. The prison of spleen (cf. "Quand le ciel bas et lourd . . .") has bars of rain: its dimensions are as vast as the universe and as limitless as the dispersed ego. In the same way, within the self, the separation becomes blurred between the locus of consciousness, responsibility, and will and the subliminal psychic region— that we know but do not acknowledge—ruled by Satan and sending up clouds of debilitating vapor. Nothing remains but a vast fog that manifests Satan's diffuse presence but hides him in the mists of unconsciousness, just as the clouded brain of the hookah smoker conceals in its depths a sadistic, satanic daydream that the dreamer's very lethargy prevents from surfacing.

Thus we see what is at stake in the disjunction brought about by "Au lecteur" between the unconscious hypocrisy of the reader (victim of Ennui and whose will has been vaporized by Satan) and the duplicity, which I will call splenetic, of the textual act of enunciation/denunciation (a duplicity governed by the conditions of Satan's reign, yet at the same time anti-satanic). The poem makes a rather desperate attempt to reestablish a certain difference—moral and metaphysical, as well as aesthetic and political—in a world threatened with vaporization and indifferentiation—in short with "in-difference" in the sense of boredom as well as indistinctness. But how can the text make this crucial difference, when it recognizes its own resemblance to the hypocritical reader, from whom it wishes to differentiate itself? "De la vaporisation et de la centralisation du Moi. Tout est là," Baudelaire would later write in *Mon cœur mis à nu*. ["It all comes down to the vaporization and the centering of the self."] But what if it is no longer possible to center the self because, on the one hand, of the *division* and, on the other, of the *diffusion* the dispersal produced within it by Satan's spell? It will be up to poetic discourse to counter the vaporized, unconscious world of hypocrisy (to which it necessarily belongs) not with centered speech, but with the duplicity of a discourse that is fully aware of the conditions of universal hypocrisy in which it is operating. It is the margin of knowledge, the consciousness in and of evil—what Baudelaire called "la conscience dans le mal"—that alone distinguishes spleen from ennui.

Spleen is thus the state of consciousness that recognizes with horror the invasion of the self and of the world by the vapors of the Devil, while ennui is the hypocritical state of those who undergo this invasion and feel its effects but are unwilling to acknowledge it—a state of blindness lucidly denounced in "Au lecteur." Satan is the name the poem gives to both the origin and the first cause of evil, to a presence that is everywhere diffuse and threatening, to a principle of undecidability and indifferentiation; and the reproach the poem addresses to all who are under Satan's power (which is everyone, including the one who says "nous") is that we feel no repugnance or "horror" at what are objectively the horrifying, repugnant conditions of our existence. For it follows from Satan's rule that we are all condemned to damnation: "Chaque jour vers l'Enfer nous descendons d'un pas" ["Each day we descend a step closer to hell"], but also that we advance "sans horreur," since our vaporized wills are incapable of alarm and cannot react against the horrifying conditions in which we live. Hypocrisy makes Satan's rule a *furtive* presence in the world, a threatening and powerful presence that is nevertheless easy to ignore.

In the two central stanzas of the poem (5 and 6), the idea of Satan's furtive presence (reformulated as the invisible entry of Death into our lungs) is consequently linked to a new theme that dominates the rest of the poem: the theme of concealed and latent cruelty. These pivotal stanzas draw together the bipartite thematics of the poem: in the first part (stanzas 1–4), hypocrisy is first defined as a loss of will resulting from the Devil's despotism, and hence as complacency toward sin and an inability to acknowledge its consequences. From this point on, however, hypocrisy appears as that which reproduces within the human psyche the structure of the Devil's reign over the universe and as a form of repression that holds in check the latent cruelty governing us. This structural homology between the Devil's unacknowledged reign over humanity and the psychic structure of repressed cruelty is what gives the poem its thematic coherence. The motif of *clandestinity* is at the heart of these central, transitional stanzas, since the secret and sinister entry of Death, "fleuve invisible," slowly flooding our lungs (the motif in stanza 6 that recapitulates the whole first part of the poem) corresponds to the furtive, sadistic cruelty of the "débauché pauvre" and the "plaisir clandestin" that we press "comme une vieille orange" (in stanza 5).

These central stanzas are remarkable for their poetic density and intensity. Sin, described as the complacent love of repugnant objects in stanza 4, is particularized in stanza 5 in the sadistic image of the "débauché pauvre" martyrizing an ancient whore; but this image is immediately generalized again through the metaphoric equivalence of the whore's martyred breast and the orange of pleasure we squeeze to the dregs. The semantic link between the verbs *presser* ("to press") and *serrer* ("to squeeze") bridges the transition to the image in stanza 6 of the brain as a place for wild revelry ("ribote"), another form of secret debauchery, while giving overtones of violence and cruelty to the tableau of debauchery. The simile of the "wriggling of a million worms" describes the head as a decaying corpse as well as a prison, so that it simultaneously recalls the martyred body of the ancient whore and Death invisibly descending into our lungs "avec de sourdes plaintes" ["with muffled moans"]. The repression implicit in this forced enclosure of the orgy within is also linked to the invisibility and furtiveness of Death's descent into our lungs, of which we are unconscious. Finally, this stanza conjures up a kind of *danse macabre*[19] while recalling the multiple images of invasion and of mental and physical dispersion by the wormlike harbingers of death that haunt the Baudelairean spleen. But it also foreshadows the furtive pleasures of the Parisian nightworld evoked in the "Tableaux parisiens"[20] while it activates a historical memory, perhaps, of the desperate orgies of those about to die in the overcrowded prisons of the Terror.

The following stanza calls attention to the fact that the sadist in us all remains clandestine. Pusillanimity corresponds to the complacency evoked earlier as another way of not acknowledging what is: "C'est que notre âme, hélas! n'est pas assez hardie" ["It is because our soul, alas, is not bold enough!"]. To the vaporization of the will (which is the source of complacency), however, cowardice adds the repression of sadistic instincts, which prevents them from surfacing into action: the inventory here, "le viol, le poison, le poignard, l'incendie" ["rape, poison, the knife, and arson"] tellingly echoes the list of sins in the opening line of the poem. Whereas complacency appears as an unconscious phenomenon, pusillanimity is characterized as a phenomenon of censorship that prevents violence from stitching its "plaisants dessins" ["ludicrous designs"] onto the embroidery of a "life canvas" that remains boring and adventureless as a result ("le canevas banal de nos piteux destins"). Thus the psychic structure of Ennui as a "banal" surface, lacking "grands gestes" and "grands cris" but harboring an unrealized dream of cruelty, is clearly prefigured here. At the same time, the text's self-figuration as an embroidery canvas on which the repressed "designs" of violence seek to express themselves anticipates the self-reflexive role played by the hookah smoker in the final stanza.

Yet we must wait a while longer for Ennui to be named and identified. It could have been named in the list of vices in the first line of the poem. But it has been postponed and is postponed again now: the menagerie image and the personification of Ennui as an Oriental potentate both intervene before Ennui is actually named and its hypocritical structure revealed. Through this strategy of postponement, the poem simulates in its own structure the return of the repressed that the imagery now begins to thematize. For not only do the wild beasts in their cages recall the image of repression present in the prison house of the brain where demons are crowded together in orgiastic revelry, this image also suggests the *need* for repression. For if these animals—these "monsters that howl and growl and squeal and crawl"—are caged, it is for fear of what would happen if they *escaped* from their prison (as does the swan in "Le Cygne," discussed in chapter 6). Here again the mechanism of self-reflexivity is at work: after the "muffled moans" of Death (figure of a poetry that seeks to be the repressed voice of "invisible" Death), these cries and crawling of wild beasts are the sign of a language traversed by a violence that seeks to *return*, of a poetry whose rhythm has taken on the sinuosity of cruel insinuation.

But menagerie animals are caged not simply to contain their ferocity, but also because they are on display; the cage serves to repress them and to prevent a return of the repressed, but also to make them visible. There is one animal, furthermore, that stands out as an exception in this catalog of venomous and wild beasts: it is the monkey, which owes its place in the menagerie exclusively to its talents as amuser and mime—the humanoid animal who, as the "hypocrite" of the animal world (in the Greek sense of *actor*), reflects back to men and women an animalized image of themselves.

The monkey not only anticipates the "hypocrite reader" of the final line but, through its role as a hypocrite on display, illuminates the self-reflexive meaning of the menagerie as a whole (picking up from the earlier figure of "the banal canvas of our pitiful destinies"). The menagerie of vices reads, then, as a figure for *Les Fleurs du mal* itself, as the textual mirror in which the unconscious "reader" is invited to contemplate his hypocrisy; but hypocrisy is given as a repressive cage whose bars hold back a ferocity of wild beasts. The *visibility* of the animals of the menagerie thus becomes a sign of the *readability* that enables the text to reveal what the "hypocrite reader" unconsciously represses and fails to recognize in himself. But at the same time, the purely symbolic character of the return of the repressed accomplished in the text is figured by the fact that the animals of the menagerie remain *behind bars*, visible but deprived of liberty, incapable of acting out their dangerous potential for violence and cruelty. The text remains hypocritical, but the spectacle it provides makes visible to the hypocritical reader the mechanisms of censorship and repression of which the reader is unconscious, just as it shows the latent ferocity that these mechanisms are designed to repress. As a return of the repressed, the text is able to outmaneuver the mechanism of censorship only by setting an example of readable hypocrisy and by exposing in that way the operation of censorship itself. Where Satan is *le maître des marionnettes* (puppet master), the poet is *un montreur de monstres* (a freak showman).[21]

As the standout in the list, hypocrisy (the monkey) is therefore already linked in advance with the vice of Ennui—that other major standout from the list, "even uglier and fouler than the rest." Ennui owes its prominence to its special monstrousness: as opposed to the wild beasts, whose ferocity is visible, Ennui is a seemingly civilized "monstre délicat," whose appearance is all quiet and stillness ("il ne pousse ni grands gestes ni grands cris"), but that conceals a violence of cosmic dimensions: "Il ferait volontiers de la terre un débris / Et dans un bâillement avalerait le monde" ["This beast would gladly bring the earth to ruin / and swallow all creation in a yawn"]. Ennui's all-encompassing violence recalls that of Saturn/Cronus, the god of melancholics and of time that eats away at life; and hence the erosive cruelty of Satan. So it is appropriate that, like the humanoid monkey, Ennui is the vice that assumes human form: the ape of hypocrisy (an animal resembling a man) and the Oriental despot (a man concealing the ferocity of an animal) have in common a deceptive structure: their human guise masks an animal nature.

Perhaps enough has now been said about the intertwining of hypocrisy and Ennui in the final lines, the similar and yet different manner in which the subject and reader are implicated by the knowledge they have of these vices, and the rhetorical function of the act of denunciation that ends the poem. I will, however, point out that the figure of the Oriental hookah smoker ties together all the images of repression and vaporization in the poem, along with the sense of the return of the repressed that emerges toward the end as a latent threat in the form of destructive desires and bloodthirsty dreams. Finally, I will call attention to a self-reflexive detail that is of particular importance if one bears in mind that the Oriental despot figures the "hypocritical" textuality of the poem, as well as the social hypocrisy, rooted in repression, which is that of the "reader." I am thinking of the "pleur involontaire" ["involuntary tear"] with which the eye of the hookah smoker is filled ("chargé")—a curiously suggestive term that literally means "loaded" or "weighed down" or even "charged with" (in the sense of "responsible for"). Because it is "involuntary," this tear contrasts with the "vils pleurs" in the second stanza—cheap, hypocritical tears that are supposed to "wash all our stains away" ("laver toutes nos taches"). The involuntary tear in the eye of the hookah smoker is a figure for the poem itself as a denunciatory sign both of the hypocrisy of society and of the return of the repressed; this tear does not wash away sin but functions as an involuntary trace of its presence. But if the poem is the "involuntary tear" of society, doesn't this figure invite us at the same time to seek *within* the poem itself—figured as it is by the hookah smoker—denunciatory tears of its own, the signs of an "involuntary" labor going on in the poem? Isn't its own face (that of the poem) also "chargé de larmes"—weighed down or *charged* with tears?

Because it is involuntary, the hookah smoker's tear is a sign of the vaporization of the will produced by the devil's alchemy. But taken as an involuntary sign, filling the eye, as if from beneath the weight of an accumulation of meaning, it becomes readable. It can be seen as a *substitute* for the violence that Ennui conceals (and hence a sign of the repression of that violence), but also as a transformed *manifestation* of that violence, welling up from the depths toward the surface, where it becomes visible (and hence a sign of the return of the repressed). Concealing and revealing violence at the same time, this "involuntary tear" has a structure of duplicity resembling that of the text itself, as a symbolic return of the repressed—that is, as a manifestation of violence that simultaneously bears witness to to the power of censorship and repression and therefore appears in the end as an "involuntary" phenomenon, itself a product of vaporized will. Unlike the animals in the menagerie, who openly display a violence whose threat is restrained by the bars, the poem-tear shows a sign that appears harmless but is actually a sign of repressed violence. And it is in this way—through this occultation of ferocity that the animals make visible—that it manifests the vaporization of the will.

But in the final analysis the involuntary tear, a product of the vaporized will as it is, itself appears as a kind of *secretion* of ennui, the product of a *condensation* of the vapors. It thus alludes to the possibility of a mode of poetic production, however involuntary, that would be capable—through a form of creation of its own—of *responding* to the "Asiatic mode" of existence led under the tyrannical rule of the Devil. If social hypocrisy is the repression of an unknowledged violence, and if textual duplicity is a vaporized anger that is readable only through a textual smoke screen, the figure of the involuntary tear also gives an image of the poem as a cold form of anger, a condensation derived from its evaporation. Such a condensation would remain within the order of the sign and the symbolic; it would always be a function of the return of the repressed and, consequently, a substitutive expression—yet this expression would derive from a mode of production that would be at the opposite pole from that promoted by Satan's alchemy. "De la vaporisation et de la centralisation du Moi. Tout est là," reads the famous saying. But condensation proposes a conception of poetic work that labors against vaporization (yet depends upon it), without being grounded in a centered self, a concept that is henceforth impossible.

As a "pleur involontaire" welling up within the eye of a hypocritical society that knows Ennui—*bearing down* on it with the weight of an unexpressed meaning but also *accusing* it, as one speaks of a *témoin à charge* (a witness called upon to give testimony)—the poem "Au lecteur" thus, in the final analysis, presents its relation to this society as an enigma. It presents itself—and indeed the whole collection of which it is the liminary piece—as a sign to be interpreted. But is it a sign of the repressed violence on which the social order, producer of ennui, is based and hence *semblable* (similar) to that society? Or is it a sign of the symbolic return of that violence, of a textual duplicity responding with violence to social hypocrisy? And in that case, is it a manifestation of vaporization, and hence subject to the reign of the Devil? Or rather is it a condensed form of violence subject to the conditions of the return of the repressed but derived from an "autonomous" mode of production and, consequently, a trace of that margin of suffering that distinguishes spleen from ennui? A sign that would escape in this way and to this extent from the control of the vaporizing tyrant of the will? *Les Fleurs du mal*, one will no doubt agree, are readable as *all of the above.*

*

In any case, the melancholy text—for melancholy, in the most conventional of codes, is what an involuntary tear signifies—presents itself as a decentered text, *containing* and consequently *revealing* an anger, a violence, a cruelty of which it is the product but not the direct expression. If social ennui results from the imposition of order, it is the sense of an absence, of a lack of ground, that marks the sorrow in Baudelaire, the presence of a vaporizing Devil implying the disappearance of the God who presided over the traditional *theatrum mundi*. To the bourgeois order, the Baudelairean text will therefore oppose a metaphysics denouncing the presence of Satan, but an erotics of lack (since, as we will see in the following chapter, the object of desire is never anything but a substitute for the Object that is henceforth unavailable) and a "depolitified" politics, which is a politics of loss (the lost enthusiasm of the 1840s, the lost causes of 1848). The vapors, the mists that invade the world, the psyche, society, and discourse manifest a presence—that of evil—but at the same time bear witness to a loss—of self, meaning, reality, God—that turns the universe into an uncentered place emptied of substance, a place of mourning.[22]

Sadism in the realm of eroticism,[23] repressed resentment and dreams of gallows in the social world, and, in the realm of poetry, the latent cruelty and violence of text and the provocative, denunciatory role it assumes as a social discourse—all these are signs of the diffuse presence of Satan in the dispersed and uncentered world of modern melancholy. What distinguishes the melancholic text is that it presents itself as readable (in the sense that its textual fog demands to be penetrated) and that consequently it seems "aware" that it possesses an unconscious. Constituted as melancholic by a desubstantializing lack, it nevertheless puts, *in place of that lack*, a frightening anger that is its source, *fons et origo*, an anger that is all the more frightening because it is latent and repressed.

Few pre-Freudian texts display themselves as so aware of the unconscious as does Baudelaire's, and few deploy their duplicitousness in ways so unhypocritical—that is, in ways that so explicitly acknowledge the knowledge they have but cannot name. Thus the rhetorical structure of "Au lecteur" demonstrates a certain duplicity; thematically, the poem is an analysis of unconscious duplicity (which it calls "hypocrisy"). But these two structures—the rhetorical structure of the denunciation and the thematic structure of the analysis—together form what I will call the "dramatic" structure of the poem, which *enacts*, performs, what it cannot name: the phenomenon of repression and the return of the repressed.

For the rhetorical "cover" provided by the deployment of the pronoun *nous* and the thematic postponement of the direct presentation of Ennui *coincide*, in such a way that the unveiling of the reader's knowledge of Ennui and the cruel (*je-tu*) denunciation of the hypocrisy of Ennui occur simultaneously in the final stanza. At the same time, the distancing figuration of violence through the use of exotic images—the displacement of responsibility for social relations onto the Devil, the stereotypically "Orientalist" personification of Ennui as an Asiatic despot—suddenly gives way to a show of violence that mobilizes instead a a relation of kinship and familiarity: the I-you (*je-tu*) relationship of brothers enacted in the words "Mon semblable, —mon frère." The alienating images are in this way unveiled and demystified; they concern a family affair. For otherness is substituted similarity—and an acknowledgment that what is at stake lies close to home. Just as the poem cruelly forces the reader to admit the knowledge he has of Ennui—"Tu le connais, lecteur"—so too its complex unveiling gesture in the closing lines represents its own way of acknowledging what all along it has known intimately but until now has not wanted *to let out of its cage*.

On the stylistic level, the text also displays evidence of the pressure of unconscious knowledge. In general terms, Baudelaire's interest in the "bizarre" can be understood as a sign of his awareness of discursive duplicity, and the stylistic bizarreness of "Au lecteur," particularly in terms of figuration, has been studied by Nathaniel Wing in a fine article.[24] But one can point also to the poem's lexical bizarreness: the sporadic use of recondite or archaic words (such as *lésine*, *lice*, and *helminthes*) in a text that otherwise makes use of a traditional, not to say threadbare, vocabulary of morality and religion. The poem also displays certain semantic or syntactic "awkwardnesses," such as the ugly chain of relatives in "C'est le Diable *qui* tient les fils *qui* nous remuent" [literally, "It is the Devil who holds the strings that move us"] or the bold telescoping of "Il ne pousse ni grands gestes ni grands cris" [literally, "He utters neither grand gestures nor loud cries"]. One can *pousser un cri* in French, but not normally *pousser un geste*. Baudelaire was an extremely self-conscious artist, however, and would certainly not have tolerated these apparent blunders (especially in so important and strategically placed a text as "Au lecteur") had he not sensed their latent expressivity. These stylistic quirks are "tears" that "charge" or "weigh down" (*charger* is another infelicity of the poem's expression) the surface of the text, evidence—whether involuntary or not—of obscure forces *pushing* through its otherwise stylistically bland exterior. But pushing also suggests a reaction or "return" of energy, a counterforce to the repressive connotations of the verbs *presser* ("to press") and *serrer* ("to squeeze") that figure at the center of the poem. Indeed, *pousser un geste* (by analogy with *pousser un cri*, which means "to utter an involuntary cry") can only signify (as *énoncé*) what it is rhetorically *performing* (as *énonciation*) in its miming of a *lapsus calami*, or slip of the pen. It signifies, in short, what it is: a "slip" or *Fehlleistung*, an error (*Fehl*) that allows the subject to accomplish (*leisten*) an expressive act—albeit involuntarily, subject as it is to the reign of vaporized will. This is true of the poem as a whole: miming the return of the repressed, *charged* with latent meaning, the poem enacts what it declares that Ennui fails to do—*pousser un geste*. Expressing what Ennui (society) represses, the poem serves a *counterrepressive* function.

But can a text "acknowledge" in such a way everything that it represses? Claude Pichois, as I mentioned earlier, calls attention to the absence of themes of the "ideal" in "Au lecteur"; and it is indeed the *absence* of a certain ideal world that is manifested by the presence of the tormented world of spleen. However, the Baudelairean "ideal" is not the world of centered plenitude that the presence of God would guarantee; such a world is definitively lost. In the Baudelairean universe, the ideal derives, like spleen, from a poetics of vaporization, but in a different manner; and if it is the case that in spleen Satan has *replaced* God, my suggestion is that it is the poetics of the ideal that spleen *represses*. Yet the repressed can always *return*. For the ideal is a poetics of resemblance, whereas (as we have seen) splenetic discourse depends crucially on disjunctive violence. Resemblance functions therefore as a return of the repressed in the poetics of spleen, acknowledged as it is on the level of rhetorical address, where it serves to motivate the disjunctive act ("Mon semblable,—mon frère!"), while it goes unackowledged on the level of the thematic structuring of the poem. In my opinion this secret or unacknowledged kinship between the poetics of spleen and ideal, that is, their joint belonging in the universe of vaporization, is betrayed by the fact that, in the Baudelairean imagery, each is figured as a function of Oriental despotism and of the "Asiatic" mode of production.

As I write, lines from another poem in *Les Fleurs du mal* (an "ideal" poem) stir my memory, as what needed to be repressed in order for Baudelaire to write: "Hypocrite lecteur,—mon semblable,—mon frère!" The lines open "L'Invitation au voyage," just as the line I have just cited closes "Au lecteur":

> Mon enfant, ma sœur,
> Songe à la douceur
> D'aller là-bas vivre ensemble. . . .
>
> [My child, my sister,
> Imagine the sweetness
> Of going there to live together. . . .][25]

In a remarkable analysis, Barbara Johnson has shown that the poetic beauty of "L'Invitation au voyage" stems from the repression of the *real*— from the absorption of the woman as addressee and referential object into the metaphoric structuring of the text: "The land in which 'tout n'est qu'ordre et beauté, luxe, calme et volupté' is not really a land that resembles the woman; it is what the 'I' would like the woman to resemble," writes Johnson. "Thus it is metaphor itself that becomes an 'invitation to travel,' a process of seduction."[26] Metaphor (by which is meant here the paradigmatic structure of the poem) has become more real than the referent; the woman addressed by the poem in the narrative function is the victim of a gesture of expropriation and exploitation that imports her into the bedchamber of the text (in stanza 2)—a clear figuration of the poem as a closed space and an autonomous world—in the same way that the ships in stanza 3 are brought by a system of colonial economy to rest on the warmly lit canals of a similarly poeticized Holland.

So it is significant that, in this bedroom, the placid bourgeois comfort of Flemish homes ("des meubles luisants, polis par les ans") is subtly metamorphosed little by little into a dream of Oriental luxury and splendor ("les riches plafonds, les miroirs profonds, la splendeur orientale"), which is itself immediately associated with the production of an ideal language that would speak the soul's native tongue:

> Des meubles luisants,
> Polis par les ans
> Décoreraient notre chambre. . . .
> Les riches plafonds,
> Les miroirs profonds,
> La splendeur orientale,
> Tout y parlerait
> A l'âme en secret
> Sa douce langue natale.

> [Gleaming furniture
> Polished by the years
> Would decorate our bedroom. . . .
> Richly decorated ceilings,
> Deep mirrors,
> Oriental splendor,
> Here all would speak
> To the soul in secret
> Her sweet native tongue.] (59)

Thus in "L'Invitation au voyage," as in "Au lecteur," the exotic is tied to the intimate and the familiar (represented here by the "native tongue").

But there is also a subterranean link between the despotism exerted *against the reader* in "Au lecteur" and the cruelty of poetic transformations in "L'Invitation au voyage"—its suppression of the referent through metaphoric transformations that correspond to the dream of an abstracted purity of language able to speak the soul's native tongue. This repression is enacted not against a male addressee (as in "Au lecteur"), but against a woman addressee—*une lectrice*. For technically, I am mistaken in speaking of the female figure in "L'Invitation au voyage" as the referential object of the text, since the referent is in fact the fictive world the poem produces. Yet Barbara Johnson is absolutely correct in identifying the woman "narratee" as a representation of the *materia poetica* that the poem seeks to transform verbally into ideal beauty through the metaphoric "transport" figured by the voyage.

Whereas the text of "Au lecteur" turns toward a social reality ("hypocrite lecteur") so as to enact a disjunctive gesture in a polemical manner, the text

of "L'Invitation au voyage" turns *away* from an eroticized reality, which it
addresses only in order to absorb it into the web of its textual construction.
The woman is in effect effaced, her reality subjugated and "infantilized" by
her absorption into the dream of an ideal language: "Mon enfant, ma
sœur, / Songe à la douceur. . . ." Unlike the politicized figure we find in
"Au lecteur," the Oriental imagery in "L'Invitation au voyage" is closer to
the ideal harem imagined by Gautier. But in each case it becomes evident
that poetic despotism responds to a desire to bring about an *autonomiza-*
tion of poetic language, whether with respect to the "hypocritical" reader
it denounces or the referent for which it substitutes the "dream" of a linguistic construct.

Although the poetic modes of both spleen and ideal are based on a despotic act of cruelty, it is clear, then, that they correspond also to two different conceptions of poetry as verbal production in a world in which words
have become vaporous under the Devil's sway. Having lost their anchor-
age, words are a bit like the seagoing vessels in "L'Invitation au voyage,"
"dont l'humeur est vagabonde" ["whose mood is roving"]; they are free to
create structures of their own that bring happiness, in the way the vessels
in the poem come from the ends of the earth "pour assouvir ton moindre
désir" ["to satisfy your slightest desire"]. But in its vaporous state, poetic
discourse is also free to answer the social duplicity of a hypocritical world
with a duplicity of its own—a duplicity both similar to and distinguishable
from that of society, in the same way that the return of the repressed is
distinguishable, and indistinguishable, from repression. In short, in the
Baudelairean universe it seems that vaporization can give rise (on the one
hand) to condensation, in the cold, rainy world of spleen in which the
"involuntary tear" betrays a sadistic dream, and (on the other) to the "tiède
atmosphère" of "Paysage," the "chaude lumière" of "L'Invitation au voyage," the luminosity, warmth, and ideal atmospherics of the imaginary that
one finds in "Parfum exotique," "La Chevelure," and numerous other
poems.

Yet these two modes of poetic discourse are mutually exclusive. One
cannot simultaneously respond to the world and leave it, absorbing it into
oneself in the "transport" of a metaphoric voyage. In the final analysis, each
form of textuality must repress the other and be haunted in turn by the
other as by its shadow. By absorbing into itself its "sister" reality, Baudelaire's poetry of the ideal turns away from the world of ennui and from
social duplicity in order to become an "invitation au voyage." In wanting
to intervene in the affairs of the world by denouncing as its "brother" the

empire of Ennui, however, poetry forgets the possibility of the "voyage," its power as a verbal artifice to forge the seductive beauty of a world that is not unreal but, as Baudelaire would say, surreal. (With Jean Baudrillard, one might suggest the word "hyperreal," so clear is it that the Baudelairean ideal is pure simulacrum, a product of signs.)

These differences in *genre* on the poetic level are signaled by the *gender* differences that mark these two modes of poetic discourse: the reader as brother in "Au lecteur," the *materia poetica* as child-sister to the poetic subject in "L'Invitation au voyage." The incestuous relation to the sister and the polemical relation to the brother, the *frère ennemi*, not only indicate the close kinship, the family resemblance between these two modes of poetic production, they also point to the whole problematics of difference and resemblance that constitutes the central dilemma of Baudelairean poetics. The *sister* is imagined as different from the poetic subject: she differs from him as nature from culture or the order of things from the order of words. It is therefore necessary to efface her difference by making her *resemble* the poetic landscape, at the cost of her own reality. Such is the power of metaphoric transformation as discursive structuring. But it gives us the measure, also, of the misogyny—of the hatred and fear of woman—that Baudelaire adopted unchallenged from his society, the "hypocritical" society that he detested so heartily in other respects. And there is indeed a strong resemblance between the *frères ennemis*, the *je* and *tu* of the textual discourse and the sociopolitical context, which is why the disjunctive power of poetic denunciation must be mobilized as a polemical (indeed political) tool to drive a wedge between the *frères ennemis* and produce poetic discourse as different. (This need for differentiation within the dynamics of mimetic desire is a central preoccupation in the work of René Girard.)[27] Here it is no longer a matter of opposing culture to nature or words to things, but instead of a polemical relation situated in the realm of language and culture alone—that is to say, where relations of a *political* order can exist.

In the realm of discourse, it is therefore between men, between brothers, that difficult dealings and complicated maneuvers are pursued. Woman is excluded, as "sister" or "child," *sœur* or *enfant* (let us recall once again the etymology *infans* = "not speaking"); or else she is absorbed, effaced by virtue of the magical power of metaphoric transformation. Through an eroticization of discourse, woman is effaced from the political sphere. And yet all this work of differentiation—between sister and brother and between brothers—is done within the intimate circle of the family, within (and against) the kinship expressed by these terms, but expressed as well by the presence of the Oriental figure in the realms of both *spleen* and *ideal*. The Oriental despot presides over poetic production, sitting alone and smoking his hookah. Is he dreaming himself—and reality—into a cloud of erotic bliss? Or is he, behind his smoke screen, dreaming of scaffolds? Either way, poetry is always despotic. The question at any given moment is, Which despot and which reign is to prevail—that of *spleen* or that of *ideal*?

To late twentieth-century readers, it is evident that the Baudelairean distinction between *le frère* (with whom the poetic subject shares access to the realm of discourse and political action) and *la sœur* (identified with a "nature" that is merely unformed matter to be transformed culturally into poetry) is itself the product of a political gesture. It is "hypocritical" in the Baudelairean sense of the term: failure to acknowledge what one *knows*, refusal to *know* (to acknowledge) the unconscious as a product of the mechanism of repression, and as a result, vulnerability to a return of the repressed. The poetics of the *ideal* can be read as the repressed unconscious of the poetics of spleen, and vice versa; which means that the relation between them is subject to the blurring and questioning of lines of separation that is precisely the business of a poem such as "Au lecteur."

The consequence is that *Les Fleurs du mal*, as a collection, defines poetic discourse as a discourse that is always *alienated*, but alienated in different ways. First, it is alienated from a "reality" or "nature" against which it constructs itself as artifice, metaphoric transformation and linguistic structuring. Second, as a communicational act, poetic discourse is alienated in relation to its social context, where it is self-defined as a return of the repressed. Finally, poetry is alienated in relation to *itself*, since it is unable to reconcile the two conflicting modes of poetic despotism that repress and exclude each other despite their close kinship. For each of these modes of discourse is a function of the same phenomenon of linguistic vaporization, a vaporization that produces these lines of separation—between repression and the return of the repressed, consciousness and the unconscious—while at the same time blurring them irrevocably.

The distinction—between address to the brother and address to the sister—on which a poem like "Au lecteur" depends, *condensing* itself coldly into an act of political hatred rather than *evaporating* warmly as an aesthetic transformation of the real (cf. a poem like "Harmonie du soir": "Les sons et les parfums tournent dans l'air du soir" ["Sounds and sweet smells waft in the evening air"]), is therefore subverted by the way the poem subverts other distinctions, denouncing as hypocrisy every refusal to acknowledge what one knows. It is in this sense that the unveiling of the familiar and the familial (*heimlich*) character of the Oriental figuration in the poem appears crucial to me.

I have chosen not to describe as "Orientalist" the Asiatic figures of the poem (the hookah smoker, the sumptuous chamber or *chambre luxueuse*)—by which the Baudelairean text designates itself self-reflexively, although they unquestionably participate in the production of the Orient as Europe's "other" excoriated by Edward Said in his memorable study.[28] It was Marx who described "Oriental despotism" as a precaptialist phenomenon of limited relevance to the industrialized world of the West, failing in this to foresee the extent to which capitalism and industrialization would themselves serve as breeding grounds for despotism in the modern world. By contrast, Baudelairean poetics produces its exotic imagery and designates the Orient as "other," but only to add—in a way that demystifies its supposed alterity—"Tu le connais, lecteur!" ["You know him, reader!"]. We in our turn can draw from this statement implications that the poem was perhaps unable to articulate or even to foresee. Yet writing in the early days of the Second Empire ("Au lecteur" dates from 1855), Baudelaire's modernity lay in the perception that Oriental despotism is a fitting figure for the alienated relationships—whether political, psychosocial, or aesthetic—that have characterized the Western world in the wake of the Industrial Revolution: the death of God, the cycle of revolution and counter-revolutionary repression, the countless alienations resulting from the development of an industrialized, urban capitalist society. Indeed, Oriental despotism is a *doubly* fitting figure for these alienated relationships, since through its "alterity" it provides the duplicity of rhetorical "cover," while through its resemblance it is consistent with its object.

In the preface to *Les Orientales*, Victor Hugo had predicted: "Pour les empires comme pour les littératures, avant peu peut-être l'Orient est appelé à jouer un rôle dans l'Occident" ["In matters of empire, as in literature, the Orient is perhaps soon destined to play a role in the West"]. When he wrote this in January 1828, Hugo could scarcely have foreseen the precise sense his vague linking of empire and literature would assume in Baudelaire's poetry, which defines itself in terms of the relation of power that links methods of social control and literary duplicity, repression and the return of the repressed. Nor could Hugo have imagined the close relation of *kinship* that the Baudelairean poetics of the "involuntary tear" would uncover between the "Asiatic mode of production," on the one hand, and modern European society and its literature, on the other.

But that is the point. Prophecies always come true in unexpected ways. They too *know* much more than they are able to *say*, and in this sense demonstrate the uncanniness or *Unheimlichkeit* of textuality. It is the Baudelairean text's acknowledgment of this latent textual knowledge that gives it its characteristic duplicity; and it is the duplicitously self-conscious "hypocrisy" it deploys in and against a hypocritical world that distinguishes *Les Fleurs du mal* as one of the key texts of modernity. It is the duplicity of *Unheimlichkeit*, if you will; but only provided that the eerie strangeness of the uncanny is understood, as Freud was later to teach, as a product of the simultaneous denial and recognition of the *heimlich*, of the familiar.

MEMORY AND MELANCHOLY

Le Cygne
A Victor Hugo

I

Andromaque, je pense à vous! Ce petit fleuve,
Pauvre et triste miroir où jadis resplendit
L'immense majesté de vos douleurs de veuve,
Ce Simoïs menteur qui par vos pleurs grandit,

A fécondé soudain ma mémoire fertile,
Comme je traversais le nouveau Carrousel.
Le vieux Paris n'est plus (la forme d'une ville
Change plus vite, hélas! que le cœur d'un mortel);

Je ne vois qu'en esprit tout ce camp de baraques,
Ces tas de chapiteaux ébauchés et de fûts,
Les herbes, les gros blocs verdis par l'eau des flaques,
Et, brillant aux carreaux, le bric-à-brac confus.

Là s'étalait jadis une ménagerie;
Là je vis, un matin, à l'heure où sous les cieux
Froids et clairs le Travail s'éveille, où la voirie
Pousse un sombre ouragan dans l'air silencieux,

Un cygne qui s'était évadé de sa cage,
Et, de ses pieds palmés frottant le pavé sec,
Sur le sol raboteux traînait son blanc plumage.
Près d'un ruisseau sans eau la bête ouvrant le bec

Baignait nerveusement ses ailes dans la poudre,
Et disait, le cœur plein de son beau lac natal:
Eau, quand donc pleuvras-tu? quand tonneras-tu, foudre?
Je vois ce malheureux, mythe étrange et fatal,

Vers le ciel quelquefois, comme l'homme d'Ovide,
Vers le ciel ironique et cruellement bleu,
Sur son cou convulsif tendant sa tête avide,
Comme s'il adressait des reproches à Dieu!

II

Paris change! mais rien dans ma mélancolie
N'a bougé! palais neufs, échafaudages, blocs,
Vieux faubourgs, tout pour moi devient allégorie,
Et mes chers souvenirs sont plus lourds que des rocs.

Aussi devant ce Louvre une image m'opprime:
Je pense à mon grand cygne, avec ses gestes fous,
Comme les exilés, ridicule et sublime,
Et rongé d'un désir sans trêve! et puis à vous,

Andromaque, des bras d'un grand époux tombée,
Vil bétail, sous la main du superbe Pyrrhus,
Auprès d'un tombeau vide en extase courbée;
Veuve d'Hector, hélas! et femme d'Hélénus!

Je pense à la négresse, amaigrie et phtisique,
Piétinant dans la boue, et cherchant, l'œil hagard,
Les cocotiers absents de la superbe Afrique
Derrière la muraille immense du brouillard;

A quiconque a perdu ce qui ne se retrouve
Jamais, jamais! à ceux qui s'abreuvent de pleurs
Et tettent la Douleur comme une bonne louve!
Aux maigres orphelins séchant comme des fleurs!

Ainsi dans la forêt où mon esprit s'exile
Un vieux Souvenir sonne à plein souffle du cor!
Je pense aux matelots oubliés dans une île,
Aux captifs, aux vaincus! . . . à bien d'autres encor!

[THE SWAN
To Victor Hugo
I

Andromache, I think of you! That stream,
Poor and sad mirror that once reflected
The immense majesty of your widow's grief,
That lying Simoïs swollen by your tears,

Suddenly watered my fertile memory,
As I crossed the new place du Carrousel.
The old Paris is gone (the face of a city
Changes faster, alas! than a human heart).

Only in my mind's eye can I still see all those builders' sheds,
Those piles of rough-hewn cornices and columns among the
    weeds,
The huge blocks of stone discolored by the puddles,
And the jumble of bric-à-brac glittering on display.

There was once a menagerie here;
There one morning, at the hour when Labor awakens,
Under the cold, clear heavens, when the street workers
Raise a somber hurricane of soot and noise in the silent air,

I saw a swan that had broken out of its cage,
And with its webbed feet scraping the dry pavement,
Dragged its white feathers across the uneven cobblestones.
Opening its beak wide in a waterless gutter in the street.

It wildly beat its wings in the grimy dust,
And cried, its heart full of memories of the lovely lake of its
    birth:
"Water! when will you rain? Thunder! when will you roll?"
I see this unhappy creature still, strange and fatal myth,

Like mankind in Ovid,
Straining its neck and turning its head imploringly
Toward the ironic and cruelly blue heavens
As if it were reproaching God!

II

Paris is changing. But nothing in my melancholy
Has changed! New mansions, scaffoldings, blocks of stone,
Old neighborhoods, everything becomes allegory for me,
And my fond memories weigh heavier than rocks.

Standing in front of the Louvre today, an image oppresses
    me:
I think of my great swan, thrashing wildly,
Like exiles, ridiculous and sublime,
And tormented by endless longing! And then I think of you,

Andromache, fallen from the arms of a great and noble
   husband,
Common chattel in the hands of haughty Pyrrhus,
Crouching, in ecstasy, over an empty tomb,
Hector's widow, alas! Now the wife of Helenus!

I think of a black woman, emaciated and consumptive,
Floundering in the mud, and searching with a haggard eye
For the missing palm trees of splendid Africa
From behind an immense wall of fog;

I think of all those who have lost what can never, never again
   be found!
Of those who slake their thirst with tears
And nurse at the she-wolf Sorrow's dugs!
I think of scrawny orphans withering like flowers!

And in the forest where my mind wanders in exile
An old Memory loudly blows its horn!
I think of sailors shipwrecked on an island,
Of prisoners, the vanquished! And so many more!]][1]

Few poems have undergone as much critical examination as "Le Cygne,"
and few are cited so often for the striking character of their modernism.[2]
In my view it is precisely the modernist traits of "Le Cygne" that explain
the large number of commentaries that the poem has generated and continues to generate. For it is a "stream poem" or *poème-fleuve*—itself a "Simoïs menteur" or lying Simoïs (why it lies, we shall see later)—that is
remarkable for the double openness of its structure.[3] Just as the poem begins by posing the problem of its starting point, it ends with the provocative exclamation "à bien d'autres encor!" ["And so many more!"] that signals an absence of closure and the possibility of an infinite extension of the
listing activity it has begun.

Is the poem's starting point when "I" crosses la place du nouveau Carrousel? Or does it begin instead with the story of Andromache and, if so,
at what *point* in her story? The figure "I" thinks about is, after all, a survivor
left over from an earlier adventure (the fall of Troy) and as such—going
from Hector to Pyrrhus and from Pyrrhus to Helenus—she is the heroine
of a biography made of multiple repetitions. Or again, is the poem's point
of departure instead the episode of the swan, the indispensable link without which the association between la place du nouveau Carrousel (on the
one hand) and Andromache and the "lying Simoïs" (on the other) could

not have occurred? Each of the three—Andromache, the swan, and the nouveau Carrousel—can for different reasons, but with equal justification, lay claim to being the text's starting point; the opening of the poem is brilliantly undecidable in this respect.

Hence the poem remains suspended in a kind of intermediary space that separates it from any absolute point of origin, as well as from any definitive ending. Just so, the swan that has "escaped from its cage" at the market can neither return to the edenic lake it came from, nor obtain from the "ironic and cruelly blue sky" the rain that would end its suffering. As John MacInnes puts it, the poem is open at both ends.[4] It starts without indicating a clear beginning and closes without really ending. Yet there it is, absurdly existing without boundaries and abuttals, as if it too had escaped from a cage (perhaps from the constraints of censorship or self-censorship, if we keep in mind the indications in "Au lecteur"), and demonstrating in its own way the impossibility of a return to the past before it was caged, while at the same time seeming to call out for someone to end its present suffering, perhaps by giving it a meaning that would close off its endless forward movement.

The flood of critical analysis that this poem has generated can be understood, precisely, as an effort to exorcise the uneasiness that a text of this kind produces, just as the sight of the struggling swan raises the question of *its* meaning. The critics' mission has been to ascribe an origin to the text, or else to try to staunch its onward flow by defining its meaning. Some evoke the conditions of urban life during the 1850s, the events of the Second Empire, or the disruption of bourgeois identity caused by memory or desire. The upshot, however, is that criticism has tended to replicate the poem's structures and to perpetuate the endless "mulling over" of things that is its most striking feature. I make no claim that my own commentary can succeed in avoiding these pitfalls, particularly since I will be reiterating some of the recent criticism of the poem. But I will try to understand why things cannot be otherwise—why any commentary on "Le Cygne" is necessarily trapped in the same revolving door as the text itself.

In their efforts to contextualize the poem in a way that would close off its meaning, commentators have been particularly attracted to the urban context evoked by the allusions to Paris. In fact, "Le Cygne" has been at the heart of an important body of thought concerning the distinctive features of city life and the type of textuality that results from contact with cities—"la fréquentation des grandes villes," as Baudelaire was to put it in the dedicatory letter that opens *Le Spleen de Paris*. I would summarize this thinking as follows: As a result of the rapid expansion of the population of Paris during the first half of the nineteenth century, the capital—in contrast to village life and to the relatively small-scale existence that still characterized provincial towns—became the locus for an experience of anonymity. People walking in the street encountered not only strangers, but strangers they were more or less certain never to see again. Out of this experience of anonymity grew a feeling of existential fragmentation.[5]

It is true that the anonymity of urban crowds made possible the exaltation that Baudelaire celebrates in poems such as "Les Petites Vieilles" and "Les Foules." There he describes a projection and an identification of self with others that leads to a euphoric experience of the crowd—the famous *bain de multitude*; for, paradoxically, it is difficult to identify with someone one knows and whose irreducible otherness is clear to us. In "Le Cygne," too, criticism has pointed to the way the "thought" of the poetic subject constructs a community of exiles[6]—a community of the nameless that brings the poem into the ambience of sympathy for *les misérables* expressed by Hugo (to whom "Le Cygne" is dedicated), as well as recalling the chorus of oppositional voices that can be heard in Nerval's writing (in "Angélique," for example).

However, the random happenings in the street—the people one passes, the things one sees, chance encounters—all have in common the remarkable and disturbing fact that they constitute discontinuous episodes in the eyes of *le flâneur* (idle stroller), who knows neither where they come from nor what happens next, and who experiences these events as a disorderly sequence of fragmentary moments. As a reader of the text of the city, *le flâneur* can take cognizance of it only as a set of fragments removed from the context that would give them meaning—his experience is that of a metonymy or *pars pro toto,* but one that lacks any sense of the *totum* and indeed any possibility of constructing such a whole. What does it mean when we see a parched swan writhing in the dust of the gutter? The bird becomes an "allegory"—that is, the starting point of a search for meaning that is carried out without any guarantee of certainty and leads to *unlimited semiosis.* As such, it is the object of "avid" desire that, like any object of desire, reveals itself to be the locus of lack (an *"objet-petit a,"* as Lacan would say), and for which are in turn substituted other objects that no less inevitably bear the trace of original lack. Critics, especially in North America, who have been influenced by Derrida and Lacan and by the understanding of allegory that one finds in the work of Paul de Man, have there-

fore viewed "Le Cygne" as a kind of "Danaides' vessel" determined by the
boundless mechanisms of desire and the endless slippage of sense.[7]

But Paris in the 1850s was also the locus for the experience of a break in
the dimension of time. The clearing of the heart of the city—neighborhoods teeming with life, and home to a huge population of artisans, shop-
keepers, workers, and *bohèmes*—had begun under the July Monarchy but
culminated in the massive urban renewal projects of the Second Empire.
These "embellissements stratégiques" ["strategic improvements"] brought
"order," replacing what Baudelaire describes in "Les Petites Vieilles" as "le
chaos des vivantes cités" ["the chaos of living cities"] and the "plis sinueux
des vieilles capitales" ["the tortuous angles of old capitals"] with a whole
system of straight, wide avenues leading to grandiose (but empty) squares
and imposing (but hollow) monuments.

One imagines that someone walking through the new quartier du
Louvre and comparing it with what had been there only recently might be
tempted to associate these vast new empty structures with the feeling of
inauthenticity produced by the pompous regime of the Second Empire,
notably in relation to the Napoleonic era that it recalled. That same person
might well experience the present as a moment *emptied* of its meaning in
relation to a rich and animated past that was now gone. Andromache,
"crouching, in ecstasy, over an empty tomb" and builder of a "lying Simoïs," thus becomes the figure for a certain sense of history—a melancholy
that turns memory into a remembrance of loss and links the present to a
feeling of repetition and inauthenticity. The fate of this widowed queen,
wrapped in the "immense majesty" of her grief but simultaneously "fallen"
with the fall of Troy into a regimen of increasingly humiliating repetitions
(Hector-Pyrrhus-Helenus) and a widowhood (*viduité*), that is inexorably
linked by an accident of the French language to a notion of emptiness
(*vide*)—all this makes of her a symbol easily applied to the recent history
of republican France. For after the exaltations and struggles of 1848, the
mood was one of sullen mourning. Republican ideals had fallen into the
temporality of postdefeat gloom and a regime of falseness that tinged all
its productions: Thus, through figurative self-reflexivity, the poem presents itself as a "lying Simoïs" and an "empty tomb."

Certain German critics confidently read "Le Cygne" as the generalized
expression of Baudelaire's "historical negativity" after he had been "physically depolitified" by the events of 2 December 1851.[8] They tend also to
view the poem as a precisely coded allusion—one that would have been

quite transparent to any well-informed contemporary of Baudelaire—to
the political events of 1848–51 and their consequences. Thus Dolf Oehler
has proposed that we should see in Baudelaire a "hermetic socialist" using
Andromache's fate as a figuration of that of the French Republic, and the
episode of the swan (which breaks out of its cage "at the hour when Labor
awakens" only to find itself abandoned and helpless in the gutter) as an
allegory of the fate of the working class between February and June of that
year.[9] Similar Trojan parallels (e.g., between France and Andromache, Pyrrhus and Cavaignac) had also been drawn by Daumier.

In more elaborate detail, Wolfgang Fietkau draws attention to the ambiguity of certain passages and the emotional ambivalence they betray.[10]
Thus, the poem's syntax justifies asking whether Andromache is "in ecstasy" ("en extase courbée") beside her husband's empty tomb or under
Pyrrhus's sway. He also calls attention to the way the poem works to bring
together the animal and the human—in the comparison of the swan to
Andromache and in the way the swan is humanized by the allusion to humanity in Ovid, while Andromache is animalized as "vil bétail" ["common
chattel"], despite her "immense majesty." The conclusion is that "Le
Cygne" poeticizes Napoléon I's remark on the occasion of the retreat from
Moscow: "Du sublime au ridicule, il n'y a qu'un pas" ["There is only a
small step from the sublime to the ridiculous"]. This theme of the closeness
of the sublime and the grotesque applies explicitly to exiles in Baudelaire's
line: "Comme les exilés, ridicule et sublime" ["Like exiles, ridiculous and
sublime"]; but it might suggest more discreetly that between the First Empire and the Second there exists a relation parallel to that between Andromache's majestic grief and the grotesque gesticulations of the swan. As
indirect support for this view, Fietkau recalls the famous passage in *Dix-
huit Brumaire* where (à propos of the same events) Marx refers in similar
terms to those who are condemned to live history twice: "the first time as
tragedy, the second time as farce." Like Baudelaire, who of course could
not have read Marx's essay, Marx alludes to the example of Troy (and specifically to the figure of the Trojan horse) to describe the undermining political effect of the liberal Republicans, the "tricolores," whose activities
between February and June prepared the way for the electoral victory of
the Prince-President and for the subsequent coup d'état.

Thus, by making use in 1859 of an iconography familiar to those who
had lived through the period 1848–51, Baudelaire gave his melancholy
poem an explicitly oppositional cast and a duplicity that made the poem
readable—despite censorship—as a disguised expression of revolutionary

regret and of solidarity shown by someone *exiled within* an oppressive regime toward those who were exiled *outside* France after 1851. The best
known of these political exiles was of course Victor Hugo, to whom the
poem was dedicated and who had just refused the prince's offer of amnesty,
confirming in a typically "magnificent" response (which Baudelaire is on
record as having approved),[11] the irreducible character of certain forms of
oppositionality and exile: "Dans la situation où est la France, protestation
absolue, inflexible, éternelle, voilà pour moi le devoir" ["Given the current
situation in France, my duty lies in absolute protest, inflexible and eternal"].[12]

But we see, therefore, that two ways of understanding allegory are possible, depending on whether one looks at political interpretations of the
poem or its interpretation in terms of the problematics of desire and the
endless "drift" of the signifier. In the face of censorship, allegory appears as
a *call for interpretation* and implies that the figures of the poem are readable,
although on another level that the poem is not in a position to state explicitly. The emblem of this way of reading would be the swan that has escaped
from its cage (as the poem evades censorship) out of faithfulness to a remembrance of past happiness—"the lovely lake of its birth," of which it
would have been reminded by the "somber hurricane" in the street at the
hour when labor awakens—but whose escape cannot be complete and cannot acquire meaning unless it encounters and recovers the water and the
thunder, the storm it desires, which would fulfil the promise of the illusory
"hurricane." By imploring the heavens, the swan becomes an emblem of
the demand for a pro-revolutionary reading, without which the allegorical
poem would itself remain forever unrealized, incomplete, and unanswered.

In that case, however, the text's insistence on the "ironic and cruelly blue
sky" and the reproaches that the bird seems to address to God merely signal the disillusioned character of the gesture enacted by the poem that "escapes from its cage" without hope of finding an answer. Indeed, the allegory implies a certain despair, since the swan's escape is presented as the
result of a complete misunderstanding: the bird's mistaking the noisy passage of the street workers in the morning silence for the "hurricane" it
hoped for (the storm is only an illusion, a *false* storm). It is almost as if the
poem functions as confirming evidence and *proof* of exile, much like a person suffering from a raging toothache who keeps touching the inflamed
tooth to verify the pain; for it knows that the heavens will never respond
to the exile's longing, that his desire for escape is destined to remain unfulfilled—"un désir sans trêve." The divinity of Ovidian man (one might

think of Jupiter Pluvius, the god of storms) no longer exists, no longer responds; the heavens are clear and therefore empty. That is why the desire for meaning—the desire for it to be possible to give a meaning to the swan, or to the poem, that would liberate it by transforming its act of escape into an act that is not absurd—cannot be fulfilled. In other words, the reading of the poem as a political allegory that can be interpreted in a way that would "close" its meaning leads instead to a realization of its openness that is more compatible with the second understanding of allegory as a matter of fragmentation, the impossibility of completeness, and the drift of the signifier. As Nathaniel Wing has pointed out, a Danaides' vessel—if one can consider it a container at all—is one whose contents (and meaning) are inevitably subject to leakage.[13]

It is precisely in the context of an evocation of the city as a locus of fragmented and incoherent juxtapositions that the poem presents itself self-reflexively as an allegory—or, more accurately, as the locus for a *process of allegorization*, since the poem does not say "tout pour moi est allégorie" ["everything is allegory for me"], but says "tout pour moi *devient* allégorie" ["everything *becomes* allegory for me"]:

> . . . palais neufs, échafaudages, blocs,
> Vieux faubourgs, tout pour moi devient allégorie.

> [. . . New mansions, scaffoldings, blocks of stone,
> Old neighborhoods, everything becomes allegory for me.]

"The prevalence of allegory always corresponds to the unveiling of an authentically temporal destiny," writes Paul de Man. "It remains necessary, if there is to be allegory, that the allegorical sign refer to another sign that precedes it."[14] The swan, then, is a figure of *allegoresis* in de Man's sense, since the subject of the poem cannot "read" it without the horn call of Memory sounding through the forest of his mind, bringing with it the slide of signifiers—fragments of an uncompletable totality—that leads from the swan in nineteenth-century Paris to the widow of classical Greece, from the widow to the consumptive *négresse* floundering in the muddy streets, and then on to a whole series of more generalized figures of loss ("whoever," "those who"): orphans, shipwrecked sailors, prisoners, the vanquished, and "so many more," who all in different ways live out their exile as an exclusion from what would give meaning to their lives.

And yet, although it is impossible to exhaust the unlimited semiosis opened up by the spectacle of the swan as allegory, the traits these figures

all share—their exile and the lack that irremediably meets their desire—
nevertheless make it possible to say that the swan has a meaning, which is
the very impossibility of closure and the lack that *has its place* in it (as Derrida puts it in his critique of Lacan's "Seminar on *The Purloined Letter*").[15]
The swan is an allegory of allegorization, as the search for missing palm
trees through "an immense wall of fog" (a fog of signs) or the forest of
exile in which the mind wanders as "an old Memory loudly blows its horn."
Whereas the "political" conception of allegory led, paradoxically, to a figuration of allegorization as endless semiosis in the face of heavens that remain "ironic and cruelly blue," this second figuration enables us, no less
paradoxically, to grasp the *meaning* of a world where "everything becomes
allegory" as that of lack, of exile, and unrelenting desire.

So it is as if the image of the swan combines a *contextualizing* conception
of allegory (according to which its meaning would lie in the historical context to which it refers) and a *textualized* conception—according to which
allegory functions as a principle of redundancy, by means of which a text is
constructed out of the void of missing meaning, through the endless and
originless addition of examples (like a "lying Simoïs" that continuously
swells with tears). One could not hope for a more apposite illustration
of my thesis that the new "open" textuality characterizing literary modernism is inseparable from a contextualizing self-referentiality, calling
on the reader to grasp this textuality itself as a function of a historical
moment.

The sky is "ironic," then, because, "cruelly blue," it produces an irony of
the sign (*signe*) or an irony of the swan (*cygne*) that leads us to read the
swan's gesticulation as a call for meaning and to view it as a sign (or a
cygne) that in turn alludes endlessly to other signs (or *cygnes*), and vice
versa. Such is the "carousel" or revolving door in which Ovidian man finds
himself engaged—in a universe in which instead of prayers it is reproaches
that one rightly addresses to God. The irony of the sign is that a swan that
has escaped from its cage is not a sign set free. Caught between the lovely
lake of an origin to which it cannot return and the empty sky that denies
all hope of an end, the sign, like the swan, is defined by *loss* in the past that
results in an irremediable *lack* in the present. As a result, it functions simultaneously as a *call for meaning* (the swan calls out for an interpretation) and
as a *denial of closure* (since the sign and the swan allude endlessly to other
signes and *cygnes*).

In this way, or rather in *both* these ways, the sign takes on historical signification. For it exhibits, in de Man's sense, an "authentically temporal

destiny," cut off from origins and endings. Yet at the same time it is linked to a historical present—a human and social context—whose main characteristic is the awareness of a break in relation to a past that is henceforth irrecoverable, since it preceded the cataclysmic "fall" into time and into "la nouveauté" (whether this break occurred at the fall of Troy or in 1848). The irony of the sign is thus determined by an irremediable absence, just as the emptiness of the heavens that were once full (but *always already* once full) makes it impossible that the escape of a swan or a political revolution should be the same thing as access to freedom. And yet the poem nevertheless does bear witness that *something has escaped from its cage*. Whereas "Au lecteur" expresses opposition to social hypocrisy (the caging of wild animals) through a denunciatory poetics figured by an "involuntary tear," "Le Cygne" explores the consequences for poetic discourse of that escape from the cage of social control and figures them as the image of an ever growing "river of tears."

*

"Le Cygne" affirms that the modern subject is inescapably the victim of a problematics of memory and melancholy, which are the joint symptoms of a *historical* identity—a postlapsarian identity that links the "I" of the poem to the temporality of a Paris undergoing rapid change. The temporal break is complete, and we find ourselves in a universe of loss, which the subject's "fertile memory" in vain tries to resist. For memory is in turn the source of an oppressive experience of heaviness and melancholy: "Une image m'opprime" ["An image oppresses me"], "Et mes chers souvenirs sont plus lourds que des rocs" ["And my fond memories weigh heavier than rocks"]. Since in general terms memory is the subject of the first part of the poem while melancholy is the concern of the second part, we can ask how the two phenomena are articulated, what revolving door of subjectivity they operate. For the poem teaches that, as signs of modernity, memory and melancholy are the psychic responses that correspond to the irony of the sign.

Confronted with the temporal break that launches history, memory presents itself in the first instance as "fertile"—it is a principle of fecundity in the face of the sterility of the new and a principle of identity and continuity in a world subject to change.[16]

> Le vieux Paris n'est plus (la forme d'une ville
> Change plus vite, hélas! que le cœur d'un mortel).

[The old Paris is gone (the face of a city
Changes faster, alas! than a human heart).]

Thinking of Andromache, the "I" of the poem finds in his memory an image from antiquity that gives meaning to the recent memory of the swan floundering in the gutter. (The precise moment of this encounter is not clear: it was sometime after the urban renewal projects had begun, but that could have been either under the July Monarchy, in 1848, or afterward.) This double memory gives the present—the moment when "I" crosses the nouveau Carrousel—a quality of euphoric discovery and almost of epiphany, in the Joycean sense of an unveiling of the self and of the world. This almost triumphal mood is indicated at the very start of the poem by the exclamation point in conjunction with the use of the present tense: "Andromaque, je pense à vous!" ["Andromache, I think of you!"].

As a consequence, the poem that presents itself, in the manner of the romantic ode, as a mimesis of the movements of a conscious mind constructs itself likewise as "fertile": it too has a memory. The reader is invited to reminisce in turn, to search for the memories that might "fertilize" the poem in the way the recollection of Andromache gives meaning to the image of the swan. And clearly, just as the memory of Andromache fertilizes the mind of the subject, so too the allusion to Virgil fecundates Baudelaire's poem, which bore an epigraph drawn from the *Aeneid*: "falsi Simoentis ad undam" ["on the banks of a lying Simoïs"] when it was first published in 1860. But the memory of recent events in the history of France might also have fertilized the minds of Baudelaire's contemporary readers as they encountered the complex allegory presented in the poem— that formed by the interrelations between the subject "I," the swan, and Andromache.

Whereas the opening line "Andromaque, je pense à vous!" conveys a joyous, even triumphant mood, this celebration of the fertile power of memory is however quickly relativized and indeed subverted in the lines that follow, so that the "je pense" of the opening line turns out to foreshadow the melancholy litany of phrases beginning with "je pense" that recur in the second part of the poem. Because of its capacity for memory, the human heart may change less quickly than a city's face; yet that heart is still "mortal" and hence still subject to change. In fact, the human heart and the face of the city differ only in their *pace* of change; both are subject to temporality and hence to death. Moreover, the time lag that arises between humans and their material milieu is itself problematic, since its effect is to isolate the subject in his heart and mind, alienating him from the material and social forms of culture (if that is what the word *ville* stands for), whose transformation is a manifestation of history: "Only in my mind's eye can I still see all those builders' sheds."

And finally, the fertile effect of memory is inevitably secondary and derivative in relation to "le nouveau," that sign of historical change. While it is true that the subject's "fertile memory" produces the rich association of Andromache and the swan, the condition for setting these memories and associations in motion was nevertheless the crossing of "the new" (in the form of the nouveau Carrousel). If Andromache and the swan are linked in the mind of the subject, it is not only because they share the status of exiles, but also and primarily because they both come to mind as, in the moment of crossing the new square, he realizes that his own situation is that of an exile. It is because the subject "I" of the poem is an exile that the joint memory of Andromache and the swan comes to him. The swan is spatially linked to la place du Carrousel because it is there that "I" remembers catching sight of it at some former time ("Là je vis . . . "). Similarly, Andromache is associated with the nouveau Carrousel because of the similarity between her "lying Simoïs" (an inadequate substitute for the real river) and the inauthenticity of the glaringly new constructions of the Second Empire. But this means that the completion of the *new* Carrousel was a necessary condition for the absurd memory of the bird, associated with the building site, to acquire meaning by being associated with Andromache.

It also means that the key to the "fertile" power of memory lies in the temporality that marks each of the three central figures with a negative sign: like the subject of the poem "I," Andromache and the swan are situated in the aftermath of a temporal break and in a time that is already dominated by newness. Andromache is a victim of the fall of Troy, and the bird was spotted at a time when the quartier du Louvre was already being renovated, with new construction sites ("those piles of rough-hewn cornices") juxtaposed with leftovers from the past ("le bric-à-brac confus" of the curio sellers' booths). Thus the swan recalls a period when the destruction of the past and the construction of the new were already under way. Although at first the fertile power of memory may seem like a means of transcending the temporal break weighing on the present, it soon comes to appear capable only of *confirming* that break, since what it generates is images evoking a time either when the fall into history had already taken place (as in Andromache's case) or when change was already under way (as in the swan's case).

For the subject of the poem who is crossing the nouveau Carrousel, memory is fertile indeed, but it can therefore be only a memory of exiles. The lack it tries to fill—the lack of continuity between past and present, the swan's lack of meaning—can be completed only by still another lack: the recollection of Andromache's widowhood and her construction of a Simoïs that is inevitably "new." All this gives a strongly negative cast to the "fertile" power of memory, the production of meaning, and the construction of identity, for such identity can only be an identity of exiles, in the way that the poem—itself a product of memory—can be made only by adding figures to other figures that resemble and recall one another, but as figures of lack. Indeed, it is only by producing the memory of a lack always already there and hence of "relentless desire" that "fecund memory" generates the poem, in the way Andromache's "lying Simoïs" swells with tears.

As a result, the poem does have other models besides the artificial river built by the widowed former queen and the new square of the Carrousel (another belated monument marked with the sign of an absence): I am thinking of the construction site and the work of the street workers evoked in stanzas 3 and 4. Like them, the poem as a work of memory is a struggle against the entropic, disordering force of time—a struggle that is by its very nature self-perpetuating and irresolvable, since it is subject to the entropy it opposes. The street workers' negentropic activities produce the noise of a storm that is as illusory for the swan as Andromache's Simoïs is artificial. Similarly, the construction site destroys the old and builds the new in all the disorder of half-begun cornices and the jumble of bric-à-brac; its work is a struggle against time that is indelibly marked with the seal of temporality. The poem too works with the bric-à-brac of chance recollections, residues of a classical education and of a life of *flâneries* (idle strolls), in order to "rough hew" the *chapiteaux* (capitals or cornices) of a "capital" monument ("capital" because it is in Paris and because, like the head, it is the center of memory). Like the "lying Simoïs," like the empty tomb, and like the scaffolding it evokes, the poem signifies not a victory over time, but *work within time*: work that implies mourning for the past, the inauthenticity of a present that is always "new," and the disorder of the unfinished.

By that measure any new construction, the nouveau Carrousel, for instance, is itself incomplete in that, as an imperfect reflection of an earlier model that has been effaced, it necessarily calls for a supplementation that can only be a new repetition. The new can never be other than a memory of the lack that brought it into being and so, like "fertile memory," an attempt to *abolish* lack that resolves into a *confirmation* of that lack. And it is because reminiscence can never discover in the past anything but post-lapsarian images of a fallen temporality that is always already in place, while in the present the new (itself a reminiscence) can function only according to the law of endless supplementation, that "fertile memory" becomes transformed into melancholy. Melancholy thus appears as the mechanism of memory itself, and of the production of meaning, when it is experienced as a phenomenon of unfinished and interminable "thought"—that is, a lengthy "mulling over" of things in a world given over to change without beginning or end.

So what is constant, what does not change in the ever changing world, is melancholy itself, the subject on which the opening lines of the poem's second part focuses, defining it as what is immovable:

> Paris change! mais rien dans ma mélancolie
> N'a bougé!

> [Paris is changing. But nothing in my melancholy
> Has changed!]

These lines clearly echo the earlier ones concerning memory:

> Le vieux Paris n'est plus (la forme d'une ville
> Change plus vite, hélas! que le cœur d'un mortel).

> [The old Paris is gone (the face of a city
> Changes faster, alas! than a human heart).]

But it is consequently the *immobility* of melancholy that causes it to be experienced as an oppressive weight: it is "fond memories" that weigh heavier than rocks and an "image" that "oppresses" the subject as he stands before the Louvre. The paradox of melancholy is that it is simultaneously an oppressive and motionless weight and a dispersion of the mind, subject to the tedious redundancy of recollection, the drift of signifiers, and the endlessness of meaning—phenomena that the second part of the poem now proceeds to mime. If it is *an* image that oppresses the subject, it is because the image of the swan—a memory heavier than a rock—like the inexhaustible Danaides' vessel, contains in itself all the others. And these are the images that are now enumerated in the second half of the poem, going back over those that were already invoked in the first part ("I think of my great swan . . . / . . . And then I think of you, / Andromache"), but so as to incorporate them now in the lengthy inventory that reproduces an inexhaustible list of figures that are the objects of the subject's "thought": the *négresse*, those who have lost what can never be found, those who slake themselves on tears, withering orphans, sailors, prisoners, the vanquished, and "so many more." Among these various exiles, the subject of the poem even includes his own mind, exiled in the forest where memory's horn sounds.

It is because it is a mulling over of this kind that melancholy is both multiple and unitary, heavy and evanescent, fog that nevertheless constitutes a wall, mud that entraps, a long sounding of the horn that is "full." And as the word "full" reminds us, it is because memory is "fertile," but at the same time fallacious, that the melancholic subject can slake himself on tears and "nurse at the she-wolf Sorrow's dugs," deriving nourishment as did the orphans who founded the *new* city of Rome—a city that inherited the power of Troy after its fall and foreshadowed future history as a series of repetitions. For it is Rome, the city that came after and so was not Troy, that furnished the model for later republics and empires.

Although "fertile" memory opens out eventually onto melancholy—as an absurd mulling over occupying the temporality of history, always incomplete and unfulfilled—melancholy ultimately reveals itself, then, to be oddly nurturing: one can live on melancholy, however poorly and painfully. One can build in melancholy, even if what one constructs is only a "lying Simoïs" that is forever swelling with tears. Such is the revolving door of the psyche, whose structure is exactly analagous to that of the ironic sign, and it is this structure that the poem in turn mimics. For the first part, as a celebration of memory's fertility and of closed meaning, is itself closed in a sense by the coupling of the swan and Andromache, each corresponding to the other so that they form a pair in the "thought" of the poetic subject. But it opens out, through the reproaches addressed by the swan, not even to but *in the direction of* ("vers") an unhearing, "ironic and cruelly blue" sky, onto the open form of the second part. Here a chain of images mimes melancholy's mournful mulling, as a kind of eternalization of pensiveness, but also its own form of "fertility" and fullness.

Thus, by affirming the nurturing character of Sorrow and the fullness of the horn blast of Memory, even as the final verses emphasize the text's incompleteness, the poem refuses to allow the reader to settle with a shrug for the negative (or at least disillusioned) view that the thought of a melancholic subject is just an endless mulling over of things. For the capital letters of the words "Souvenir" ["Memory"] and "Douleur" ["Sorrow"] send us back to the first part of the poem, where the only other capitalized noun is found (other than proper names): "Travail" ["Labor"]. Labor (in the form of the noisy street workers with their din) is the only form of life—besides the poet—that is awake at the hour when the bourgeois is still sleeping. This stanza parallels the last two lines of "Crépuscule du matin" which, in the edition of 1861, ends the section of *Les Fleurs du mal* titled "Tableaux parisiens" (which of course also includes "Le Cygne"). There again we find the word *sombre*, associated in "Le Cygne" with the "hurricane" produced by the street workers, but used in "Crépuscule du matin" to describe Paris itself, personified as "un vieillard laborieux," a hardworking old man gathering up his tools for the day's labor.

Whereas the city is new in "Le Cygne," in "Crépuscule du matin" it has become old. Whereas in "Le Cygne" the city is a place of melancholy, in "Crépuscule du matin" it figures a certain daily courage, hard work, and lucidity—the last suggested perhaps by the line "en se frottant les yeux" ["rubbing his eyes"]. This is not to say that the thematics of melancholy is completely absent from the poem:

> Le chant du coq au loin déchirait l'air brumeux;
> Une mer de brouillards baignait des édifices,
> Et les agonisants dans le fond des hospices
> Poussaient leur dernier râle en hoquets inégaux.

> [The crow of a cock from far away pierced the misty air,
> A sea of fog swirled around the buildings,
> And the dying in the hospitals for the poor
> Gasped their last choppy breath.][17]

Yet in "Crépuscule du matin," as in "Le Cygne," work appears "under the heavens / Cold and clear" as the sole positive recourse available in this universe of melancholy and the irony of the sign.

The way the "carousel" of the poem leads us from memory to melancholy and then from melancholy to work no doubt constitutes a discreet tribute to the values of February and the uprising of the working class. Since the poet-*flâneur* is also up "at the hour when Labor awakes," however, the poem is about another kind of work as well: that of *Trauerarbeit*, the work of grief-stricken thought the poem calls melancholy—work that is no less relentless and heartbreaking than the labors of the worker end-lessly caught up in the daily grind. Against a gaping backdrop of loss and in the aftermath of an irreversible fall, in a time of repetition and inauth-enticity, poetic labor—which "Le Cygne" both illustrates and embodies—is defined as a tireless activity of thought that goes on and on, cut off from any beginning and advancing toward no end. Its conditions are those of absurd temporality: the irony of the sign, the revolving door of memory and melancholy, a negentropy that (like the work of the street workers) produces disorder in combating it—whether in the form of the revolution-ary hurricane, the grimy dust in which the swan flounders, the mud in which the black woman is trapped, or the perpetual construction site of the modern city. Or, finally, the poet's thoughts (*pensées*).

The verb *penser* ("to think") appears for the first time, somewhat trium-phantly, in the opening line of the poem. It then recurs and is repeated three times (always in the first-person indicative) in the second part of the poem, but now in a more muted register. This shift in tone seems to sug-gest that, though the *Aeneid* is the main text recalled by the poem in its fertile memory, quite a different subtext underlies its melancholy: the Cartesian *cogito*. For the labor of thought constituting the discourse of melancholy forms a contrast to the rational analysis of the Cartesian dis-course of method, just as the classical "self" (autonomous, compact, and centered on the presence of God) contrasts with the melancholic subject, whose exiled identity, consumed by lack and dispersed in the endless ru-minations of memory, is shared with the vast community of exiles.

The poem is anti-Cartesian, however, not only in its construction of a melancholic identity, but also in the antihypocritical understanding it has of the nature of the sign. Here we may recall "Crépuscule du matin," where the daily morning departure of Labor (the working class) is juxtaposed symmetrically with the return home of Vice ("Les débauchés rentraient, brisés par leurs travaux"), as well as "Au lecteur," where "la ménagerie in-fâme de nos vices" is a figuration of repression and censorship. (See the discussion of "Au lecteur" in chapter 5.) In "Le Cygne" we also find a ménagerie; the line "Là s'étendait jadis une ménagerie" provides material motivation for the image of the swan that breaks out of its cage. But the lesson of "Au lecteur" is that our main vice is ennui when it is combined with hypocrisy. In contrast, the swan that has escaped from its cage is the figure of a laborious melancholy of work, free of the unconscious duplicity that is Baudelaire's definition of hypocrisy. Despite the vices that work away at our passive selves—the "stupidity, error, sin, and stinginess [that] occupy our minds and work away at our bodies," despite our hypocritical preoccupation with remorse (which we sustain "as a beggar nourishes his lice"), we can still break out of the cage of hypocrisy that imprisons us and thereby reverse the bourgeois order of things. At that point we can nurture ourselves, instead of nourishing the vermin of our hypocrisy, even if we must feed on our sorrows; and by becoming active workers in the labors of melancholy, conscious of the absurd conditions in which we must persevere, we can replace "the debauched who return home, exhausted by their exertions" ("brisés par leurs travaux").

Although "Le Cygne" is characterized by duplicity, it is anything but a hypocritical poem, if by hypocritical we mean "unconscious of its own duplicity." Its duplicity is the generic duplicity of all allegory, condemned never to coincide with its meaning, but also the particular duplicity of a poetic allegory eluding censorship through the use of a figurative language decipherable for some readers but not for others. Finally, "Le Cygne" is duplicitous (in the sense of double) because the combination of its generic allegoresis and its particular political allegory engenders the dual structure of a closed meaning coinciding with the drift of the signifier, as well as the copresence of the irony of the sign and the revolving psychic mechanism of memory and melancholy.

But quite openly the poem figures these various forms of duplicity in the image of a bird that has escaped from its cage, as if to say that certain forms of hypocrisy—exactly those described in "Au lecteur" by the metaphor of "the squalid menagerie of our vices"—are no longer possible. For what "Le Cygne" demonstrates, proclaims, and almost flaunts—what at the very least it admits without hypocrisy—is the duplicitous character of signs, of which the text is itself an exemplary manifestation. This is the awareness that has broken out of its cage with the appearance of this poem and that can no longer be suppressed, repressed, or caged again. Antihypocritical in this sense, the poem further confirms its anti-Cartesianism by offering as the principle of modern textuality a view of discourse as the work of signs in full knowledge of their unfathomable duplicity—a conception that is the polar opposite of classical views of language as the transparent expression of a meaning clearly conceived by an autonomous subject. In place of these traditional conceptions, what emerges is the understanding of discourse as a task unflaggedly pursued under conditions of "désir sans trêve," or relentless desire.

The lucidity of "Le Cygne" is most apparent in what it deduces from the irony of signs. That the bird has broken out of its cage does not mean human beings are free; like the swan, they are instead condemned to desire. This postlapsarian knowledge implies recognition of the inevitability of work—of the work of signs in memory and in the endless, mulling labor of melancholy. Work for Baudelaire is identified, in short, with the anxious consciousness of a fall into historical time, a fall that was always already in progress and that does not have an end. Thus the *nouveauté*, newness, or novelty characteristic of the textual forms implied by the work of signs cannot be in any way a source of pride or satisfaction; quite the contrary, it can only be the clearest evidence of the sad conditions under which the work is pursued.

What then are we to think of critical discourse expounding on the *nouveauté* of this poem, analyzing its insuperable themes, prolonging its painful mulling over of things through a tireless repetition of its obsessions? What more striking evidence could one imagine of what the poem itself gives us to understand? The work of the melancholic text is never finished; modern thought is exiled thought that, having no option, is continually propelled forward, never ceasing its mulling over of things. The critical work on "Le Cygne," to which I have just added another page, bears witness to this fact. "Absolute protest, inflexible, and eternal," was Victor Hugo's phrase.[18]

SEVEN

REPETITION AND IRONY

"Disparition élocutoire" ["elocutionary disappearance"]: Mallarmé's famous term in "Crise de vers"[1] is ambiguous, as has sometimes been remarked. "Disappearance" may indicate a *result* (that the poet is absent, no longer present in the texts), or else a *process*—a progressive fading of the subject, performed "illocutionarily" (i.e., enunciatively) by texts. It is clearly this second meaning of the phrase that describes the phenomenon I have been tracing in the preceding chapters: the fading of the narrator (or more precisely of the narrative function) that can be observed in the texts of Nerval and Baudelaire. In "Sylvie" the narrator is the blurred, suicidal subject of the practice of irony as "permanent digression." In Baudelaire, on the other hand, the poetic subject tends to disappear in a discourse of duplicity (itself a brother to social hypocrisy) or else to be emptied of presence (presence to self and presence to the present moment) in the repetitiveness of memory, allegory, and melancholy.

It is in Flaubert's *Madame Bovary*, however, that we specifically witness a disappearance of the narrator in the sense that the text enunciatively mimes his disappearing act. After calling attention to his presence in the "we" that opens the novel ("We were in class, . . . "), and after again employing a "we" that implies an "I" a few pages later in the imperturbably contradictory statement, "It would now be impossible for any of us to remember anything about him,"[2] the narrator suddenly stops referring to himself pronominally. (There is a universal, impersonal "we" in the description of Emma's funeral.)[3] The narrative function thus shifts to a "zero degree"; its place is a void. Begun in a narrative perspective that is clearly characterized as that of a classmate, the story of Charles's life continues in a supposedly "objective" mode that dominates the rest of the novel. Moreover, with his courtship, marriage, and move to Tostes, the center of interest soon shifts from Charles to Emma, while free indirect style now allows the privilege of focalizing the narrative to move freely between the official narrative instance (now apparently quite neutral) and (mainly) this new character, Emma. As a result, the narrative is rather oddly focalized, both on and through the woman whose fate consists in marrying Charles, whom we already know (after his brief initial appearance as a model of "ideal idiocy") as an incarnation of uniformity, conformity, routine, monotony, repetition—of everything in the novel that represents the power of the social order. (See the discussion of Charles in chapter 1.)

One could argue, then, that the textual discourse has itself "espoused Charles," in the sense that it adopts a degraded discourse and mindless points of view; for the narrator's elocutionary disappearance has given rise to a narration whose "idiocy" (or absence of a distinct or specific point of view) implies an alliance with *la bêtise*—the stupidity, banality, pettiness, and conformism of the social order—embodied by the characters (by Emma as well as Charles). It is as if the text's desire for distinction (the "not being present" of idiocy) has led it into a fate that merges with the fate of its heroine, for she too tries to find happiness in ways that inexorably lead her back to the very same social "law" she is seeking to escape. Free indirect style, in which the "stupidity" of the characters and the "distinction" of idiotic writing mingle in equal and perhaps indissociable parts, is the terrain on which we can point out some of the implications of this problematic.

The free indirect style in *Madame Bovary* forces the text to "repeat" the social discourse embedded in the discourse of the characters, and in this novel, as in "Le Cygne," "reality" is defined as a degraded domain, because it is subject to a law of repetition. We have seen that it is Charles's utter emptiness (even after his death, we read that "[M. Canivet] opened him up but found nothing") that enables this *déclassé* to "fit in"—to absorb, so quickly and so completely, conventional "wisdom" and, by means of mindless repetitions (repeating his name, writing lines, memorizing the questions on his exams) to become a perfect incarnation of banality and stupidity. Charles himself, of course, wants nothing better, but as a model for the novel, his example is a problematic one, since it illustrates the dangerous kinship of idiocy and the mindless conformity of *la bêtise*. In this chapter I want therefore to continue the analysis of Charles begun in chapter 1, but I will shift my focus (as does the novel itself) to Emma (and through Emma back to Charles), since she represents in a more active manner the text's own desire for autonomy: the desire of the *déclassé* to remain outside the norms (*hors-classe*) and to cling to a self-definition in those terms. Emma's dreams of distinction and happiness do indeed distinguish her, in the name of a desire for an intense and well-filled existence, from the torpor and platitude of provincial life; yet she is totally unaware of her own *bêtise*, which in her case is sentimental rather than intellectual. She seems not to realize that in trying to escape banality and in searching for something "new" she is only condemning herself to an existence of repetitions. Consequently the model Emma provides, in relation to the problematics of the text, is less positive than ironic.

A victim of a bourgeois education that has given her a romantic ideal of individual self-fulfillment, Emma then marries a man whose education, no less bourgeois, has made him an embodiment of regularity, platitude, and clichés. She in fact becomes his possession: "Now he possessed for life this beautiful woman whom he adored" (p. 24; p. 32 of French). This marriage is, as I have said, the central fact that defines the novel, and it simultaneously points to a fundamental but not arbitrary contradiction in the social order and defines the discursive situation of the text, which, like Emma, is socially conditioned to desire a distinct identity while nevertheless having to "marry" Charles (to "espouse" what he represents). "By dint of hard work," Charles had succeeded in becoming a kind of "mill-horse, who goes round and round with his eyes bandaged, not knowing what work it is grinding out" (pp. 6–7; p. 9). The personage who rides to his fatal meeting with Emma is consequently a completely submissive and deadened character half asleep on his horse: "Still sleepy from the warmth of his bed, he let himself be lulled by the quiet trot of his horse" (p. 9; p. 12). (The twofold assimilation of Charles to his horse, *sa bête*, is hardly accidental.) Emma, for her part, also appears in complementary fashion as a being who is always already social (raised to become "Madame Bovary") and necessarily social (already "possessed" by her husband), but one whose desire, itself socially determined, is to experience the necessarily impossible adventure of an intensely and passionately individual life.

Charles's socialization involved a difficult apprenticeship, which is why his *bêtise* is never without a compensatory idiocy, of which it is the sign. Emma, on the other hand, is easily socialized; and she emerges from her education with a passionate character and an individualizing energy that is, for this very reason, ironically subverted by the banality, the mediocrity, and the conventional character of her desire for happiness and distinction. In this sense there is little to choose between the two spouses—Charles with his desire to *conform*, Emma with her desire to *distinguish* herself (a desire to rise above normal classifications that allows us, in fact, to classify her). The novel that figures its own situation in their marriage struggles within the same vicious circle of a desire for self-fulfillment, self-distinction, and novelty that necessarily demonstrates its involvement in the banality of the social condition it is trying to escape. This is the basis of the text's kinship with Emma.[4] But it cannot evade the implication that is firmly established from the beginning by its initial identification with Charles, that the deepest desire of "a book about nothing"—of an "idiot" novel—is perhaps simply to fill itself with the banality of *bêtise*.

For with respect to writing, the narrator's fading out or "disparition élocutoire" poses a crucial question: What happens when a text is emptied of its subject and loses the distinctive and "individual" voice that constitutes the narrative function? What happens when a text becomes an "idiot"? Is the writing that remains or that substitutes itself for the narrative function able to achieve a distinctiveness of its own? Or is it condemned instead to absolute nondistinctiveness, to "in-difference," since it has no option but to repeat conventional discourses of social provenance, that is, discourses that are already stale and hackneyed through endless repetition? Emma, we read, "ne croyait pas que les choses pussent se représenter les mêmes à des places nouvelles" (p. 61) ["did not believe that things could remain the same in different places"] (p. 80). Yet the text itself has good reasons not to share this belief: just as, for Emma, Yonville will turn out to be a repetition of Tostes—and therefore worse than Tostes—the literary representation of things can only be a degraded repetition of them, despite the change of "place" produced by the textual transcription of social discourses. Such a discovery can only induce "that depression caused by the repetition of the same life, with no interest to inspire and no hope to sustain it" (p. 84; p. 110). Even a partial loss of the means of control and individual characterization offered by the narrative function means that writing must reproduce in absolutely unmediated fashion the raw material of social discourse—whether the banal thoughts and perceptions of the different characters reproduced in free indirect discourse or whether typical forms of speech, emptied of meaning by the invasion of clichés and either quoted in dialogue or taken up directly into the text in what is the equivalent for speech of free indirect discourse for mental activity. Thus we get the rustic letters from Emma's father, Monsieur Homais's Parisian slang and pseudoscientific jargon, the priest's religious babbling, Emma's sentimental prattle, Rodolphe's cynically seductive lexicon, Charles's platitudes, and the tedious official phraseology of the speeches at the agricultural fair (*les Comices*)—all of it (not just the speeches and Rodolphe's pseudosentiment at the fair) more or less likened to the bleating of sheep, the lowing of cattle, or the cackle of chickens in a barnyard.

Perhaps, however, there *is* some "interest" to "inspire" all this, some "hope" to "sustain" it and permit the text to escape from the "depression" caused by this oppressive and mindless repetition? The problem posed by Baudelairean textuality and the violent disjunction that it strives to produce between its own duplicity and the hypocrisy of social discourse have their counterparts in Flaubert's writing. But they are transposed into another register (that of the problematics of *la bêtise*) and are rendered more acute by the fading of the narrator. In denying itself most of the standard resources of narrativity, the Flaubertian text loses the means (such as any type of "I-you" denunciation) to directly confront the oppressive social discourse by which it is invaded. In order to determine its autonomy in relation to that invasive discourse, the text must therefore rely on the reader, on the *other* instance that is so indispensable to its existence as a text and that it would like to be not "other than itself" but "an other self." It is because the textual function implies an instance of reading that the Flaubertian representation of banality can count on there being some "interest" to inspire it and some "hope" that would permit it to escape the banality it reproduces.

As narrative statement (*énoncé*), Flaubertian textuality is indeed difficult to distinguish from the repetitive discourses that constitute both its material and its referential object; indeed, it comes close to a dangerous degree of indistinctiveness. It is only as an enunciative act—as a relational phenomenon between writing and reading, text and reader—that it can begin to come into its own. Condemned as *énoncé* merely to repeat (to reproduce or represent) a "reality" that is already defined as repetition, the text can find a certain measure of autonomy and a form of distinction that is free of the *bovarysme* it portrays only by relying on the judgment of a third party. However, such a third party must be sufficiently sensitive to irony to insert the missing quotation marks in crucial places where they are needed and to realize that the various dialogues and other passages where quotation marks do in fact appear are not objective or neutral reproductions but are being ironically "mentioned." To the extent that the text is indeed fundamentally indistinguishable from its raw material of social discourse, such a reader might ultimately put quotation marks around the *entire novel* and sustain an ironic reading, sentence by sentence and without the slightest lapse, from beginning to end. But that would be no small feat.

Yet a simple ironic reading (or a reading that is simply ironic), assuming it were indeed possible, would not even suffice to resolve the problem of textual differentiation. We will see that irony does not rescue the text from *la bêtise* any more than adultery rescues Emma from the degradation of marriage. A different type of irony becomes necessary—one that fosters the recognition of a certain textual sincerity and simplicity that I will refer to as a "demand for love." For if the quotation marks of irony are so often or so easily suppressed in the text of *Madame Bovary*, the reasons for their suppression need to be considered quite carefully. They may well go beyond any simple notion of irony, such as would make the Flaubertian text comparable, for instance, to the blatantly ironic discourse that Hugo brandishes like a sword in *Les Châtiments*. In *Madame Bovary* one certainly finds an irony that is signed and authorial, a satiric irony, but it is not only that. Irony with an ironic subject is not, strictly speaking, *textual* irony, which relates more to a problematics of reading than to a phenomenon of "expression." It is as a demand for reading—indeed for a *simple* reading— that one ultimately needs to understand the ironic writing of free indirect style, which is technically so complex. And my purpose in what follows is to draw on the example of free indirect discourse, not to demonstrate so much as to begin to probe the discursive complexities that a text like *Madame Bovary* reveals in its textual function and hence on the enunciatory plane, as the relation of a reading to a writing.

*

I should stress that what I am presenting here is the *radical* version of the problematics of elocutionary disappearance. Yet it is only logical that whenever this problematics arises, it does so radically. In Flaubert's novel, the narrator's "fade-out" does not imply the elimination of all narrative function; quite the contrary. The narrator's own presence continues to be apparent throughout the entire text, even if he no longer says "we" or "I," and this is the case quite independent of the sense in which, by definition, there can be no narration without a narrative subject, nor any story without a teller. Observations and all-purpose judgments appear here and there, concerning "that peculiar brutality that stems from a steady command over half-tame things" (p. 36; p. 48) (these are horses and women, admittedly loose ones); the role of the window in provincial life, where it replaces the theater and "promenading" in Paris; or speech that is described as "un laminoir qui allonge tous les sentiments" (p. 218)—["like a rolling machine that always stretches the sentiment it expresses"] (p. 169). This intermittent commentary, linked in obvious ways to certain fundamental themes of

the text, can scarcely be attributed to anyone but the character of the narrator. Similarly, from time to time a *vous* ["you"] occurs that is distinct
from the self-adressing *vous* of certain characters in free indirect discourse—as when the maître d'hôtel at the Vaubyessard manor "faisait sau-
ter pour vous le morceau qu'on choisissait" (p. 45) ["loosened for you the
chosen morsel"], as Emma observes, reflecting on the service at dinner before the ball. Thus a narratee might well be addressed in the following
sentence: "The orator painted for you those fierce times when men lived
on acorns" (p. 106; p. 138). That a narrative instance has been active
throughout the text is indicated quite clearly by a shift to the present tense
at various points in the novel. Toward the end of part 1, we find an isolated
present-tense verb: "Amidst the grass of the ditches grow long reeds with
sharp-edged leaves that cut you" (p. 31; p. 41); there is a longer present-
tense passage at the beginning of part 2: "Yonville-l'Abbaye . . . is a
market-town . . . . Since the events about to be related, nothing in fact has
changed at Yonville" (pp. 49–52; pp. 65–68); and finally, there is a return
to the present in the last sentence of the novel: "He has just been given the
cross of the Legion of Honor" (p. 255; p. 324).

But setting aside a certain taste for moral maxims—"But casting asper-
sions on those we love always does something to loosen our ties" (p. 205;
p. 262); "of all the icy blasts that blow on love, a request for money is the
most chilling and havoc-wreaking" (p. 227; p. 289)—what the narrator of
Madame Bovary does lack after the opening pages is a distinct, *describable*
personality.[5] Or rather, what characterizes the narrator most clearly is his
detachment as an observer and his seemingly objective attitude concerning
the life of the characters, which incidentally clashes somewhat with the
intimate knowledge that he seems to have—with a few exceptions—of
their thoughts, emotions, and best-kept secrets.[6] The narrator presents the
characters; but as James Reid has observed, he also serves as their secretary.[7] In both roles, he generally abstains from expressing his individual
point of view concerning what he is relating. Through him a story gets
told and the narratee, who is provided with so much information, is deprived of all guidance when it comes to interpreting it.

The narrator thus becomes a kind of neutral agent through whom narrative takes place and who transmits a mass of information that it is then
the reader's job to process, since the *narratee* necessarily fades away at the
same time as the *narrator*. The facts are communicated, dialogues are reported, the characters' thoughts are relayed, on their own terms; but—

inhabiting as he does in turn Emma, Charles, the village gossips, père Rouault, or Mme Bovary senior—the narrator has little opportunity to show a personality of his own. The writing itself, largely given over to reproducing the interior or exterior discourse of the characters, tends to become the locus of a multiplicity of "presences" among which the narrator's own personality is increasingly dubious. For as soon as one realizes that this writing is permeable to the outside presences that continually pass through it, it becomes impossible to be absolutely sure that a particular statement, stock phrase, or seemingly neutral word cannot similarly be viewed as a "quotation without quotation marks" made by the narrator in his self-assigned and very obvious role as secretary to the characters. And yet the problem is as follows: No alert reader fails to recognize that while the effacement of the narrator opens the text to what is potentially a total invasion of discourses, these same discourses remain identifiable as *alien* to the text; they are ascribable to the characters themselves and not to the literary enunciation that is a kind of empty vehicle for them. The fading of the narrative function and the consequent task of processing the raw information that is transmitted forces on the reader a highly active role; but this role, it seems, simultaneously involves a responsibility for making the necessary distinctions that permit the text to *be* a text and not simply to blend indiscriminately into the different discourses constituting it.

How is this reading effect achieved? The discourses invading the text are by definition typical; reproducibility is their characteristic. They are easily recognized, which makes them all more or less clichés. Yet the text that reproduces them manages to do it in such a way that the repetition changes signs: *its* repetition is no longer taken as cliché but is considered an original enunciative act.[8] As has often been observed, the problem is to understand the "creative" use of a language that, as the medium of communication, has been made banal and worn out by social use. In *Madame Bovary*, the adventure of the text diverges in one respect from Emma's adventure; for Emma rebels against the law that determines her existence as a woman, only to find herself always conditioned by the same law in the very forms taken by her revolt. It is a law of repetition that is indistinguishable from the law of the symbolic: the law of the father, according to which she is passed from one man (her father) to another man (Charles) who possesses her, and then on to a series of lovers (from Léon I to Rodolphe, and then from Rodolphe to Léon II) so that, in her adulterous affairs, Emma undergoes the *same* passing on from one man to another (but with a repetition in the chain of repetitions itself). Each affair leads her back to the calm monotony of marriage: after six months with Rodolphe, "they were to one another like a married couple, tranquilly keeping up a domestic flame" (p. 123; p. 159), and with Léon "Emma found again in adultery all the platitudes of marriage" (p. 211; p. 269). And finally, exploited erotically as she is by men, Emma's desire simultaneously makes her vulnerable to the commercial seductions of Lheureux.[9]

Does the symbolic order give advantages to a text that it denies to a woman like Emma? Does the "success" of the text depend to a certain extent (and if so, how?) on the failure of the character? Does the phenomenon of reading make available valuable resources of which the characters are unaware? Does it amount to what Shoshana Felman calls "dé-lire textuel" ["textual delirium"]—a rhetoric whose ironic law is to outmaneuver the law?[10] As is perhaps already evident, we will need to try to understand that Emma serves as a dual model for the text, or more precisely, as both an antimodel and a positive model. We will need to consider the different ways the fate of the text is linked to Emma's fate: how it reproduces her failure, yet how (in the very act of replicating that failure) it invites reading and, in so doing, ventures on a relation that might accomplish what Emma is unable to achieve and might answer the desire she embodies.

*

Something crucial is at stake: the social status of the literary. John Frow has argued in a book of fundamental importance that it is by means of intertextuality, and not directly, that literary discourse exhibits its opposition to the dominant social discourse.[11] And it is indeed clear that the problematics of Flaubertian writing is inscribed in the intertextual relations displayed by *Madame Bovary* and particularly in the newness—or only the novelty—that the text aims at in relation to the generic models offered to it by the novel, tragedy, and opera. There is no need to dwell on the romantic reading matter of Emma's youth, or on the alternately pious and salacious reading of her adulthood, from which the text has no trouble in ironically distancing itself. But what are we to make of the conventional scenario the novel itself follows of a "fallen" woman and bad mother, who falls into adultery and pays for it with a horrible death? What of the third act of *Lucia de Lammermoor*, which Emma misses at the theater, only to fall into a madness of her own in the third part of the novel, in the feverish affair with Léon and its outcome? And what of the tragic pathos of "fatality" that is clearly evoked by the prophetic but unrecognized role of the blind man—even if such pathos is demystified by the cynical or inane references to fate on the part of certain characters? We see how the text distances itself from these models: the theater is not real life—a fact Emma herself is well aware of, since she notices the banality of passions that art makes so much of: "Elle connaissait à présent la petitesse des passions que l'art exagérait" (p. 210). "Fatality" is in fact *engineered* by men such as Rodolphe and Lheureux. "Fallen" women are not so much fallen as they are "half-tame things" like horses, victimized by the brutal domination of males. (Charles and Rodolphe are both linked, although differently, to horseback riding).[12]

The text cannot take its distance from these models without submitting to them, however. By redefining the romantic or tragic heroine and the "fallen" woman as a social victim, the novel (like Emma) merely confirms the vicious circle in which it finds itself trapped in relation to social discourse and the problematics of repetition; for, like Emma, the text is itself a "victim of society." As a genre, the novel is historically linked, as the French word *roman* recalls, to vernacular language and everyday discourse; it is *sermo* and not *oratio*, or at most it is a *sermo* tending toward the condition of *oratio*. It cannot deny this link without denying its generic identity as a novel (rather than as *unmarked* discourse). Yet, at the same time, a novel cannot fully realize the condition of its generic identity (as does *Madame Bovary*) without jeopardizing its oppositional autonomy—without undergoing the consequence, as Anne Freadman might say, of the proximity of Mount Olympus and Mount Parnassus (i.e., the domination of the latter by the former).[13] Like horses and women, literature appears to be one of those "half-tame things" that are *trained* in a way that preserves a bit of their spirit of independence only to better subjugate them in the end.

Following Frow's line of thought, I would argue that the modernist texts of the 1850s share a common system of intertextual reference through which their oppositional relation to the dominant social discourse becomes readable. The interconnectedness of their opposition is a function of their treatment of narrative. The forms of textuality developed by Nerval, Baudelaire, and Flaubert all relativize the narrative function as a form of discourse that privileges the relation among coherent, autonomous subjects, characterized by their self-presence and their control of language (another "half-tame thing"); this is the dominance they struggle against. But these new forms of textuality are themselves thought of and readable as directly derived from the social, so that they are in danger of becoming indistinguishable in turn from the prevailing "in-difference." This is a consequence of the Nervalian "blur," and it arises both in the duplicity entailed by Baudelairean antihypocrisy (as a return of the repressed) and in Flaubertian "idiocy," which is so easily permeated by the stupidity of *bêtise*. It is in this context that the abandoning of narrativity—the "elocutionary disappearance" of the narrator dramatized in *Madame Bovary*—can be seen as a threat to the identity and the autonomy of literary writing.

In other words, the text becomes melancholic when it can no longer be centered on a self that, like the bourgeois self, is master of the communicational act and free to mark it with the seal of its "originality." As a result, the melancholic text becomes the locus of an anguish of identity, since all boundaries become blurred between textual discourse and social discourse, which share the same language. In this way these antibourgeois texts unwittingly confirm the bourgeois hegemony they oppose. Unable to completely stop conceiving of identity in terms of individuality and originality (that is, in terms of *difference*), and unable as a result to completely renounce the narrative function (the mark of the autonomous subject), the "new" writing of the 1850s had to guarantee itself a certain form of difference in the textual function as well—a new identity that appears as an appeal for reading. Let the act of reading confer on me the differentiated identity, the very distinction that is thrown into question by my nature as a melancholic and undifferentiated textual production!

Such at least is the hope in Flaubert. In the writings of Nerval and Baudelaire, the problem of melancholic textual identity arises less urgently, since Nerval is more at home in a regressive and narcissistic textual paradise, while Baudelaire is more attracted to the violent disjunctions of a provocative, confrontational style. We have nevertheless seen what stakes are attached to the "right" reading that is required by texts like "Sylvie" or "Au lecteur" (and by extension *Les Fleurs du mal* as a whole). However, *Madame Bovary* stands out among these texts by the urgency with which it poses the problem of textual identity in relation to social discourse. From this will arise, as we are about to see, a special complexity and a particular form of duplicity, which is a double one, since to the duplicity of a narration "doubled" and, in this case, to a large extent *swamped* by the textual function is added, *within the textual function itself*, another kind of duplicity involving the act of reading: beyond a first level of irony, the reading instance is asked to take account of a second and superior irony.

As in Baudelaire, the Flaubertian text is able to counter social hypocrisy with textual duplicity—taking the form in Flaubert of irony, and in Baudelaire of "knowledge" of the unconscious. Against Lheureux, Homais, or

Binet as representations of the social order, the writing of *Madame Bovary* exploits depths and nuances that are figured, for me, by the changing color of Emma's eyes: "Black in the shade, dark blue in broad daylight, they seemed to contain layer upon layer of color, more opaque at the back, lighter and more transparent toward the lustrous surface" (p. 23; p. 31). This can be read as a metaphoric definition of irony, as it was to function as Flaubert's textual weapon against the world of those who defend the moral order while breaking the law, who line their pockets by means of lies and manipulation, and who repress love in the way they shut up a gangrenous leg in a cruel box. Yet what are we to think of irony that is aimed not at social hypocrisy, but at a *victim* such as Emma? By distinguishing the text from the kind of *bêtise* Emma represents in order to ensure its individuality and "difference," doesn't this irony have the effect of causing the text to relapse into certain bourgeois failings, and particularly into a certain kind of egotistic individualism that is not easy to distinguish from the smug satisfaction demonstrated by seducers, exploiters, and hypocrites— indeed, the whole gang of people the novel angrily exposes? Irony reveals itself in this way to be a double-edged sword, which serves to protect the text against one form of *bêtise* only to undermine it with another less innocuous and more threatening form. Irony is *necessary* in order to distinguish the text from its characters; but it cannot save the text from the problem of indifferentiation because it demonstrates an indifference of its own.

For Flaubert as for Baudelaire, indifference (which again can be written "in-difference") is a greater danger than hypocrisy. It takes the form of a hardness of heart (like that of Rodophe, who cynically manipulates his relation with Emma), but also of feigned, hypocritical indifference, at which Lheureux is the past master, using it as a means of commercial manipulation. But this indifference on the part of the exploitative characters throws into question the "impassiveness" of Flaubert's text—for which the figure is once again in Emma, after her wedding night: "the bride gave no sign that revealed anything" (p. 21; p. 28). How to ensure that this impassiveness will not be viewed as cynicism like Rodolphe's, that the "presentational" style of the narration will not be confused with the "delicate" art of discreet salesmanship exhibited by Lheureux? "Today, then, he had come to show madame, *in passing*, various articles he *happened* to have by an unusual stroke of luck. . . . Then Monsieur Lheureux delicately exhibited three Algerian scarves, . . . etc." (p. 74; p. 97; emphasis mine). In such a context, textual irony can only make matters worse by tending to confirm the diagnosis of real or feigned indifference to which the discourse of *Madame Bovary* is in any case vulnerable and, consequently, to confuse it with the exploitative world that it represents and of which Emma is the victim.

The text must therefore be able to offer itself—*irony included*—to be read as a text that is *not* indifferent. This can be its way of differentiating itself in relation to the indifference that prevails among those who surround Emma and, by extension, in the society they represent. In other words, since Emma herself is clearly the opposite of an indifferent character, the text should pattern itself after this character that it otherwise presents in an ironic fashion. Like Emma, the text will draw on passion in order to fight ennui, that invasive and generalized form of indifference that is the clearest sign of the social order's victory over individual desire. But how can it achieve this? How can the text resemble in this way the passionate character of Emma without succumbing to her fate as a blind, exploited victim who flees the monotony of her existence as a bride only to realize bitterly later on, as a "woman of experience," the unsatisfactory nature of life—"cette insuffisance de la vie" (p. 263)? Is it possible for the text to demonstrate (as Emma does) that it is not heartless, without falling (as she does) into banal romantic phraseology and stupid, sentimental cliché and without designating itself as a social victim? For the text to escape that fate, it must employ a second, superior form of irony, an *other* irony, that differs from Emma's vulnerable *bêtise* by its lucidity without being confused with indifference, and whose clear-sightedness does not prevent it from expressing an authentic passion that distinguishes it from society's indifference. Such an irony would not be unlike a certain type of *sincerity* that could be confused neither with Emma's naïveté nor with the hypocrisy of the people of Yonville and that would simultaneously contrast with the indifference characteristic in such a society of the worst exploiters. It would be an impassioned irony that the vaporized text of melancholy makes readable as a latent anger, but that also (as we will see) has another aspect, that of a demand for love.

But irony and sincerity are both effects of reading and therefore cannot be *proved*—by textual analysis, for instance. They are commonly viewed, moreover, as mutually exclusive opposites, like complexity and simplicity. I will try to show, however, that *Madame Bovary* is a text that requires to be read as simultaneously ironic and sincere, as sincere in its irony and simple in its complexity. For it is this secret affinity between irony and sincerity that constitutes the text's best chance for an autonomous identity,

since from it the text derives its duplicity as a melancholic text—a duplicity
through which it resists the invasive force of social ennui and the blurring
of differences that ennui produces.

*

In the course of their horseback ride, Emma and Rodolphe arrive at the
top of a hill:

> On était aux premiers jours d'octobre. Il y avait du brouillard
> sur la campagne. Des vapeurs s'allongeaient à l'horizon, contre
> le contour des collines; et d'autres, se déchirant, montaient, se
> perdaient. Quelquefois, dans un écartement des nuées, sous un
> rayon de soleil, on apercevait au loin les toits d'Yonville, avec
> les jardins au bord de l'eau, les cours, les murs et le clocher de
> l'église. Emma fermait à demi les paupières pour reconnaître sa
> maison, et jamais ce pauvre village où elle vivait ne lui avait
> semblé si petit. De la hauteur où ils étaient, toute la vallée pa-
> raissait un immense lac pâle, s'évaporant à l'air. Les massifs
> d'arbres de place en place saillissaient comme des rochers noirs;
> et les hautes lignes des peupliers, qui dépassaient la brume, fi-
> guraient des grèves que le vent remuait. (pp. 147–48)

> It was early in October. There was fog over the land. Hazy
> clouds hovered on the horizon between the outlines of the
> hills; others, rent asunder, floated up and disappeared. Some-
> times, through a rift in the clouds, beneath a ray of sunshine,
> gleamed from afar the roofs of Yonville, with the gardens at the
> water's edge, the yards, the walls and the church steeple. Emma
> half closed her eyes to pick out her house, and never had this
> poor village where she lived appeared so small. From the
> height on which they were the whole valley seemed an im-
> mense pale lake sending off its vapour into the air. Clumps of
> trees here and there stood out like black rocks, and the tall lines
> of the poplars that rose above the mist were like a beach stirred
> by the wind. (p. 114)

Beneath Emma's gaze, the mist transforms the Yonville countryside into
the scenery of a lake. At the same time, the smallness of the village is
heightened by the distance, even if the heroine can still make out her
house. This smallness is real, but it is also subjective, just as the objective
weather conditions contribute to the work of the imagination, to which
the text draws attention by underlining the metaphoricity of the vision:
"Clumps of trees . . . stood out *like* black rocks, and the tall lines of the

poplars that rose above the mist were *like* a beach stirred by the wind" (p.
114; p. 148; italics mine). Without leaving the familiar, Emma has man-
aged to create around her something that distances her from the village
where she is imprisoned and brings her closer to what she loves best:
the sea.

From the account of her time at the convent school, we learn that Emma
"knew the country too well; she knew the lowing of cattle, the milking,
the ploughs. Accustomed to the quieter aspects of life, she turned instead
to its tumultuous parts. She loved the sea only for the sake of its storms"
(pp. 26–27; p. 34). But by the time of her first conversation with Léon,
she is capable of invoking the sea in purest romantic style:

> "And doesn't it seem to you," continued Madame Bovary, "that
> the mind travels more freely on this limitless expanse, of which
> the contemplation elevates the soul, gives ideas of the infinite,
> the ideal?" (p. 58; p. 76)

Later, it is natural for her to dream of her departure with Rodolphe as a
departure for some Italian fishing village—that is, a sort of Yonville in
which farming and livestock raising would have been replaced by fishing:
"C'est là qu'ils s'arrêteraient pour vivre . . . au fond d'un golfe, au bord de
la mer" (p. 183) ["It was there that they would stay . . . in the heart of a
gulf, by the sea" (p. 141). So the lake scenery created by Emma's vision is
only an intermediary phase between what she knows (the countryside of
Normandy, the lowing of cattle) and what she dreams of; and indeed, the
landscape as it is described to us does lie somewhere between imagination
and reality. In it we still recognize "from afar the roofs of Yonville, with its
gardens at the water's edge," while the "immense pale lake sending off its
vapor into the air," into which the heroine's imagination would like to
transform the valley, cannot achieve fully convincing existence. For how
exactly can a pebbly beach (*une grève*) be "stirred by the wind"?

It is important, however, that in her effort to realize an ideal landscape
(if not exactly a mental one), Emma has a powerful ally in actual weather
conditions: the fog, the hazy clouds hovering and rising, the mist that aids
the metaphoric transformation of the trees into rocks and beaches. For this
external fog corresponds to a fog in her head. Emma's mother-in-law has
always viewed Emma as a flighty "évaporée" (p. 180) and recommends
vigorous treatment for "these vapors, that come to her from a lot of ideas
she stuffs into her head, and from the idleness in which she lives" (p. 90;

p. 117). The bourgeoises of Yonville had also noticed her "vaporish airs" or "airs évaporés" (p. 89; p. 117). Emma is in short a victim of melancholia; we recognize all its classic symptoms—the dispersal of the self, the torpor and listlessness, and the sense of temporal break—in the description of her psychological state following Léon's departure, when his memory remains only as a void "at the heart of her ennui":

> The next day was a dreary one for Emma. Everything seemed shrouded in an atmosphere of bleakness that hung darkly over the outward aspect of things, and sorrow blew into her soul with gentle moans, as the winter wind makes in ruined castles. Her reverie was that of things gone forever, the exhaustion that seizes you after everything is done; the pain, in short, caused by the interruption of a familiar motion, the sudden halting of a long drawn out vibration. (p. 88; p. 115)

In fact, in the course of one of Emma's earlier attacks, Félicité her maid had already pronounced what amounted to a categorical diagnosis:

> "Ah! yes," Félicité went on, "you are just like La Guérine. . . . She was so sad, so sad. . . . Her illness, it appears, was a kind of fog that she had in the head. . . . Then, after her marriage, it stopped, they say."
> "But with me," replied Emma, "it was after marriage that it began." (p. 78; p. 102)

It would not be entirely accurate to say that Emma's "vapors"—the "kind of fog" she has in her head—are the result of marriage; the frustrations that produce her ennui come instead from the disparity between the romantic desires inculcated in her by society (notably during her education at the convent) and the social law she is condemned to live by (symbolized by her marriage with Charles). Although her malady has the appearance of individual suffering, it is nevertheless social, therefore, in origin; that is why it is important to see that the "vapors" Emma has in her head have an equivalent in the real vapors hovering in the air of the region where she lives, and notably in Yonville.

Shortly after their arrival, the Bovarys had been warned of the bad air in the area by the pharmacist Homais in his pseudoscientific jargon (although Emma, completely absorbed by Léon, had of course not paid any attention):

and this heat, moreover, which, on account of the watery va-
pours given off by the river and the considerable number of
cattle in the fields, which, as you know, exhale much ammonia,
that is to say, nitrogen, hydrogen, and oxygen (no, nitrogen
and hydrogen alone), and which sucking up the humus from
the soil, mixing together all those different emanations, unites
them into a single bundle, so to speak, and combining with the
electricity diffused through the atmosphere, when there is any,
might in the long-run, as in the tropical countries, engender
poisonous fumes . . . (p. 57; p. 76)

The awkward and interminable sentence (of which I am citing only a portion), with its ungainly vocabulary and labyrinthine structure, mimes a decentered, degraded language that is itself vaporized. But the composition
of the fumes infecting the air of Yonville warrants a closer look: they are
composed partly of "natural" water vapors or fog, partly of the exhalations
of the cattle and the "humus" of the fields where they graze, combined
with the electricity in the atmosphere. Like Emma's imagination, which
transforms the valley into a lake, Flaubert's writing invests nature with
meaning by means of a metaphoric operation. For in a place like Yonville,
where people have names like Tuvache, Lebœuf, and Bovary, and where
the lowing of cattle and the bleating of sheep are practically indistinguishable from human speech, the vapor emanating from the animals clearly
figures a stupid, animalized society with a noxious discourse. (Similarly,
the electricity might stand for the role of desire, capable as it is of transforming this heavy and unhealthy atmosphere of the area into a stormy
drama.)

Indeed, descriptions of vapor are frequently associated in *Madame Bovary* with evocations of animality. For example, in a passage that begins: "It
was the beginning of April . . ." (and that therefore anticipates the passage
we are studying: "It was early in October . . ."), a poetic evocation similar
to Emma's vision on the hill is accompanied by a reminder of the presence
of cattle; for here we are in the village, not blissfully "afar":

The evening vapors rose between the leafless poplars, touching
their outlines with a violet tint, paler and more transparent
than a subtle gauze caught amidst their branches. Cattle moved
around in the distance. (p. 78; p. 103)

Similarly, in the description of the coarse banquet that closes the agricultural fair, the "vapors" that hover in the air are clearly of animal prove-

nance, even though they are described as steam: "Sweat stood on every brow, and a whitish steam, like the vapor of a stream on an autumn morning, floated above the table between the hanging lamps" (p. 109; p. 142). (Flaubert uses the word *buée*, which by phonetic contamination, suggests the bovine.)

In the social "fog" that Emma inhales, we can pick out more specific elements as well. For example, the description of the evening in early April stands out because, like the village itself in October, the animals are at a distance and hence cannot be heard. This silence allows Emma to hear the tolling of the angelus, which carries her back in a nostalgic reverie to her days in the convent: "She remembered the great candlesticks, . . . she saw the gentle face of the Virgin amid the swirling blue smoke of the rising incense" (p. 79; p. 103). These mystic inclinations were alluded to as well in the earlier passages describing her life at the convent, where "she was softly lulled by the mystic languor exhaled in the perfumes of the altar" (p. 25; p. 33). But to Emma's mystical vapors must be added the poisonous fumes that Homais complains of living among in his pharmacy (p. 255), since it is from Homais's poison that, in a sense that is obviously very broadly symbolic, Emma dies in the end. The poisonous vapors thus symbolize not only the scientific knowledge of which the pharmacist gives so false an image, alongside the religion so poorly represented by Father Bournisien, but ultimately all the social forces that enable a man like Homais to prosper yet to Emma are fatal. In the death chamber, sprinkled by turns with chlorine by the pharmacist and with holy water by the priest, the two men are finally reconciled, in a crucial image, through the sleep induced by the "heavy atmosphere" of the room in which "bluish vapor" rises like incense from the pharmacist's aromatic herbs, while the fog seeps in from the window. There the odor of putrefaction rising from Emma's body and the emanations of the "social body" are irrevocably blended.

Not surprisingly, it is at this moment that Charles has the vision of Emma evaporating in the shimmer of her dress:

> The watered satin of her gown shimmered white as moonlight. Emma was lost beneath it; and it seemed to him that, spreading beyond her own self, she blended confusedly with everything around her—the silence, the night, the passing wind, the damp odors rising from the ground. (p. 243; p. 309)

In the "opium fumes" (p. 182; p. 234) that numb the minds of the inhabitants of Yonville and from which Emma alone tries to escape, there is a concealed agent of uniformity, indistinctness, and indifferentiation that is the source of a collective disease of identity. Melancholy is not simply a contagious illness that is caught through contact with such a society; it is a disease of the system, an ecological disease.[14] Does the valley appear like a lake to Emma because the mists of her imagination are reinforced by real external fogs, or because the vapors from outside have entered her mind and inspired her with a transformed vision of reality? The ambiguity of the passage we are considering makes this question difficult to answer, since it strikes an even balance between external vapors (figuring a sick society) and diseased vision (the symptom of an impaired individuality).

The irony is of course that the person who tries the hardest to escape infection and to distinguish herself from the poisoned atmosphere of her social environment is the one who succumbs to it in the most "fatal" if not tragic manner. The people of Yonville, like good herbivores, tranquilly follow the herd, blindly submitting to social uniformity and a routine existence that consume them without their even noticing. The disease is much worse for those (such as Emma and, to a lesser extent, Léon) who feel themselves infected by ennui and try to resist it. Emma has no way of fleeing the poisonous exhalations of society except by taking refuge in the "warm atmosphere" and "hothouse air" of imaginary pleasures—in short, in other forms of vapor.

These Baudelairean phrases ("tiède atmosphère" and "air chaud") are in the text of *Madame Bovary* in the passages describing Emma's convent (pp. 25–27; pp. 33–36) and the ball at the château de la Vaubyessard respectively—two of the main sites where the romantic reveries and unquenchable desires of her *bovarysme* are first fostered. It is during the whirlwind waltz with the viscount—"they turned; everything around them was turning" (p. 38; p. 50)—that Emma first experiences the dizziness of love to which she later abandons herself with such intense pleasure when Rodolphe woos her:

> . . . it seemed to her that she was again turning in the waltz under the light of the lustres on the arm of the Viscount, and that Léon was not far away, that he was coming . . . and yet all the time she was conscious of Rodolphe's head by her side. The sweetness of this sensation revived her past desires, and like grains of sand under a gust of wind, they swirled around in the subtle breath of the perfume that diffused over her soul. (p. 106; p. 137)

To the extent that this whirlwind image is a figure for the repetitive structure of the novel (the viscount, Léon I, Rodolphe, Léon II) and foreshadows Emma's "fall" (for during the waltz with the viscount, we learn that "a
torpor seized her" and "panting, she almost fell" [p. 38; p. 50]), the vapors
of pleasure are superimposed on, and identified with, the episodic form of
a text itself caught up in a vertiginous whirlwind of repetition. Similarly,
the "tourbillons bleuâtres"—the bluish circles of incense that had numbed
her mind in the convent chapel as a girl (p. 79; p. 103)—anticipate the
mystic vapors in which Emma tries to console herself after Léon's departure: "it seemed to her that her being, mounting toward God, would be
annihilated in that love like a burning incense that melts into vapor" (p.
154; p. 199). Finally, it is the overheated, stuffy atmosphere of the opera
house in Rouen that controls Emma's reunion with Léon as well as moti-
vating it (since the heat impels Charles to go out to the lobby in search of
refreshments, whence he returns with Léon). The oppressive air of the theater sets in train the feverish atmosphere of the whole third part of the
novel:

> Then Léon sighed: "Don't you find it hot?"
> "Unbearably so! Yes!"
> "Don't you feel well?" Bovary inquired.
> "Yes, I am stifling; let's go."
>
> (p. 165; pp. 212–13)

It is an atmosphere of deception and theatricality (at the theater, Emma
and Léon are already in collusion to deceive Charles) and one that (like the
whirlwind waltz) is full of self-reflexive implications for the text itself. For
Emma becomes, in a sense, the *romancière* ("novel writer") of her own
existence—that is, until Lheureux proves to be an even better constructor
of plots than herself. And the text will have to struggle to distinguish between the pathos of Emma's fall and the deceptions of tragic theater with
its insistence on "fate."

So it makes sense in this third part that the fogs of Rouen should appear
to Emma as the visible breath of pleasure:

> At every turn, they could see more and more of the city be-
> low, forming a vast luminous mist above the blurred mass of
> houses. Emma knelt on the cushions, and let her eyes wander
> over the dazzling light. She sobbed, called to Léon, sent him

tender words and kisses which were lost in the wind. (p. 193;
p. 248)

This dazzle in turn foreshadows the dizzy luminosity of the hallucinatory
view of the houses of Yonville in the fog that Emma experiences after her
final, heartbreaking meeting with Rodolphe: "Suddenly it seemed to her
that fiery spheres were exploding in the air like bullets when they strike,
and were whirling, whirling. . . . In the midst of each of them appeared the
face of Rodolphe" (p. 228; p. 291).

The novel's diagnosis concerning its heroine is thus very clear. Emma
cannot escape the poisonous fumes of society in the "tiède atmosphère" of
passion or fulfill her desires by pursuing imaginary pleasures. Quite to the
contrary, she only aggravates her problem and confirms her status as a victim as the fog surrounding her becomes a whirlwind, her melancholy turns
to hysteria, and her vertigo rushes her to her downfall. Emma's fatal blindness, caused by the fog in her head, lies in her failure to grasp the social
origin and function of the malady that has been carefully inculcated in her.
The reader, however, recognizes that Emma's upbringing and education
have made her vulnerable to seduction and hence to exploitation, and that
in this sense the manipulations of men like Rodolphe and Lheureux are
strikingly equivalent.

Looking down from the hills above Yonville, from where the village appears so small and the landscape of Normandy seems so close to her dream
of happiness, Emma knows then that she is moving toward love; but she
does not see that she is also moving toward a fall that is the consequence
of an act of seduction and exploitation:

> "Oh! Rodolphe!" she said slowly and . . . she abandoned
> herself to him. . . . Then far away, beyond the wood, on the
> other hills, she heard a vague prolonged cry, a voice which lin-
> gered, and in silence she heard it mingling like music with the
> last pulsations of her throbbing nerves. Rodolphe, a cigar be-
> tween his lips, was mending one of the two broken bridles with
> his penknife. (p. 116; p. 150)

Absorbed by the "pulsations of her throbbing nerves," Emma perceives as
music this faraway cry that the reader in contrast perceives as a cry of warning, lament, and impending danger. She does not realize the implications
of the calm indifference in Rodolphe's attitude as he triumphantly manipulates phallic attributes (the cigar and knife) and imperturbably repairs the
bridle—a broken instrument of control that seems to symbolize Emma's

infraction of conjugal fidelity but that he (in taking possession of Emma) clearly intends to make use of for purposes of his own. Nor does she perceive the parallel between the calm indifference of satisfied male lust exhibited by Rodolphe and the feigned indifference—masking what Marx claimed was the only bourgeois passion, the passion for money—that serves as an instrument of seduction for the merchant Lheureux. The genuine indifference Lheureux will display to her in due course consequently comes as a total surprise to her:

> She was sobbing. . . . "You'll drive me to do something desperate!"
> "Don't make me laugh!" said he, shutting the door.(p. 215; p. 274)

On the one hand, then, Emma's naïveté and blindness; on the other, irony on the part of the text: Emma makes her horse prance in the street when she and Rodolphe return from their tryst in the woods: "En entrant dans Yonville, elle caracola sur les pavés" (p. 151). I have noted in passing some possible points of comparison between Emma's malady and the discursive features of the text that point to the fact that, like its heroine, the text of *Madame Bovary* is invaded and its identity blurred by the "fogs" of social discourse. But the difference between them, if there is one, seems at first glance to derive from the character's deep blindness by contrast with the relative lucidity one can attribute to the text. Emma's triumph is ingenuous, but the passage describing her joyous prancing in the street calls for a reading that is both perspicacious and ironic, thereby implying a lucidity at the level of the reading-writing relation that the heroine herself lacks. Emma lives out her *bêtise*; the text in contrast draws attention to it and, in so doing, distinguishes itself from her naive stupidity.

There are two problems with irony, however. First, irony can be confused with *bêtise*, of which it is in a sense the "intelligent" version. Second, directed at Emma—and establishing the novel's identity and individual autonomy at the expense of its "half-tame" heroine—the irony of the text risks associating the novel with the exploitative and somewhat cruel indifference exhibited by the male seducers, who profit from her naive gullibility. Furthermore, following Roland Barthes's analysis in *S/Z*,[15] irony shares with Emma's vertigo a structure of perpetual regression—it has the characteristics of a "flight toward." As a "quotation" of the codes of others, irony is itself governed by a cultural code that is that of "intelligence"; and the ironist, presenting himself as "intelligent" in the face of stupidity, is therefore obliged to ironize his own recourse to this conventional code as just another manifestation of *bêtise*. And so on. For this new irony will have to be ironized in turn, in another attempt to escape irony's *bêtise*, so that an endless mechanism of ironizing irony and ironizing the ironizing of irony is set in motion. Emma falls unintentionally into the intensification of *bêtise* that is the "vaporizing" of her being in melancholy. But the ironic text is itself caught up in a kind of vertigo, not simply a vertigo of repetition like that of its heroine, but also a vertigo caused by its own efforts to distance itself from her fate, to pull back from the *bêtise* it cannot fully escape. In this sense irony might be defined as the form of hysteria to which textual melancholy leads.

So irony is necessary, since it contrasts with the blindness of the characters and preserves the text from being confused, as is always possible, with their discourses and their fate. Yet it does not liberate the text in its search for a mark of identity that would distinguish it from the world of *bêtise* and from the vertigo of vaporization; quite the contrary, irony shows the text to be, albeit at one degree removed, immersed in this world. There is, however, another another way out that is available to the text and for which Emma offers not a negative but a positive model: that of sincerity, which is not quite the same thing as naïveté. Totally devoid as she is of a sense of irony, Emma easily mistakes words of seduction for sincerity; even later, when she is more experienced and recognizes Léon's manipulations, she remains utterly taken in by Lheureux. That is Emma's error, but the error of seducers like Rodolphe and Lheureux is that, because of their own cynical indifference, they either fail to recognize (in Rodolphe's case) or else coldly exploit (in Lheureux's case) the sincerity visible in her—sincerity that signifies the authenticity of desire, even when it is inextricably bound up with the kitsch and *bêtise* that speak of society's ascendancy.

In the presence of Emma, then, and of *Madame Bovary*, it is for the reader not to resemble, in their different forms of cynicism, characters like Léon, Rodolphe, and Lheureux. Yet there are no markers that would permit one to distinguish sincerity from a hypocritical or self-interested discourse, any more than it is possible to distinguish irony from an impassibility that comes close to a seductive or exploitative indifference. Irony and sincerity are moreover inextricably intertwined at the level of the passion—the anger, if one will—that they convey. The task of the reader is nevertheless not only to distinguish the irony of the text (which distinguishes it from Emma's *bêtise*), but also and simultaneously to remain sensitive to a sincerity of expression and an authenticity of emotion that the ironic text conveys, like Emma, in its very *bêtise*. For it is this sincerity that distinguishes her—and with her the text—from all the hypocritical or indifferent characters who (with a few exceptions, such as Charles and Justin) surround her.

In reading the description of Emma's horseback ride with Rodolphe, one must therefore distance oneself ironically from Emma, noting, for example, how the work of her imagination conceals reality from her—the reality of the landscape and that of Rodolphe's intentions, in particular. Yet at the same time one must empathize, against Rodolphe, with her desire, which is a desire for happiness and love—a desire that is in no way deceptive or hypocritical, and certainly not indifferent, even if we view it as foolish and naive. The text's free indirect style is the vehicle for this double reading. By inseparably linking the narrative voice to the character's vision of things, the text presumes and calls for an ironic reading that is capable of dissociating the narrative voice from the vision it conveys. By giving access to Emma's subjective vision in a direct and "unmediated" manner (i.e., without commentary), however, the text permits and even encourages a nonironic reading, indeed an *identificatory* reading. This is of course inevitably a mediated and hence indirect reading, taking for its object, as it does, that of which the blind warping vision is itself an expression: a desiring subject, a subject defined by her desire.

I will return in a moment to the discussion of the text's free indirect style. In the meantime, to give an example of the type of reading *Madame Bovary* calls for, let me refer briefly to the epitaph Homais devises for Emma: "Sta viator, amabilem conjugem calcas" ["Traveler, stay: your feet trample the lovely spouse"] (p. 252; p. 320). The epitaph clearly has an ironic sense, owing to its unexpected accuracy, of which Homais is of course unaware, but which a reader should not fail to grasp; for no one more than Homais has "trampled on" this woman, who was scarcely a "lovely wife" ("épouse aimable") in the sense of the piously conventional phrase—the cliché—he chooses to describe her. As a self-reflexive figure of textual address to the reader, however, the epitaph has the value of a piece of negative advice. One needs to have first grasped its irony in order to understand its sincerity, the sense in which it is nonironic. Read in this way, the epitaph admonishes: "Reader, do not trample on Emma—or *Madame Bovary*—as did those of her milieu; respect the character's sincerity (and likewise that of the text), which is the sincerity of desire. Do not trample (*fouler*), but become the agent of her/its *défoulement* or liberation from repression."

The problem in reading posed by *Madame Bovary* is that this demand for a "sincere" reading is accomplished by means of a positive statement (the epitaph) that implies a negative injunction, the positive statement being itself an ironic quotation, the textual repetition of a cliché taken from the banal discourse of epitaphs—a genre to which the novel (itself an epitaph to Emma) consequently acknowledges its own belonging and whose banality it thus shares. Although the melancholic text, invaded by the *bêtise* of society, may vaunt the originality of its irony, it is nevertheless through this same irony that the text most resembles the characters it portrays. If such a text has any chance of differentiating itself from social discourse, it is through its duplicity as an ironic text conveying a sincere desire—the desire that its own deepest desire, for which its irony is only a vehicle, not be repressed (*refoulé*) in the way that Emma was trampled (*foulée*) underfoot. (I know that I am lapsing into tautology or repetition.) But how many layers of *bêtise* must be penetrated before this desire is recognized? Will *Madame Bovary* be able to find a reader able to truly *love* it if Emma was never able to find a lover able to truly *read* her?

*

Let us now reread our passage:

> It was early in October. There was fog over the land. Hazy clouds hovered on the horizon between the outlines of the hills; others, rent asunder, floated up and disappeared. Sometimes, through a rift in the clouds, beneath a ray of sunshine, gleamed from afar the roofs of Yonville, with the gardens at the water's edge, the yards, the walls and the church steeple. Emma half closed her eyes to pick out her house, and never had this poor village where she lived appeared so small. From the height on which they were the whole valley seemed an immense pale lake sending off its vapour into the air. Clumps of trees here and there stood out like black rocks, and the tall lines of the poplars that rose above the mist were like a beach stirred by the wind. (p. 114; pp. 147–48)

This passage conveys a strong impression of beauty, happiness, and plenitude. Even the hastiest reader cannot remain insensitive to this impression or fail to recognize the precision, rhythm, and firmness of the prose. But how are we to *understand* the impression conveyed by the passage? Is it Emma's impression alone, for which she is solely responsible? Or is the text associating itself with Emma's impression and taking responsibility for it on its own behalf? And what of the reader? Should one share in Emma's joy and abandon oneself to it, as she does? Or should one distance oneself from her feelings, treating them cautiously as a mere consequence of her blindness? But then why should a text communicate a feeling of happiness that the reader should *not* trust? Beauty cannot be proved (any more than irony or sincerity), so I will not try to analyze it here. I will, however, ask what *meaning* it might have in a passage such as this one.

The whole first half of the passage is enunciated, or seems to be enunciated, in a tone of absolute objectivity: the voice that indicates the date ("It was early in October") and describes the weather ("There was fog over the land") and the landscape ("the outline of the hills" and the village in the distance) communicates information that the reader is obligated to accept with confidence as true. (For example, one can hardly imagine that Emma and Rodolphe actually stayed in the village, or that it was really August instead of October.) The use of neutral pronouns—*on* in the French, "it" and "there" in the English translation—seems to guarantee this objectivity. Yet who exactly is *on*? Early October is neither the time of the narration nor that of the reading; it is the moment in time in which the characters find themselves. Moreover, the way the narrating *on* progresses from banal observations and general perceptions concerning the date and weather to more nuanced and detailed glimpses concerning the landscape ("Hazy clouds hovered . . . ; others, rent asunder, floated up and disappeared. Sometimes through a rift in the clouds, . . . gleamed from afar the roofs of Yonville, with the gardens at the water's edge, the yards, the walls and the church steeple") mimes the movements of a consciousness whose vision goes from a general impression to more specific observations and from the foggy countryside back to the village the couple have only recently left. (So there is a backward glance: Why is it looking back?)

As one reaches the second half of the passage, the focalization suddenly sharpens: "Emma half closed her eyes to pick out her house." Now the descriptions explicitly take on the quality of personal judgments: "never had this *poor* village where she lived appeared so *small*" (italics mine), while the subjectivity of the observation is underlined by the use of the verb "appear." The whole rest of the passage—a long, extended metaphor over which the narrating *on* seems to linger lovingly, turning the valley into a lake, clumps of trees into rocks, and lines of poplars into a beach—can therefore be ascribed to Emma. Her embellishing perception and the effort it deploys to transform land into a near seascape are readable, as I have mentioned, both in the verbs *sembler* ("to seem"), *paraître* ("to appear"), and *figurer* ("to figure") and in the implausibility of the comparisons, especially the last (beaches fluttering in the breeze).

Thus the reader is imperceptibly led from an objective point of view on the landscape that he or she is encouraged to accept with confidence to a view that is clearly "subjective" and that one would be wrong not to be wary of. But also, the text does everything in its power to combine these two visions. The effect of the attribution to Emma's point of view in the middle of the passage is not only that it leads the reader to take the description with a grain of salt but also that it casts a certain retrospective doubt over the seeming objectivity of the first part of the passage. If one naturally identifies the consciousness that looks back on the gardens, courtyards, walls, and steeple of Yonville as the same subjectivity (Emma's) that tries to make out Emma's house, the same identification must be valid as well for all the preceding observations. Someone *thinks*, "it is early October" and *notices*, "there is fog over the land," and so on. This is the case even as the imperfect-tense verbs signal that this individual, subjective consciousness is being assumed by a narrative instance that does not lose its authority and indeed continues to exercise it through the second half of the text, where the perceptions are explicitly produced as Emma's. It is perhaps at the moment when "Emma half closed her eyes" that the narrative voice distances itself most clearly from the character's perception (but it is quite imaginable that Emma's self-consciousness is such as to lead her to think: "I am half-closing my eyes to pick out, . . . etc.").

But whereas at the beginning of the passage the narrative voice supports Emma's perceptions and gives them a certain authority, so that no reader doubts the veracity of the information, it is not the same once the text identifies her as the source of those perceptions. Does the text approve the comparison of the valley to a lake, or does it merely attribute the comparison to Emma? Who is responsible for the verbs *sembler* ("to seem"), *paraître* ("to appear"), and *figurer* ("to figure")? Is it Emma, who would then be conscious (the verb *figurer* is particularly explicit in this respect) of the imaging work of her imagination? Or is it the text, which would thereby acknowledge the illusory quality of this metaphoric transformation but, at the same time, lend its authority to the cogency of the illusion? Or again, is it that the text is distancing itself from the character's perceptions the better to underline their illusory quality and hence the force of the desire that deflects her vision? And what of the final line: ". . . and the tall lines of the poplars that rose above the mist were like a beach stirred by the wind"?

Does it humorously show Emma herself humorously poking fun at her own fantasy, or is the text ironically mocking the excesses of her imagination?

Such are the well-known effects of free indirect style. Claude Perruchot has demonstrated very effectively that it is a form of writing that irremediably subverts any notion of a coherent, autonomous subject,[16] and our passage is one of the moments in the novel in which the effect of "disparition élocutoire," the absorption of narrativity by a textuality that invades it instead of falling under its control, can be most easily grasped. But what I have tried to give a sense of, in my discussion of this passage, is how the solidarity of the narrative voice and the character's perception functions in a double way. This solidarity impels the reader, on the one hand, to make an ironic and distanced reading, conscious that all the information conveyed by the text is filtered through the subjectivity of a desiring subject. On the other hand, it requires a reading that is complicitous with the character and simultaneously with the text in which that character's vision is fully assumed, and with it her emotions and desires. Citing the content of Emma's consciousness without quotation marks, the text ironically distinguishes itself from it; and it is for the reader to grasp this ironic mentioning and, in agreement with the text, to distance himself or herself in turn. But in transmitting, without the distancing effect normally produced by quotation marks, a vision of the world informed by the transformative power of desire, it also calls for a sympathetic understanding of that vision. It leads the reader to "espouse" the immense demand for happiness that is readable in the character's very *bêtise* and blindness. One should at one and the same time be wary of the seductive beauty of the passage as a manifestation of the *bêtise* that one should resist and be receptive of it, supported as it is by the full force of textual diction.

And it is because textual "saying" associates itself with Emma's "seeing" at the same time as it distances itself therefrom that it becomes possible to claim that the text's demand for sympathy for Emma functions simultaneously as a call for a sympathetic reading of the text itself. Neither Charles, nor Rodolphe, nor Léon—and certainly not Lheureux—is able to respond with appropriate love to Emma's passionate demand for happiness. As a self-reflexive figure of the text, whose heroine she is and whose title is furnished by her own alienated name (as a woman married to Charles), Emma formulates through the readability of her own desire a demand for happiness to which the reader is encouraged to respond with more imagination than Charles and with more generosity and less egoism than Rodolphe, Léon, or Homais. We are called upon to grasp Emma's *bêtise* and that of the text—that is, to read ironically, without blinding our-selves like Emma—but also to read without cynicism and, above all, *with-out indifference*. On this depends the text's own possibility of being differ-entiated from the social milieu it "portrays" and by the *bêtise* with which it is invaded. Unlike Emma, and thanks to the irony realized by the reader, it will not be blind to the meaning of its own desire—its own desire for "happiness" and originality being, like Emma's, social in origin and hence a form of *bêtise*. But in contradistinction to the indifferent, it will also show itself to be in possession (as the husbands, seducers, and exploiters are not) of a "soul" and a "heart" that have the power to respond with a sincere desire of their own to the intensity of Emma's desire for happiness. All this is a function of identificatory reading.

The passage where the text formulates its own demand for happiness and for an understanding, sympathetic reading is well known. In account-ing for Rodolphe's hardness of heart, the uncharacterized (and uncharac-terizable) narrator of *Madame Bovary* suddenly chooses to express himself in explicit and personal terms:

> He had so often heard these things said that they did not strike him as original. Emma was like all his mistresses; and the charm of novelty, gradually falling away like a garment, laid bare the eternal monotony of passion, that has always the same shape and the same language. He was unable to see, this man so full of experience, the variety of feelings hidden within the expressions. Since libertine or venal lips had murmured similar phrases, he only faintly believed in the candor of Emma's; he thought one should be aware of exaggerated declarations which only serve to cloak a tepid love; as though the abundance of one's soul did not sometimes overflow with metaphors, since no one is ever able to give the exact measure of his needs, his concepts, or his sorrows. The human tongue is like a cracked cauldron on which we beat out tunes to set a bear dancing when we would make the stars weep with our melodies. (p. 138; pp. 178–79)

That this passage has become a commonplace of Flaubert criticism does not mean we can afford to ignore it. For it is, as we can see, an eloquent plea for the possibility of there being authenticity, sincerity, originality, and *nouveauté* beneath "la parité des expressions"—the sameness of expression. And the condemnation of Rodolphe's cynical reading of Emma does not imply the superiority of an ironic reading. Rodolphe is as incapable of an ironic reading (for which he substitutes self-interest and exploitation) as he is of a sympathetic reading (which he replaces by indifference and a kind of lassitude toward the "eternal monotony of passion"). A man of experience dulled by the repetitiveness of life ("Emma was the same as all his mistresses," "always the same shape and the same language"), he is incapable of seeing that repetitions can sometimes express something genuine, straightforward, and original. And yet, if there is in life any possibility of "charm" that is likely to survive the "eternal monotony of passion," it lies on the one hand in the existence of an impassioned sincerity such as Emma's and on the other in finding a reader who, unlike Rodolphe, is able to resist the temptations of indifferentiation and remain prepared to distinguish on occasion between "libertine or venal lips" and the "abundance of one's soul." And since "no one is ever able to give the exact measure of his needs," it follows that this analysis applies to the most intelligent and self-conscious of discourses (*Madame Bovary*, for example) as much as to the sentimental clichés that fall from the lips of its heroine.

My colleague Marcel Muller points out to me that whereas Rodolphe's cynical manner of reading is described by a metonymy, the kind of reading demanded by the text (for Emma and for itself) can be formulated only by indirection and through metaphor: "the human tongue is like a cracked cauldron," and so on. More specifically, a "good" reading must itself be metaphoric, perceiving in the "emptiest metaphors" an "abundance of the soul" that spills over and fills their emptiness. In contrast, a "bad" reading is metonymic, deducing from the venality or libertinage of lips the degraded character of their message. It is through contiguity and a reading sensitive to contiguity that language becomes degraded; thus the discourse of *Madame Bovary* suffers from its metonymic pars pro toto contiguity with the social discourse that furnishes its substance. Yet a metaphoric reading of this same language, while recognizing its emptiness, would be attentive to the unsaid and the unsayable—"the needs, concepts, and sorrows" of which that language cannot give an "exact measure"—and would be able to recognize, in the "same shape and the same language," something vital: the "variety of feelings." Rodolphe's error is to practice a reading that, from the "sameness of expressions," deduces textual indifferentiation; what is required of the good reader, on the other hand, is an act of differentiation and the ability to recognize in *Madame Bovary* the "abundance of [its] soul" and its desire to "make the stars weep."

Such a reading would be ironic in the broadest sense of the term. For there are two kinds of irony. There is an irony of intelligent superiority that distances text and reader from the characters without rescuing them from *bêtise* (and indeed succeeds only in plunging them further into it). This kind of irony is grounded in a considerable sense of certainty: I can agree quite easily with other readers of the novel that Emma is frequently the butt of its irony, and other characters even more so. The understanding is between the text and reader, at the expense of the character. The second kind of irony is a matter of communicational uncertainty (is one really *communicating* or just exchanging words?); paradoxically, it brings together the character, the text, and the reader in the same possibility of error. It is an irony that recognizes that sincerity itself—a phenomenon generally thought contrary to irony—is a rhetorical matter and is therefore subject to the hazardous conditions of ironic communication. To say "I am being ironic" or "I am being sincere" does not in itself ensure that one is read as ironic or sincere, for it is perfectly possible to be ironic in saying "I am ironic" and insincere in saying "I am being sincere." But saying so also does not exclude the possibility of one's being ironic or sincere as claimed. Irony and sincerity are alike in that one must always read them between the lines; that is why one is always in danger of failing to perceive them, just as there is a certain risk of error in recognizing them.

In the letters from her father, despite all the spelling errors, Emma can follow "the kindly thought that cackled right through it like a hen half hidden in a hedge of thorns" (p. 124; p. 161). Yet she is able to spend her whole life with Justin without ever suspecting the sincere love that the boy feels for her—a love that readers clearly perceive, even if they put it in the category of "puppy love" and therefore consider it another form of *bêtise*. She is so absorbed by her exalted, bookish, and sentimental fantasies that she is unable also to appreciate or even perceive the depth of feelings that Charles's gauche banality hides from her—not so much an error of "reading," perhaps, like Rodolphe's in his relation to her, as an error of evaluation. But this error serves as a warning for the reader who recalls that Charles is a textual figure as much as Emma herself. And yet it is so easy to fall into the opposite trap—as does Emma in the presence of seducers and exploiters, or like Charles when confronted with Emma's lies—that is, to believe in sincerity where there is only venality, hypocrisy, egoism, and indifference. This too is a lesson for the reader to ponder. Why should one necessarily believe a text like *Madame Bovary* simply because it makes a claim of sincerity? Even if it is not consciously trying to deceive the reader, isn't a text capable of deceiving itself? Sincerity is always a risky bet, whether one claims it for oneself or believes in it in others; that is why it can be approached only with an ironic consciousness of the possibility (and, it seems, the probability) of error.

Charles and Emma have one thing in common, that their subjectivity is defined by a demand for love, a search for a sincerity equal to their own, that is quasi-absolute and in both cases goes unfulfilled. As in Racinean tragedy, Charles presents Emma with a demand for love to which she remains insensitive, so absorbed is she in her own demand for the love of others, each of whom profits from it in his own way without ever truly responding to it. As in "Le Cygne," desire implies not fulfillment, but endless exile and an existence of deprivation and repetitions. Long before Lacan, *Madame Bovary* taught that desire arises in the interstice between need and demand, between what can be fulfilled and what remains, of necessity, unfulfillable.[17] For the birth of desire, which is a birth to the substitutive structure of the *objet-a*, constitutes an entrance into the symbolic order, whereas demand belongs to the narcissistic order of the imaginary.[18] As Lacan observes, "the priority given by the *neurotic* to demand hides his anxiety concerning the desire of the Other" (my emphasis).[19] In this sense Charles's unshakable fidelity and Emma's increasingly desperate adventures come together in the end as symptoms of the same obstinacy in their demand and the same neurotic frustration. Each consequently dies in the same paroxysm of unfulfilled love, and at the end Emma's melancholia is echoed in the lonely and quite romantic mourning of her widower, "this long-bearded, shabbily clothed, wild figure of a man, who wept aloud as he walked up and down" (p. 254; p. 322).

To the characters' demand for love corresponds exactly the demand for reading conveyed by the novel, aware as it is of the ironic conditions of any act of communication and of the fact that "no one is ever able to give the exact measure of his needs, his conceptions, or his sorrows" (p. 138; pp. 178–79). This means that any empirical reading the text may encounter can only belong to the uncertain domain of the symbolic and constitute a substitute object, whereas the reading it demands, which is of the order of the imaginary, is therefore unattainable because it is strictly speaking impossible. The text foretells that its demand for love will be read as Charles's and Justin's are by Emma or as Emma's is by Rodolphe: it will be misread or pass unnoticed, or else it will be perceived but answered with cold, manipulative, and calculating egoism. For example, who can say, perusing the present "reading" of *Madame Bovary*, to what extent it can be ascribed to love for the text and to what degree it is a manifestation of egoism, whether in the form of subjective projection or of professional calculation and ambition. (Am I not, after all, simply adding another stone to the construction of an "enviable critical career"?) The text's desire for happiness and fulfillment, altogether like Emma's, is therefore doomed to defeat. Moreover, in both cases the instrument of defeat is ultimately represented by the triumphant figure at the end: Homais, provider of poison and master of a degraded, journalistic slang that is filled with pretension, vulgarity, clichés, and lies.

The analysis made by the text of the conditions of its readability strikes me as entirely relevant to the practice that we now call interpretation: that is, a response that is constitutively inadequate because it is linked to the substitutive and repetitive structure of desire, to the infinite and ever recurrent demand for reading that, for us, makes a text a text. The bears dance, but the text wants to make the stars weep—whence the melancholic, that is, neurotic character of modern textuality but also of its reading. Both text and reading can discover their identity only in a consciousness of lack; their access to the symbolic order—that is, to the real, the only reality we have—is conditioned on the recognition of their own exclusion and exile from "happiness," from Rimbaud's *vraie vie*, a true life that is always already elsewhere.

This is the neurosis, the "anxiety concerning the desire of the Other" in which we live; and the conclusion with respect to criticism must be that it can hardly be neutral. Quite to the contrary, criticism is deeply and intimately involved in the work of mourning and "eternal protest" that is melancholy. As this book itself illustrates, a critic cannot "comment on" or "interpret" a melancholy text without adopting a discursive practice that is itself melancholy and without failing to put an end to the appeal of texts for an end to be put to their appeal for reading.[20]

IN/CONCLUSION:

READING THE BLUR

Apatheia, acedia, *tedium vitae, mal du siècle,* ennui, spleen. . . . In the course of its long history, before it became known as "depression" and "the blues" as it is today, melancholy has assumed a wide variety of forms and been known under many names. But such is the very nature of melancholy, if it can be said to have a nature, for it is a sense of lack and a failure of being that plunges any "individual" into dizzying multiplicity, diversity, and drift, on the one hand, and into an equally disconcerting indeterminacy and "in-difference," on the other.

Why then have I chosen to privilege one particular moment, and at first glance a not especially remarkable one, in the history of melancholy, and one particular form of this malady that has so many others? Doesn't this approach risk doing violence to what might be called the "general economy" of this ecological disease? I do not think so, if one considers that it was in the 1850s that people began to view the melancholic experience not simply as an illness, which it continued to be, but also as a way of experiencing truth—an oppositional truth, to be sure, but truth all the same. In that sense "Aurélia" was perhaps the founding text, since in it we can watch Nerval's straining to ground conviction in illusion and to make the "impressions of a long illness" the occasion of an encounter with truth.[1] But Nerval was wrong to search for the truth of his experience of melancholy in the content and "meaning" of his dreams, whereas it might be situated instead in the very shiftiness of that experience itself and in the forms of dialogic textuality it generates. By contrast, in "Le Cygne" Baudelaire mobilizes the dialogic resources of intertextuality in order to reassess the Cartesian *cogito* in the context of melancholy and to propound the truth of the melancholic subject, dissolved in pensiveness, as the modern successor of an outdated classical *self*, the subject of thought. We had still to await Freud, the Freud of "Mourning and Melancholy" (1916), however, for this sense of the dependency of truth on what is nevertheless an illness to

207

find its definitive expression, especially when he asked: "We only wonder why one must first become ill in order to have access to such a truth."[2]

That is the question that haunts this book. Our truth is an invalid's truth, and clear-sightedness is a function of alienation. As early as 1847, Freud's question underlay the famous phrase of the *Communist Manifesto*, in which the "vaporization" of all that is solid, itself consequent on the ascendancy of the bourgeoisie, was held to condemn humanity henceforth to see without illusion ("mit nüchternen Augen") the true condition of its existence ("Lebensstellung"), the actuality of social relations. Thus, on either side of the texts from the 1850s that I have been concerned with, the two great thinkers of modernity agree that to be lost in fog is to be on the way to truth. In turn, Walter Benjamin was to write in "Theses on the Philosophy of History" that "the exceptional state in which we live is the rule."[3] In the terms used in the present study, the matter could be put this way: the "fogs" (*brouillards*) of melancholy are responsible for a perception of the scrambling (*brouillages*) of reality—in indistinct identities, blurred discourses, false consciousness, a haunting presentiment of the unconscious—and with it a knowledge of the infinite interpretability of any and all human discourse.

The identity of the melancholic, which consists in a sense of the failure of solidity, has thus become the truth of modernism. (What we call "postmodernism" is perhaps only a nonmelancholic, not to say joyful, manner of *assuming* the consequences of melancholic experience—a kind of modernism without the pathos of lack.) Nothing is now self-identical: the *one* turns out to be multiple, and conversely the diverse boils down to indifferentiation. Moreover, this unhealthy situation is henceforth for us the norm, the rule. We have become resigned to living in fog.

So it should be no surprise to realize that what I have called throughout this study *the* melancholic text is not one and the same. From Nerval to Baudelaire to Flaubert, it shifts and changes, drifting as a cloud drifts. Here it is nostalgic for a lost happiness of undifferentiated harmony, while yet oppositional by virtue of that nostalgia; elsewhere, and by contrast, it becomes aggressive and denunciatory, only to resolve into the endless mulling over of thought, the ceaseless substitutions induced by the irony of the sign. Struggling likewise with repetition, with the iterativity that is the symptom of an unquenchable desire, it shows itself in a third instance less obstinate and less prone to obsession, yet more anxiety-ridden and laden with irony, to the point of vertigo and hysteria. . . .

But this diversity of melancholic expression is to be expected; change-ability is the "nature" of melancholic texts. If the writing of melancholy is always in flux, and always different from itself, it is because the being of the melancholic lies in lack of being. That is why the melancholic text can be recognized even as it changes, like itself in its dispersal, and in the problematics of uncentered identity that it tirelessly turns into writing. The fog is constantly shifting, but we are always in fog. Indeed, the swamping of narrativity by a newly predominant textuality and the duplicity of writing that is its consequence are constant from text to text and form the most characteristic feature of each. Infinitely variable as this feature may be in the forms it takes, its structure is always identical, miming as it does an impaired identity and a sense of being that is subject to vaporization and hence endangered by the blur of indifferentiation.

For in all these texts of the mid-nineteenth century, the real problem—far more than the diversity of textual productions, which is easily recuper-able as a sign of individual "originality"—is posed by the indeterminacy of the individual text in relation to the general discourse of a society itself infected with ennui. Even partial abandonment of "narrative" identity opens the text to the threat of blur and confusion, to a dangerous lack of boundaries in relation to the discourse of a society it wishes nevertheless to oppose and from which it must therefore first distinguish itself. The newness of these texts, in which modern writerliness is being invented, cannot suffice to distinguish them, since it knows itself as historical and consequently as only relatively new—a newness that has an intertext and so forms part of the universal mechanism of repetitions that go from bad to worse. At the same time, such newness sees itself destined to occupy a ready-made place in a society that *lives* on novelty—on fashion and moder-nity—and turns it to profit.

In this respect, too, one finds significant differences among the three authors. Writerly suicide, in Nerval, identifies its subject as a man of his time, even as it demonstrates his rejection of its values and his belatedness, his nostalgic desire for withdrawal into the blur that, for him, signifies happiness; as a Werther he is necessarily a modern one, "without pistols." In contrast, the Baudelairean text is threatened by the blur of indifferentia-tion, but in its duplicity it recognizes itself as the "brother" and "twin" of social hypocrisy; hence it enacts disjunctive gestures only at the price of a repression of sameness that always threatens to return. Finally, the Flau-bertian ideal of "idiocy" is a textual vacuum (in contrast to the *fullness* of

Nervalian harmony), whose emptiness is constantly in danger of being invaded and filled by the *bêtise* that surrounds it. Yet in each case the identity of the text is vaporized and no longer has distinct boundaries that would separate it from other discourses, whether literary or social. In these circumstances, "originality" is no longer possible, at least in the traditional sense of the word. Where then does one draw the line of separation, if such a line exists, that would give textual discourse an identity of its own?

It is not that these texts do not lay claim to positive values that produce them as *not indifferent* in a world that threatens them with in-difference. Happiness in Nerval, work in Baudelaire, and the demand for love in Flaubert all function as potential sources of redemption—desperate last hopes to which each is reduced and that distinguish them not only from each other, but also collectively in relation to a society that they are unanimous in judging negatively. Their complaints are accusations, as Freud was to observe regarding the psychic symptoms of melancholics: "Ihre Klagen sind Anklagen."[4] These texts *accuse* in-difference, in the double sense the verb *accuser* has in French: in the sense of showing signs of indifferentiation themselves and suffering from it, but also in the sense of challenging and opposing it,[5] the sense on which they rely to distance themselves from in-difference and claim an identity of their own. Moreover, it is in the text's oppositional stance as a "charge"—in the weight of meaning that it accumulates through readability, but also in its function as witness for the prosecution—that we can locate the "interest" and "hope" that will perhaps save it from the despair, the *accablement* that was mentioned in *Madame Bovary* as the wages of a world given over to repetition.

Not everyone is able to perceive such a "charge" of meaning, however, since it stems from a secondary textual duplicity that results from the first but is nonetheless distinguishable from it, or that it is at least worthwhile attempting to distinguish (for here too there is a blur). In addition to the primary duplicity (the "play" resulting from a split between the narrative and textual functions), there is also a secondary duplicity: that of a text that knows more than it is capable of saying and whose unspoken message (*le non-dit*) calls out to be read. It was Freud who taught us that melancholy demands reading and that only interpretation allows us to read the complaints (*Klagen*) of melancholy as accusations (*Anklagen*) and the indifference it displays as something that is not indifferent, but a "charge" of anger. So it is not altogether by chance that I have described melancholy partly in terms of *brouillard* or "fog" (according to the classical medical theory of humors) and partly in terms of a blurring and jamming of discourses—a *brouillage* that we can nevertheless try to decode (*débrouiller*) to the extent that it might yield to a science of the unconscious. It is as if, through the first type of duplicity (the "split" between the narrative and textual functions), the modernist text becomes a discursive fog, while the blurring and jamming of messages that results from the second kind of duplicity can be decoded only through the active intervention of reading. But let us not forget that, before Freud, Marx taught that the relations between consciousness and the social order can be as foggy as those between consciousness and the personal unconscious. That teaching has been the justification for the social reading I have been developing of the historical phenomenon that was the modernist discovery of melancholy as a text to be read.

Since texts depend in this way on an act of reading to restore their identity, threatened as it is with a failure of differentiation, they can no longer claim an identity that is "proper" to them. It grows instead out of the unpredictable and poorly understood relation that is the reading relation, or what I call the "textual function." Objectively undifferentiated as an *énoncé* in relation to the prevailing discourse(s), the text of melancholy can distinguish itself and show its nonindifference only as a textual enunciation, that is, as a function of its readability.[6] Its problematic identity resides in a "silent" protest, a "vaporized" anger that can be perceived only through the act of reading. In other words, the "interest" and the "hope" of the text are entrusted to an instance that the text itself calls for, but that is by definition positioned as a stranger—the unknown reader. Here too, in short, the situation is nebulous.

To put it more technically, while activating a pun latent in the French word *adresse*, the melancholy text's hope for differentiation depends therefore on its enunciatory skill (*adresse*) in *addressing* itself to the right readers, in *distinguishing* readers (from among all the indifferent ones) who will in turn *distinguish* the text. The "right" reader of "Sylvie" is one who, like the ideal addressee of a suicide note, is able to appreciate the oppositional significance of the narrative's renunciation of discursive control, despite the semantic indeterminacy—the verbal haze—to which that renunciation itself gives rise. The "right" reader of *Les Fleurs du mal* (unlike the reader-narratee defined in the poem "Au lecteur") is one who will apprehend the text as *unlike* that with which it claims a fraternal relationship—unlike in the way that the telltale return of the repressed is unlike the "hypocrisy" of repression. Finally, *Madame Bovary*, as we have seen, is the site of a demand for reading that entails a reader able to distinguish what the text itself is unable to say: its irony, its sincerity, that "other irony" that ensures that the text has nothing in common with the indifference and *bêtise* of others. But in the end, then, *all* these texts formulate a demand for reading to the extent that their identity depends on what they are unable to say—that is, on a *constitutive* duplicity.

Through this duplicity, the text of melancholy abandons the fate of its identity to an instance of reading that the context of its production as it is evoked in the text—repressive, hypocritical, stupid, and conformist— seems unlikely to provide. The reader's responsibility is therefore to pene- trate the text's duplicity in order to perceive the demand for reading that it conveys; yet it is for the text to make possible, by means of its duplicity, a particular form of readability—one that will sort out ordinary readers (those who belong to its context of production) from the "right" readers, who will have the perspicacity to penetrate textual duplicity in order to uncover the text's "truth." That "truth" is to establish the identity of the text in relation to social discourses, but it is by definition of the order of the unsaid and unsayable; it can obviously be neither formulated nor de- fined except by contrast with what it is *not* (social discourse), that is, as a matter of relation. The truth of the melancholy text is emblematized by the epitaph Homais chooses for Emma: a positive statement (*énoncé*) that one must read ironically in order to understand it as an utterance (*énonciation*), specifically an injunction, that has negative force.

Without duplicity, then, there is no reading in the "right" sense of the term. Nor, conversely, is there reading unless it be the perception of some kind of textual duplicity. An empirical reader must first feel that he or she is *not the narratee*[7] in order to be constituted as the reading instance that the text calls for, as a function of another duplicity—that of its hidden "meaning," its textual "truth." This "second" duplicity takes many forms from text to text, but they all have in common that the "meaning" or "truth" of the text is always defined, *within* the symbolic order, as existing *outside* the order of the symbolic.

In "Sylvie," the negative constitution of textual truth as that which the text is most fundamentally "about" without its being able to *say*, lies in the novella's production of happiness as the unattainable origin that phenom- ena of indeterminacy—the shared identity of women, the hazy diction of folk song, the misty landscapes of the Valois—and the textual blur of which they are all figurations, can *refer* to but cannot reproduce. Writerly suicide, as a *process* of "elocutionary disappearance," thus implies an effort of readerly empathy if the happiness it "indicates" is to be realized. In Baudelaire, "meaning" is even more clearly of the order of that which escapes formulation, since it is constituted, prepsychoanalytically, as the form of "knowledge" a text can have when what it knows is more than it can say, and is subject, therefore, to the conditions—the sliding and drifting of the signifier—that are defined by the irony of the sign and the melancholy pensiveness, the mulling over that such irony determines. Finally, in the world of inexorable repetition that is also the Flaubertian representation of reality, the hope for a certain measure of textual autonomy, the margin of independence claimed for literature, has become no more than a "rhetorical" matter, a pure demand for reading about which all that can be known is that it cannot be satisfied, since it can be responded to only within the laws of desire, which are those of substitution and repetition.

By situating the *object* of reading *outside* the symbolic order and thus marking any empirical, punctual reading as necessarily inadequate, the demand for reading demonstrates that it is governed by the order of the imaginary. But the fact that the demand for reading is by definition unfulfillable should not lead us to misjudge or dismiss it: its imaginary status does not prevent it from determining the oppositional text's identity and from distinguishing it—with its constitutive duplicity—from the whole set of "other" discourses that make up its context of production. For any demand for reading that could (by some miracle) be fulfilled would put an *end* to the process of reading, whereas it is precisely the readability consequent on the inevitable failure of the demand for reading to be satisfied that has made the text a text in the first place and permits its differentiation amid the prevailing in-difference. Such readability itself stems from the order of the symbolic and from desire—desire that resurfaces as soon as it is satisfied, as textual interpretations follow each other and pile up, without ever exhausting the demand for reading of which texts are the vehicle. Such readability therefore is open and unlimited; it does not admit of closure.

Such is the neurotic situation, as Lacan might say, the disease of discourse that has become for us today a norm, our truth—a truth that the melancholy texts of the 1850s have succeeded in imposing by virtue of their resistance to an invasion of in-difference.

*

Recent criticism has been engaged in a vast project of critical renovation of nineteenth-century texts. This book is one of a number of works that have in common the fact that they discover our own literary and philosophical concerns in the writing of the previous century, which is regularly understood as somewhat ambiguous: still classical, but already modern. Critical discourse is no more capable of "originality" than any other. I am not really innovating, therefore (except in terminology), when I propose that the "play" of narrative and textual functions is characteristic of the melancholic text of the 1850s. Yet the resulting *readability* still needed, it seems, to be brought out, judging by the critical works with which I feel the strongest affinity, which nevertheless underestimate, to my mind, this crucial phenomenon.

Nathaniel Wing has illustrated with great precision the discursive ambivalence of the major texts of the mid-nineteenth century that subscribe to the centered forms of traditional narrativity and simultaneously to the more subversive operations of textual writerliness—thus calling into question "the ideological status of literary texts, which both reproduce dominant culture and subvert the dominant which inhabits them."[8] I could not have formulated more accurately my own view of the situation of the great modernist texts of the 1850s. The oppositional character of these texts had already been captured in the seminal concepts of "antibourgeois aesthetics" and "counter-discourse" proposed by Dolf Oehler and Richard Terdiman, respectively.[9] In principle, such analyses leave nothing to add concerning the duplicity of nineteenth-century texts.

Yet antibourgeois aesthetics and counterdiscourse both situate the text in a kind of vicious circle or impasse, since the first is conceived of as a criticism of bourgeois society that has no audience other than the bourgeoisie, while the second is an oppositional discourse whose forms are determined by the hegemonic discourse of which, in the final analysis, it is therefore an expression. I am in no way proposing that the readability resulting from the duplicity of these texts functions as a "way out," since, precisely, readability has no exit. But it is the element that is neglected in analyses that hasten to confine textuality within a historically defined context of production. When one reduces literary discourse to the hegemonic social discourse from which—"objectively," I agree—it cannot be distinguished, or when one limits its readership to the public of its own time, one misrecognizes a whole potential for always future readings, a whole apparatus of address that also defines the text, but the text taken now in its enunciatory aspect as the site of a demand for reading, a demand that is not "objective." And yet it is this very potentiality for reading—never satisfied, but always *demanded*—that gives a text its distinctive identity.

We tend perhaps to think of the historicity of texts too readily in terms of *bearing witness* to a given set of social conditions, whereas it might be more appropriate to read them instead as *traces*. A witnessing text says: *"I was there; I saw; this is the way things were."* A trace text, strictly speaking, *says* nothing; one must make it speak by *reading* it. Then it signifies something like: *"I was there; I bear the imprint of the experience, and that imprint can tell you of that experience even now."* A text bearing witness to a particular set of historical circumstances is in the same relation to its context of production as a sign to its referent: it produces the referent as preceding discourse, as if it existed independent of that discourse. Viewed in this perspective, *Madame Bovary* would indeed have to be understood as if the social discourses reproduced in the text determined the text's own discursive status.

A trace text is not in a relation of referentiality with respect to its context, however, but in a relation of interpretability with respect to its reader, who proceeds to produce the context as a function of an interpretative act that seeks to grasp the meaning of the trace. In other words, the trace text gives itself to be read in a "here and now" in which the "there and then" (i.e., the context of production) are to be *produced*, but produced on the basis of the discursive characteristics of the text. The context of production is defined in this case as the condition of possibility of the "fingerprints" that the trace gives us to decipher. *This* context of production is therefore only a hypothesis: the one that best explains the characteristics of the trace as they are available to be read in the context of reception.

But the most important of these characteristics—indeed, the constitutive characteristic of a trace—is the fact of its having *survived* the past so as to be able to offer to readers in the present the elements of readability that make the text a trace of its context of production. In that sense it is the text that determines the status of its context of production, not the context that determines the status of the text. When viewing nineteenth-century texts as *traces* of the past rather than as *witnesses* to it, the first question to be asked is therefore the question of their readability in the present, given that they have survived the revolving doors and vicious circles by which they too (like certain contemporary critics) describe their context of production. This is the question I have tried to begin addressing in the preceding chapters.[10]

Let me close, then, by reiterating a few crucial points. If a text survives so as to figure as a trace of its context of production, it is thanks to its readability in the sense of its skill (*adresse*) at duplicitous address. In other words, it is as text that it escapes the understandings of its discourse that would tend to confine it within the vicious circles of its own time—

whether by according the hegemonic discourse of its period fully determinant status (which amounts to producing the context of its production as a referent that controls the discursive character of the text) or by limiting its readership to its contemporaries (which is another way of reducing the context of the text to the hegemonic discourse of the period). Both these understandings underestimate the oppositional force, the potential of a text, which lies in its ultimately inexhaustible duplicity.

Moreover—the point is obvious, but should still be made—if indeed a text has "survived" thus far thanks to its inexhaustible demand for reading, then our current conceptual tools, our interpretative apparatus, and our reading habits are not likely to exhaust the limitless potential for reading, a potential always renewed and always renewable, by which the text is defined as a text. By defining itself as virtuality, the text acquires an identity that is *inalienable* (since it always preserves a margin of "independence") and at the same time *unrealizable* (since its demand for reading can never be satisfied, and its infinite interpretability cannot be halted).

*

The play of narrative and textual functions and the relative importance given to the latter in modernist texts correspond, then, to a shift in the conception of textual identity—a shift that became apparent in the years around 1850, as the melancholy text emerged. Here textual identity no longer depends (or begins no longer to depend) on a "voice" attributable to the simulacrum that is a coherent, autonomous, and therefore particularizable subject. Henceforth the textual subject tends to merge with the social chorus, and identity can consequently derive no longer from an individual subjectivity. It becomes relational and derives now from the interpretative relation that we call reading, a relation that implies that the text should be viewed as a locus of duplicity. Such a relation produces the principle of textual identity, which resides in virtuality.

In the identity of the melancholy text, there is therefore a lack, which is at the place of the narrative function and which determines the text as indeterminate, undifferentiated, in-different. But this lack—a spatial concept recording the "elocutionary disappearance" of the Cartesian subject—will henceforth be replaced by an energy, a dynamics of oppositionality that is certainly generated by anger with respect to the context of production, but that also relates to the instance of reading as a demand for love.

Such an identity stems from an economy of desire, from the libidinal subject. It is therefore a situational or ecological identity, which determines the text as different from its context, because not in-different, only at the price of forcing it to become, through endless interpretability, endlessly different from itself. "L'être du mélancolique, c'est de n'être pas" ["The being of the melancholic subject consists of *not* being"], as Jean Starobinski (I believe) has put it.[11] But the being of the melancholic text, it seems, lies in *not yet*—forever not yet—being. This is the truth that became accessible to us only through the malady of melancholia.[12] And that is why, when writing of the writing of melancholy, one should not set much store by conclusions.

NOTES

CHAPTER ONE

1. See Gerald Prince, "Introduction à l'étude du narrataire," *Poétique* 14 (1975): 178–96.

2. See Gérard Genette, "Discours du récit," in *Figures*, vol. 3 (Paris: Editions du Seuil, 1972), pp. 65–273, translated by Jane E. Lewin as *Narrative Discourse* (Ithaca, N.Y.: Cornell University Press, 1980).

3. The standard translations for the terms *énoncé* and *énonciation*—"statement" and "utterance"—are inadequate for our purposes here. Basically, *énoncé* refers to discourse-as-structure (i.e., to statements subject to grammatical analysis), whereas *énonciation* refers to discourse-as-event (or the "speech act"). Since the two terms are so difficult to translate, I have generally chosen to use the French terms or else English paraphrases that fit the particular context. [Translator's note]

4. See Jonathan Culler, *Structuralist Poetics: Structuralism, Linguistics, and the Study of Literature* (Ithaca, N.Y.: Cornell University Press, 1975), pp. 177–78.

5. See *Story and Situation: Narrative Seduction and the Power of Fiction* (Minneapolis: University of Minnesota Press, 1984).

6. For further discussion of this point, see in particular Paul de Man, "The Rhetoric of Temporality," in *Blindness and Insight: Essays in the Rhetoric of Contemporary Criticism*, 2d ed. (Minneapolis: University of Minnesota Press, 1983), pp. 187–228. The notion of "readability" that I am proposing here should not be confused with the notion of the *texte lisible* ("the readerly text"), as opposed to the *texte scriptible* ("the writerly text"), proposed by Roland Barthes in *S/Z* (Paris: Editions du Seuil, 1970), pp. 9–10; English translation by Richard Miller, *S/Z* (New York: Farrar, Straus, and Giroux, 1974), pp. 4–5.

7. Gustave Flaubert, *Madame Bovary*, ed. Edouard Maynial (Paris: Garnier, 1961), p. 3. English translation by Eleanor Marx Aveling, revised and edited by Paul de Man in *Madame Bovary: Backgrounds and Sources. Essays in Criticism* (New York: Norton, 1965), pp. 1–2. All subsequent references to *Madame Bovary* will be to these editions, which will be cited parenthetically in the text.

8. The term "modernism" is not often used in studies relating to the French nineteenth century, where the phenomenon it covers is generally designated instead by a wide range of terms that vary according to the genre and period in question: *réalisme, symbolisme, décadentisme, avant-garde*, and so on. However, Baudelaire and Flaubert were certainly to be recognized by the great European modernists as among their most influential models. (Nerval had a smaller audience.) In my opinion, the advantage of the term "modernism" is that it calls attention to features common to texts of different genres: poetry such as *Les Fleurs du*

mal, novels such as *Madame Bovary*, and autobiographical works such as "Sylvie" or "Aurélia." Baudelaire's *Petits Poèmes en prose* (or *Spleen de Paris*) would also have a place in my discussion if their formidable complexity did not call for a separate study.

9. See the discussion of Gautier in chapter 2.

10. See Michel de Certeau, *L'Invention du quotidien, I: Arts de faire* (Paris: 10/18, 1980), translated by Steven F. Rendall as *The Practice of Everyday Life* (Berkeley and Los Angeles: University of California Press, 1984). Also see Certeau's article "On the Oppositional Practices of Everyday Life," *Social Text* 3 (Fall 1980): 3–43.

11. Baudelaire, "Une Mort héroique," in *Petits Poèmes en prose* (Paris: Garnier, 1962), p. 130. Translated into English as "A Heroic Death" by Edward K. Kaplan in *The Parisian Prowler: Le Spleen de Paris, Petits Poèmes en Prose* (Athens: University of Georgia Press, 1989), p. 65. All subsequent references to the *Petits Poèmes en prose* will be to these editions and will be given parenthetically in the text.

12. On the inevitable co-optation of any "counterdiscourse" by the dominant or "hegemonic" discourse, see Richard Terdiman, *Discourse/Counter-Discourse: The Theory and Practice of Symbolic Resistance in Nineteenth-Century France* (Ithaca, N.Y.: Cornell University Press, 1985).

13. Gustave Flaubert, letter of 16 January 1852 to Louise Colet, in *Correspondance* (Paris: Conard, 1926), 2:345. English translation by Francis Steegmuller in *The Letters of Gustave Flaubert, 1830–1857* (Cambridge: Harvard University Press, 1980), 1:154.

14. Baudelaire, "Théophile Gautier" (1859) in *Œuvres complètes* (Paris: Gallimard, Bibliothèque de la Pléiade, 1976), 2:113. In this passage Baudelaire was in fact citing his earlier preface to the French translation of Poe's *Tales of the Grotesque and Arabesque*, published in 1857 as *Histoires extraordinaires*.

15. See Dominick LaCapra, *"Madame Bovary" on Trial* (Ithaca, N.Y.: Cornell University Press, 1982).

16. Flaubert, letter of 16 January 1852 to Louise Colet, in *Correspondance*, 2:345. English translation by Steegmuller in *Letters of Gustave Flaubert*, 1:154.

17. Ibid.

18. Charles Baudelaire, "Au lecteur," in *Les Fleurs du mal* (Paris: Garnier, 1961), ed. Antoine Adam, p. 5. English translation by Richard Howard in *Les Fleurs du Mal: The Flowers of Evil* (Boston: David R. Godine, 1982), p. 5.

CHAPTER TWO

1. "Gautier transcende, avec quel art! le mal de mer en mal du siècle." See Madeleine Cottin's introduction to her edition of Gautier's *Emaux et camées* (Paris: Minard, 1968), p. 83.

2. Gérard de Nerval, "El Desdichado," in *Chimères* (Paris: Garnier-Flammarion, 1965), p. 239. The English translation is that of Peter Jay in *Les Chimères: The Chimeras* (London: Anvil Press Poetry, 1984), p. 15.

3. Arden Reed, *Romantic Weather: The Climates of Coleridge and Baudelaire* (Hanover, N.H.: University Press of New England, 1983). See esp. "The Climates of Baudelaire," pp. 229–313.

4. Charles Baudelaire, "Les Septs Vieillards," in *Les Fleurs du mal*, ed. Antoine Adam (Paris: Garnier, 1961), pp. 97–98. English translation by Mary Trouille.

5. See Donald Charlton, *Secular Religions in France, 1815–1870* (London: Oxford University Press, 1963).

6. Baudelaire, letter of 5 March 1852 to Narcisse Ancelle, in *Correspondance*, ed. Claude Pichois (Paris: Bibliothèque de la Pléiade, 1973), p. 188. English translation by Rosemary Lloyd in *Selected Letters of Charles Baudelaire: The Conquest of Solitude* (Chicago: University of Chicago Press, 1986), p. 45. The italics and capital letters were added by Baudelaire. Lloyd translates *dépolitiqué* as "depoliticized," which I have changed to "depolitified" to fit the discussion. [Translator's note]

7. Ibid.

8. Baudelaire, "Le Voyage," in *Les Fleurs du mal* (Paris: Garnier, 1961), p. 156. English translation by Mary Trouille.

9. Ibid., p. 155.

10. Baudelaire, "Spleen" 76 ("J'ai plus de souvenirs que si j'avais mille ans"), in *Les Fleurs du mal*, p. 79. English translation by Mary Trouille.

11. Baudelaire, "Le Cygne," in *Les Fleurs du mal*, pp. 95–96. English translation by Mary Trouille.

12. Ibid., p. 96.

13. See Baudelaire, "Mon cœur mis à nu," in *Œuvres complètes* (Paris: Gallimard, Bibliothèque de la Pléiade, 1975), 1:679.

14. Reed, pp. 256–67.

15. Théophile Gautier, "Tristesse en mer," in *Emaux et camées* (Paris: Librairie Droz, 1945), pp. 50–52. English translation by Mary Trouille.

16. For analogous recourse to gender difference in Nerval and Baudelaire, see chapters 4 and 5, respectively. The frequency of this retreat from the implications of the melancholic dissolution of "social" identity seems to be a sign that what was ultimately at stake was the order of a phallocratic society. When the chips are down, even the most oppositional and marginalized male poets rally in support of the gendered distinctions that their writing nevertheless questions.

17. According to an etymology that many poets are conscious of, a verse is "that which turns," from the Latin noun *versus* ("the turning of a plow") and the verb *vertere* ("to turn"); both allude to the movement of the farmer plowing his field, turning his plow around when he arrives at the end of a furrow in order to begin another one.

18. Since the attractively heaving breast is gendered male ("ami") while the figure of salvation is female, one could appropriately read the poem in the light of Gautier's bisexuality. On the blurring of sexual distinctions (and the maintenance of gender difference) in Nerval, see chapter 4. Note especially the comparison in this respect of "Sylvie" with Gautier's "Contralto," in which the figures of "ami" and "maîtresse," male friend and mistress, recur.

19. Gautier, "Préface," in *Emaux et camées*, p. 3. English translation by Mary Trouille.

20. See Michel Serres, *Hermès* (Paris: Editions de Minuit, 1968), vol. 1, *La Communication*, esp. "Le Dialogue platonicien et l'origine intersubjective de l'abstraction." Translated into English as "Platonic Dialogue," in *Hermes—Literature, Science, Philosophy*, ed. Josué Harrai and David F. Bell (Baltimore: Johns Hopkins University Press, 1982). Also see Serres' *Le Parasite* (Paris: Grasset, 1980), translated into English as *The Parasite* by Lawrence R. Schehr (Baltimore: Johns Hopkins University Press, 1982).

21. Like "shipwreck," French *naufrage* (etymologically *navis* + *frangere*) implies fracture and breaking.

22. Victor Hugo, "Au peuple," from *Les Châtiments* (Paris: Garnier-Flammarion, 1979), p. 255. The English translation is adapted from Henry Car-

rington's "To the People," in *Translations from the Poems of Victor Hugo* (London: W. Scott, 1887), 2:653–54.

23. See Dan Sperber and Deirdre Wilson, "Les ironies comme mentions," *Poétique* 38 (November 1978): 399–412.

24. Hugo, "Nox," in *Les Châtiments*, pp. 57–58. English translation by Mary Trouille.

25. I will not be dealing with the *Contemplations* in this book, although that collection—(de)centered as it is around (by) the void created by Léopoldine's drowning and the tomb at Villequier—might be considered a melancholic text. For these are the "Memoirs of a Soul" ("Mémoires d'une âme"), as Hugo calls them in his preface. As such, they trace the story of the relation of a human subject to God and produce through poetic seerdom a universe of plenitude that is diametrically opposed to the destabilized world of the melancholic subject.

26. Baudelaire, "Mon cœur mis à nu," p. 676.

27. See Gérard de Nerval, "Les Faux-Saulniers," in *Le National*, 21 November 1850; reprinted in *Œuvres de Gérard de Nerval*, ed. Jean Richer (Paris: Bibliothèque de la Pléiade, 1966), 1:458.

CHAPTER THREE

1. *Œuvres complémentaires de Gérard de Nerval*, vol. 4, *Léo Burckart*, ed. Jean Richer (Paris: Minard, 1981), pp. xxxviii–ix. The official censor's report is cited in its entirety by Richer, ibid., pp. xxxv–ix. All parenthetical page references in the text are to this edition. English translations by Mary Trouille.

2. Victor Hallays-Dabot, *Histoire de la censure théâtrale* (1862), cited by Jean Richer in *Léo Burckart*, p. xxi.

3. Gérard de Nerval, "La Censure—Masques d'Harlequin," *Le National*, 31 October–1 November 1850. Reprinted in *Œuvres complémentaires de Gérard de Nerval*, vol. 8, *Variété et fantaisies*, ed. Jean Richer (Paris: Minard, 1964), p. 243.

4. See René Girard, *Mensonge romantique et vérité romanesque* (Paris: Grasset, 1961).Translated by Yvonne Freccero as *Deceit, Desire, and the Novel: Self and Other in Literary Structure* (Baltimore: Johns Hopkins University Press, 1965).

5. Peter Brooks, *The Melodramatic Imagination: Balzac, Henry James, Melodrama, and the Mode of Excess* (New Haven: Yale University Press, 1976).

6. For a more complete discussion of this argument, see chapter 5 of Ross Chambers, *Story and Situation* (Minneapolis: University of Minnesota Press, 1984), pp. 97–122, as well as chapter 4 of the present volume.

CHAPTER FOUR

1. This chapter on "Sylvie" replaces chapter 4 of *Mélancolie et opposition*, which was devoted to Nerval's "Angélique" and "Aurélia" and which, in English translation, now forms part of chapter 3 ("The Suicide Tactic") of *Room for Maneuver* (pp. 112–43). I draw on, but do not reproduce, two pieces of work that were roughly contemporaneous with the writing of *Mélancolie et opposition*: "On the Suicidal Style in Modern Literature (Goethe, Nerval, Flaubert)," *Cincinnati Romance Review* 6, 9 (1987): 9–41; and "Brouillards nervaliens, brouillards baudelairiens," in *L'Imaginaire nervalien: L'Espace de l'Italie*, ed. Monique Streiff-Moretti (Napoli: Edizioni Scientifiche Italiane, 1988), pp.181–95.

2. Quotations are taken from Gérard de Nerval, *Les Filles du feu, suivi de Aurélia*,

ed. Béatrice Didier (Paris: Gallimard [Coll. "Folio"], 1972). Translations by Ross Chambers. In view of the many available editions of "Sylvie" and the brevity of its chapters, reference is made in parentheses to chapters, not page numbers.

3. Gabrielle Malandain, *Nerval, ou L'Incendie du théâtre: Identité et littérature dans l'œuvre en prose de Gérard de Nerval* (Paris: Corti, 1986), chap. 4.

4. See my reading of this passage in Ross Chambers, *Story and Situation* (Minneapolis: University of Minnesota Press, 1984), 118–19. The present chapter, which reads the figuration of writing in "Sylvie," is a companion piece to the essay on "Sylvie" in chapter 5 ("Seduction Renounced") of *Story and Situation*, which is a reading of the figuration of reading in the novella.

5. See Margaret Waller, *The Male Malady: Fictions of Impotence in the French Romantic Novel* (New Brunswick, N.J.: Rutgers University Press, forthcoming).

6. See especially pp. 9–10.

7. On Schlegelian irony in Nerval see Kurt Scherer, "Nerval et l'ironie lyrique,'" in *Nerval: Une Poétique du rêve*, ed. Jacques Huré (Paris: Honoré Champion, 1989), pp.153–64.

8. Stéphane Mallarmé, *Œuvres complètes*, ed. H. Mondor and G. Jean-Aubry (Paris: Bibliothèque de la Pléiade, 1945), p. 366.

9. See Gaston Bachelard, *L'Eau et les rêves* (Paris: Corti, 1942).

10. Jeanne Bem, "L'autre de la chanson dans le texte nervalien," in *Nerval: Une Poétique du rêve*, pp. 133–41. Quotation on p. 137.

11. "Angélique," letter 5 (in Nerval, *Les filles du feu suivi de Aurélia*, p. 71).

12. On the fading of narrative voice into collective enunciation in "Angélique," see *Room for Maneuver*, pp. 118–21.

13. On the writing tactics of "Aurélia," see *Room for Maneuver*, pp.123–42.

14. Bem, p. 138.

15. Gérard de Nerval, "Promenades et souvenirs," chap. 4 (*Œuvres*, vol. 1, ed. A. Béguin and J. Richer (Paris: Bibliothèque de la Pléiade, 1966), p. 135.

16. I am grateful to unpublished work by Marie Maclean for this understanding of the "name of the mother" as an oppositional option with respect to the *nom/non du Père*.

17. Felicia Miller, "The Mechanical Song: Voice and the Artificial in Modern French Narrative," Ph.D. diss., University of California–Berkeley, 1989.

18. "Angélique," letter 11 (in Nerval, *Les Filles du feu suivi de Aurélia*, p. 119).

19. See especially Kari Lokke, *Gérard de Nerval: The Poet as Social Visionary* (Lexington, Ky.: French Forum Monographs, 1987).

20. On this point, see *Room for Maneuver*. In stressing the politics of gender in "Sylvie," I am not unmindful of questions of class, which have their own role to play in the novella (notably in the portrayal of tensions that arise between the protagonist and Sylvie). But class differences in nineteenth-century France appear to have been so naturalized that they do not raise questions, and much middle-class literature simply ignores them. It is the importance of affirming gender difference that is so striking in this literature, suggesting simultaneously that gender was crucially important and that it was not so easy to naturalize.

21. See his letter to his legal guardian, Narcisse Ancelle, of 30 June 1845, which starts, canonically: "When Miss Jeanne Lemer hands this letter to you, I shall be dead" (Charles Baudelaire, *Correspondance*, vol. 1, ed. Claude Pichois [Paris: Bibliothèque de la Pléiade, 1973], pp.124–26).

22. On Aquin, see *Room for Maneuver*, pp.143–74.

23. Charles Baudelaire, *Les Fleurs du mal*, trans. Richard Howard (Boston: God-

ine, 1982), p. 93. Other translations of Baudelaire in this chapter are by Ross Chambers.

24. On "Les Sept Vieillards" as an allegory of its own poetic practice, see Ross Chambers, "Are Baudelaire's *Tableaux Parisiens* about Paris?" in *On Referring in Literature*, ed. Michel Issacharoff and Anne Whiteside (Bloomington: Indiana University Press, 1987), pp. 95–110.

CHAPTER FIVE

1. See "The British Rule in India," in *The Portable Karl Marx*, ed. Eugene Kamenka (Harmondsworth, Eng.: Penguin Books, 1983), pp. 329–41.

2. I have already discussed this point in "Baudelaire et l'espace poétique: A propos du 'Soleil,'" in *Le Lieu et la formule: Hommage à Marc Eigeldinger* (Neufchâtel: La Baconnière, 1978), pp. 111–20; and especially in "Trois paysages urbains: Les Poèmes liminaires des 'Tableaux parisiens,'" *Modern Philology* 80, 4 (May 1983): 372–89.

3. Charles Baudelaire, "Paysage," in *Les Fleurs du mal*, ed. Antoine Adam (Paris: Garnier, 1961), p. 91. English translation by Mary Trouille.

4. An earlier version of this chapter appeared in *Yale French Studies* under the title "Poetry in the Asiatic Mode: Baudelaire's 'Au lecteur,'" 74 (1988): 97–116.

5. See Walter Benjamin, *Charles Baudelaire: A Lyric Poet in the Era of High Capitalism* (London: Verso Press, 1977); originally published in German as *Charles Baudelaire: Ein Lyriker im Zeitalter des Hochkapitalismus* (Frankfurt: Suhrkamp, 1969).

6. French text from Charles Baudelaire, "Au lecteur," in *Les Fleurs du mal*, ed. Antoine Adam, pp. 5–6. English translation adapted from Richard Howard, "To the Reader," in *Les Fleurs du Mal: The Flowers of Evil* (Boston: David R. Godine, 1982), pp. 5–6. I have taken the liberty of retranslating certain words and phrases in a more literal fashion for the purposes of our discussion. [Translator's note]

7. See Ross Chambers, *Room for Maneuver: Reading (the) Oppositional (in) Narrative* (Chicago: University of Chicago Press, 1991), pp. 125–43.

8. See Michael Taussig, *The Devil and Commodity Fetishism in South America* (Chapel Hill: University of North Carolina Press, 1980), especially chapter 5, "The Devil and the Cosmogenesis of Capitalism."

9. In his letter to his mother (Caroline Aupick) of 27 July 1857, Baudelaire writes: "Je suis l'occasion d'un conflit entre trois ministres" ["I'm the cause of a conflict between three ministers"]. See *Correspondance*, ed. Claude Pichois (Paris: Bibliothèque de la Pléiade, 1973), p. 417. English translation by Rosemary Lloyd in *Selected Letters of Charles Baudelaire: The Conquest of Solitude* (Chicago: University of Chicago Press, 1986), p. 99.

10. See Dominick LaCapra, *"Madame Bovary" on Trial* (Ithaca, N.Y.: Cornell University Press, 1982).

11. See Richard Sieburth, "Poetry and Obscurity: Baudelaire and Swinburne," *Comparative Literature* 36, 4 (fall 1984): 343–53, and Nathaniel Wing, *The Limits of Narrative: Essays on Baudelaire, Flaubert, Rimbaud, and Mallarmé* (Cambridge: Cambridge University Press, 1986), especially chapter 6, "The Trials of Authority under Louis Napoleon."

12. See Jules Barbey d'Aurévilly, "Articles justificatifs pour Charles Baudelaire"

(1857): "Il y a ici une architecture secrète, un plan calculé par le poète, méditatif et volontaire" ["There is here a secret architecture, a calculated plan, meditative and willed by the poet"]. (Quoted in Charles Baudelaire, *Œuvres complètes*, vol. 1 (Paris: Bibliothèque de la Pléiade, 1975), p. 1196.)

13. Claude Pichois in his notes to Baudelaire's *Œuvres complètes*, 1:830.

14. Richard Howard's translation of these lines reads: "Although the least flamboyant of the lot; / this beast would gladly undermine the earth" (p. 6). A more literal translation seemed more appropriate for our purposes here and in a few other cases. [Translator's note]

15. Felix Leakey, "Baudelaire: The Poet as Moralist," in *Studies in Modern French Literature Presented to P. Mansell Jones*, ed. L. J. Austin et al. (Manchester: Manchester University Press, 1961), pp. 196–219.

16. See Dolf Oehler, *Pariser Bilder I (1830–1848): Antibourgeoise Ästhetik bei Baudelaire, Daumier und Heine* (Frankfurt: Suhrkamp, 1979), pp. 69 and 150. See especially p. 69: "Erinnert Baudelaire in beiden Widmungstexten an das Elend der Bürgerexistenz, seine Leere, Unausgefülltheit und Unausfüllbarkeit."

17. See Arden Reed, *Romantic Weather: The Climates of Coleridge and Baudelaire* (Hanover, N.H.: University Press of New England, 1983).

18. Charles Baudelaire, "La Pipe," in *Les Fleurs du mal*, ed. Antoine Adam, pp. 73–74. English translation by Richard Howard, "The Pipe," in *The Flowers of Evil*, pp. 70–71.

19. See Baudelaire's poems "Danse macabre" and "Spleen: Quand le ciel bas et lourd pèse comme un couvercle," in *Les Fleurs du mal*, ed. Antoine Adam, pp. 108–10 and pp. 80–81, respectively (English translations by Richard Howard in *The Flowers of Evil*, pp. 101–3 and 76–77). See especially the final stanza of the latter poem, which begins: "— Et de longs corbillards, sans tambours ni musique, / Défilent lentement dans mon âme" ["—And giant hearses, without dirge or drums, / parade at half-step in my soul"].

20. See especially the poem in that section titled "Crépuscule du soir" that mobilizes the Baudelairean thematics of the city, with its images of prostitution, corruption ("démons malsains"), and furtive pleasures: "Partout [la Prostitution] se fraye un occulte chemin, / . . . Elle remue au sein de la cité de fange / Comme un ver qui dérobe à l'Homme ce qu'il mange" ["Everywhere Prostitution opens up a secret path. / . . . It wriggles in the bosom of the filthy city / Like a worm that steals from Man what he eats"] (*Les Fleurs du mal*, p. 106; translation by Mary Trouille).

21. Baudelaire's affinity for *les forains* is well known. It is less well known that traveling showmen, under the Second Empire, were subject to intense police control as possible agents of subversion. See T. J. Clark, *The Absolute Bourgeois: Artists and Politics in France, 1848–1851* (London: Thames and Hudson, 1973), pp. 120–22.

22. See Richard Stamelman, "The Shroud of Allegory: Death, Mourning, and Melancholy in Baudelaire's Work," *Texas Studies in Literature and Language* 25, 3 (fall 1983): 390–409. This remarkable essay has been a source of great inspiration to me on this project.

23. The classic study of sadism in Baudelaire is, of course, Georges Blin, *Le Sadisme de Baudelaire* (Paris: Corti, 1948).

24. Nathaniel Wing, "The Stylistic Functions of Rhetoric in Baudelaire's *Au lecteur*," *Kentucky Romance Quarterly* 4 (1972): 447–60.

25. Charles Baudelaire, "L'Invitation au voyage," in *Les Fleurs du mal*, ed. Antoine Adam, p. 58. English translation by Mary Trouille.

26. Barbara Johnson, *Défigurations du langage poétique* (Paris: Flammarion, 1979), p. 111. English translation by Ross Chambers.

27. See in particular René Girard, *Deceit, Desire, and the Novel: Self and Other in Literary Structure*, trans. Yvonne Freccero (Baltimore: Johns Hopkins University Press, 1966).

28. See Edward Said, *Orientalism* (New York: Vintage Books, 1979).

CHAPTER SIX

1. French text from Baudelaire, "Le Cygne," in *Les Fleurs du mal* (Paris: Garnier, 1961), pp. 95–96. English translation by Mary Trouille. I am indebted to Richard Howard for his translation of the third line in the penultimate stanza of the poem: "And nurse at the she-wolf Sorrow's dugs" (in *Les Fleurs du Mal: The Flowers of Evil* [Boston: David R. Godine, 1982], p. 91.) [Translator's note]

2. I have surveyed the critical studies of "Le Cygne" for the period 1970–80 in my article "Du temps des 'Chats' au temps du 'Cygne,'" *Œuvres et Critiques* 9, 2 (1984): 11–26.

3. Its duality is mirrored in the opening allusion to the Simoïs, the artificial stream that Andromache had built in her captivity to remind her of the river of her homeland, the stream Virgil refers to as "falsi Simoentis" ["false Simoïs"] and that Baudelaire calls "ce Simoïs menteur" [literally "that liar Simoïs"], thereby calling attention to the connotations of deception and artifice embedded in the Latin word *falsi*. In his rendition of the poem, Richard Howard translates this phrase as "that mimic Simoïs"—a rich and suggestive reading, but one that strays too far from the literal sense of the poem to be useful for our purposes here. See Howard, *The Flowers of Evil*, p. 91. [Translator's note]

4. See John MacInnes, *The Comical as Textual Practice in "Les Fleurs du mal"* (Gainesville: University Presses of Florida, 1988).

5. The fundamental study of the urban inspiration for Baudelaire's poetry remains, of course, Walter Benjamin's *Charles Baudelaire: A Lyric Poet in the Era of High Capitalism* (London: Verso Press, 1977), originally published in German as *Charles Baudelaire: Ein Lyriker im Zeitalter des Hochkapitalismus* (Frankfurt: Suhrkamp, 1969). See also, for a more general study, Marshall Berman, *All That Is Solid Melts into Air* (New York: Simon and Schuster, 1982). For a more specific examination of nineteenth-century urban poetry, see Edward Ahearn, *Rimbaud: Visions and Habitations* (Berkeley and Los Angeles: University of California Press, 1983), pp. 239–350. Finally, for a careful situation of "Le Cygne" in both literary and historical terms, see Richard D. Burton, *The Context of Baudelaire's "Le Cygne"* (Durham, Eng.: University of Durham Press, 1980).

6. See Victor Brombert, "'Le Cygne' de Baudelaire: Douleur, souvenir, travail," in *Etudes baudelairiennes III* (Neuchâtel: La Baconnière, 1973), pp. 254–61.

7. See Paul de Man, "The Rhetoric of Temporality," in *Blindness and Insight: Essays in the Rhetoric of Contemporary Criticism*, 2d ed. (Minneapolis: University of Minnesota Press, 1983), pp. 187–228. See also Nathaniel Wing, "The Danaides' Vessel: On Reading Baudelaire's Allegories," in *The Limits of Narrative* (Cambridge: Cambridge University Press, 1986), pp. 8–18, and Christopher Miller, *Blank Darkness: Africanist Discourse in French* (Chicago: University of Chicago Press, 1985), pp. 115–38.

8. Baudelaire, letter of 5 March 1852 to Narcisse Ancelle, in *Correspondance*, ed. Claude Pichois (Paris: Bibliothèque de la Pléiade, 1973), p. 188. See English translation by Rosemary Lloyd in *Selected Letters of Charles Baudelaire: The Conquest of Solitude* (Chicago: University of Chicago Press, 1986), p. 45.

9. Dolf Oehler, "Ein hermetischer Sozialist: Zur Baudelaire-Kontroverse zwischen Walter Benjamin und Bert Brecht," *Diskussion Deutsch* 26 (December 1975): 569–84.

10. Wolfgang Fietkau, *Schwanengesang auf 1848: Ein Rendez-vous am Louvre: Baudelaire, Marx, Proudhon und Victor Hugo* (Reinbek bei Hamburg: Rowohlt, 1978), pp. 19–120.

11. Baudelaire, letter of [23?] September 1859 to Victor Hugo, in *Correspondance*, pp. 586–99. See English translation by Rosemary Lloyd in *Selected Letters of Charles Baudelaire*, pp. 134–36.

12. Victor Hugo, letter to Napoléon III, quoted in Baudelaire, *Correspondance*, p. 1037.

13. See Wing, "The Danaides' Vessel," pp. 8–18,

14. De Man, "The Rhetoric of Temporality," pp. 206–7.

15. See Jacques Derrida, "Le Facteur de la vérité," in *The Postcard: From Socrates to Freud and Beyond*, trans. Alan Bass (Chicago: University of Chicago Press, 1987), pp. 413–96; esp. p. 425.

16. See the seminal essay by Richard Terdiman, "Deconstructing Memory: On Representing the Past and Theorizing Culture in France since the Revolution," *Diacritics*, winter 1985, 13–36.

17. French text from Baudelaire, "Crépuscule du matin," in *Les Fleurs du mal*, p. 116. English translation by Mary Trouille.

18. For a partial response to the argument of this chapter, see Gérard Gasarian, "La Figure du poète hystérique," *Poétique* 86 (April 1991): 177–91. Gasarian understands the function of allegorization to be the construction of a poetic identity for the subject; he consequently reads Andromache and the swan more positively than I do. In "The *Flâneur* as Hero (on Baudelaire)," to appear in the *Australian Journal of French Studies*, I have gone on to explore the rhetorical consequences of the proximity of the sublime and the ridiculous.

Chapter Seven

1. Stéphane Mallarmé, "Crise de vers," in *Variations sur un sujet*, in *Œuvres complètes* (Paris: Gallimard, Bibliothèque de la Pléiade, 1945), pp. 363–64.

2. The French in these two passages reads: "Nous étions à l'étude, . . . " and "Il serait maintenant impossible à aucun de nous de se rien rappeler de lui." See Gustave Flaubert, *Madame Bovary*, ed. Edouard Maynial (Paris: Garnier, 1961), pp. 3 and 8. English translation by Eleanor Marx Aveling, revised and edited by Paul de Man in *Madame Bovary: Backgrounds and Sources. Essays in Criticism* (New York: Norton, 1965), pp. 1 and 6. All subsequent references to *Madame Bovary* will be to these editions and will be indicated parenthetically in the text—first the translation, then the French edition. The English version has at times been modified in passages where the discussion called for a more literal translation. [Translator's note]

The "contradictory" sentence shows that the narration has been double from the start: there is a particularized *narrator* (whose point of view the text espouses), but he is himself a vehicle of focalization for a more neutral, "omniscient" *narration*, as in free indirect style. The contradiction arises from the coincidence of a "neutral" judgment (Charles was eminently forgettable) with a particular perspective that implies his continued presence in someone's memory; and the "disappearing narrator" is therefore best viewed as a character in the novel whose perspective will no longer be adopted after this point.

3. ". . . et le bois du cercueil, heurté par les cailloux, fit ce bruit formidable qui nous semble être le retentissement de l'éternité" (p. 314) ["and the wood of the coffin, struck by the pebbles, gave forth that dread sound that seems to us the reverberation of eternity"] (p. 247).

4. For an excellent discussion of the mutual entailment between the narratives of Emma's desire and that of *Madame Bovary*, see Nathaniel Wing, "Emma's Stories," chapter 3 in *The Limits of Narrative: Essays on Baudelaire, Flaubert, Rimbaud and Mallarmé* (Cambridge: Cambridge University Press, 1986), pp. 41–77.

5. For a study of narration in *Madame Bovary*, see Jonathan Culler's *Flaubert: The Uses of Uncertainty* (London: Paul Elek, 1974), pp. 109–22.

6. I am thinking of the last conversation between Emma and Binet, which is distanced by being presented through the eyes of Mme Tuvache and Mme Caron.

7. See James Reid, *Grammars of Temporality: Balzac, Flaubert, Zola* (Cambridge: Cambridge University Press, forthcoming).

8. For a discussion of the literary status of the cliché, see the excellent study by Ruth Amossy and Elisheva Rosen, *Les Discours du cliché* (Paris: SEDES, 1982).

9. See Tony Tanner, *Adultery in the Novel* (Baltimore: Johns Hopkins University Press, 1979).

10. See Shoshana Felman, *La Folie et la chose littéraire* (Paris: Editions du Seuil, 1978), esp. "Gustave Flaubert: Folie et cliché," pp. 157–213. Translated into English by Martha Noel Evans and the author with the assistance of Brian Massumi as *Writing and Madness: Literature/Philosophy/Psychoanalysis* (Ithaca, N.Y.: Cornell University Press, 1979).

11. See John Frow, *Marxism and Literary History* (Cambridge: Harvard University Press, 1986), esp. chap. 6.

12. Charles not only makes his rounds on horseback but is also compared to a mill horse. But the master of horses, and of women, is obviously Rodolphe. Beginning with Emma's first encounter with Charles (p. 16), the riding whip (*la cravache*) functions for her as a sign of phallic power. This explains her joy to be dressed *en amazone* (in a riding habit) and to be able herself to make gestures with the knob of her riding whip (p. 157), as well as the symbolic meaning behind the gift she makes to Rodolphe "d'une fort belle cravache" (p. 176). Similarly, Léon charms Emma by flexing his *badine* (a light weight cane that doubles as a horse switch), by contrast with Charles, who carries a pocket knife "like a peasant" (p. 95).

13. See Anne Freadman, "Le genre humain," *Australian Journal of French Studies* 23, 3 (1986): 309–74.

14. The "frightful taste of ink" (p. 230; p. 293), and the "rush of black liquid" that pours from Emma's mouth after she is dead as if she were vomiting (p. 242; p. 307) are often linked with the symbolic poison provided by Homais, in relation to the problematics of language and writing. But these images should also be read as an allusion to black bile, which in classical medicine was thought to provoke melancholy when present in excess.

15. See Roland Barthes, *S/Z* (Paris: Editions du Seuil, 1970), 21, 59, and 87. English translation by Richard Miller: *S/Z* (New York: Farrar, Straus, and Giroux,

1974). Flaubert is explicitly exempted from Barthes's analysis: "Flaubert, . . . working with an irony impregnated with uncertainty, achieves a salutary discomfort of writing: he does not stop the play of codes (or stops it only partially), so that (and this is indubitably the *proof* of writing) *one never knows if he is responsible for what he writes* (if there is a subject *behind* the language)" (p. 140). But this oversimplifies the issue; my purpose is to show that Flaubertian writing does, in the first instance, conform to the type of irony that has the characteristics of *bêtise* but constructs also, by means of writing "impregnated with uncertainty," an *other* irony to which Barthes's account *is* relevant.

16. Claude Perruchot, "Le Style indirect libre et la question du sujet dans *Madame Bovary*," in *La Production du sens chez Flaubert: Colloque de Cerisy*, ed. Claudine Gothot-Meersch (Paris: 10/18, 1975), pp. 253–85.

17. The needs of Emma and Charles are largely satisfied (at least on a purely material level); it is their demand (for happiness, for love) that goes forever unsatisfied. In contrast, it is their daughter Berthe who, falling into the working class, is obliged to bear the burden of material deprivation—a living witness to the bankruptcy of her parents and their generation.

18. Regarding the narcissism of Emma's reveries, see Michal Peled Ginsburg, *Flaubert Writing: A Study of Narrative Strategies* (Stanford: Stanford University Press, 1986), pp. 87–91.

19. Jacques Lacan, "Subversion du sujet et dialectique du désir," in *Ecrits* (Paris: Editions du Seuil, 1966), pp. 793–827. (The quotation is from pp. 823–24.) English translation by Alan Sheridan in *Ecrits: A Selection* (New York: Norton, 1977), p. 321 (translation modified). Cf. also "The neurotic, whether hysteric, obsessional, or more radically phobic, is he who identifies the lack of the Other with his demand" (ibid.). Regarding Flaubert's neurosis, one should of course also see Jean-Paul Sartre's *L'Idiot de la famille: Gustave Flaubert de 1821 à 1857* (Paris: Gallimard, 1971), translated into English by Carol Cosman as *The Family Idiot: Gustave Flaubert, 1821–1857* (Chicago: University of Chicago Press, 1981); but also Dolf Oehler, "Art-névrose: Soziopsychanalyse einer gescheiterten Revolution bei Flaubert und Baudelaire," *Akzente* 27 (1980): 113–30.

20. For an important study of discursive indirection that shows that irony and "free" indirection are structurally related, see Vaheed Ramazani, *The Free Indirect Mode: Flaubert and the Poetics of Irony* (Charlottesville: University Press of Virginia, 1988).

In/conclusion

1. For a reading of "Aurélia" that fleshes out this claim, see Ross Chambers, *Room for Maneuver* (Chicago: University of Chicago Press, 1991), pp. 125–42.

2. The original German reads: "Wir fragen uns nur, warum man erst krank werden muß, um solcher Wahrheit zugänglich zu sein." See Sigmund Freud, "Trauer und Melancholie," in *Gesammelte Werke*, vol. 10, *Werke aus den Jahren 1913–17* (London: Imago, 1946), p. 428. Translated into English by James Strachey et al. as "Mourning and Melancholy," in *The Standard Edition of the Complete Psychological Works of Sigmund Freud* (London: Hogarth Press, 1953–74), 14:239.

3. "Der 'Ausnahmezustand' in dem wir leben, [ist] die Regel," in Walter Benjamin, *Illuminationen* (Frankfurt: Suhrkamp, 1977), p. 254. Translated into English by Harry Zohn as "Theses on the Philosophy of History," in *Illuminations*, ed. Hannah Arendt (New York: Harcourt, Brace, and World, 1968), p. 257.

4. Freud, "Trauer und Melancholie," p. 428.

5. *Accuser*, in French, can have the sense of acknowledging, owning up to, displaying signs of something on one's own behalf, as well as of accusing another. [Translator's note.]

6. As I mentioned in chapter 1, the term "readability" as I am using it here does not refer to the dichotomy of *le texte lisible* ("readerly text") and *le texte scriptible* ("writerly text") proposed by Roland Barthes in *S/Z* (Paris: Editions du Seuil, 1970), pp. 9–10; English translation by Richard Miller: *S/Z* (New York: Farrar, Straus, and Giroux, 1974), pp. 4–5. In my usage, "readability" designates unlimited interpretability as a characteristic of texts.

7. A luminous essay by Franc Schuerewegen suggests that what I refer to in this book as the "narrative function" might best be understood as a form of apostrophe, which he defines (following Fontanier) as a turning away on the part of textual address, or a turning in on itself, such that the reader is produced as excluded third instead of addressee. See Franc Schuerewegen, "Le Texte du narrataire," *Texte* 5–6 (1986–87): 211–33.

8. Nathaniel Wing, *The Limits of Narrative: Essays on Baudelaire, Flaubert, Rimbaud and Mallarmé* (Cambridge: Cambridge University Press, 1986), p. 6.

9. See Dolf Oehler, *Pariser Bilder I (1830–1848): Antibourgeoise Ästhetik bei Baudelaire, Daumier, und Heine* (Frankfurt: Suhrkamp, 1979); and Richard Terdiman, *Discourse/Counter-Discourse: The Theory and Practice of Symbolic Resistance in Nineteenth-Century France* (Ithaca, N.Y.: Cornell University Press, 1985).

10. Another aspect of this question that merits further discussion concerns the emergence of specialized institutions designed both to ensure the readability of texts and to determine which discourses are to be treated as texts. Criticism, which arose in nineteenth-century journalism but has increasingly become the preserve of the university, is one such institution. One would also need to examine the political implications of this whole phenomenon of readability: What interests are served by this production of the literary as a locus of inalienable freedom grounded in an economy of desire?

11. I have not been able to locate the phrase exactly. But see, for the idea, Starobinski's "Ironie et mélancolie: Le Théâtre de Carlo Gozzi," *Critique* 227 (April 1966): 291–308 and its companion piece "Ironie et mélancolie: 'La Princesse Brambilla' de E. T. A. Hoffmann," *Critique* 228 (May 1966): 438–57; see also his essay "Naissance du clown tragique," in *Portrait de l'artiste en saltimbanque* (Geneva: Skira, 1970), pp. 83–99, and cf. p. 92: "[Fancioulle] subit le manque d'être qui s'attache à la nature illusoire de l'art" ["Fancioulle suffers from a lack of *being* that stems from the illusory nature of art"].

12. For an important analysis of the lucidity of melancholic individuals and their privileged access to truth, see Julia Kristeva, *Soleil noir: Dépression et mélancolie* (Paris: Gallimard, 1987). Translated into English by Leon S. Roudiez as *Black Sun: Depression and Melancholia* (New York: Columbia University Press, 1989). My own book was already in production when Kristeva's study appeared.

INDEX